Additional Praise for *After Fidel*

"*After Fidel* is the first complete and detailed analysis available on the impenetrable world of the leaders of Cuba. Latell succeeds in putting together the puzzle that ten American administrations have been trying to decipher. This is an invaluable work for those trying to understand Cuba and its future—the result of Brian Latell's decades of dedication, discipline and sacrifice."
—Brigadier Rafael del Pino, highest ranking defector of the Cuban military

"*After Fidel* reflects the unusual imagination and clarity of the author who thinks and writes powerfully."
—Jeane J. Kirkpatrick, former U.S. Ambassador to the U.N., member of President Ronald Reagan's Cabinet

After Fidel

The Inside Story of Castro's Regime and Cuba's Next Leader

Brian Latell

palgrave
macmillan

AFTER FIDEL
© Brian Latell, 2005.

First published in 2002 by
PALGRAVE MACMILLAN™
175 Fifth Avenue, New York, N.Y. 10010 and
Houndmills, Basingstoke, Hampshire, England RG21 6XS
Companies and representatives throughout the world.

PALGRAVE MACMILLAN is the global academic imprint of the Palgrave Macmillan division of St. Martin's Press, LLC and of Palgrave Macmillan Ltd. Macmillan® is a registered trademark in the United States, United Kingdom and other countries. Palgrave is a registered trademark in the European Union and other countries.

ISBN 1–4039–6943–4

Library of Congress Cataloging-in-Publication Data

After Fidel : the inside story of Castro's regime and Cuba's next leader / Brian Latell.
    p. cm.
Includes bibliographical references and index.
ISBN 1–4039–6943–4
    1. Castro Ruz, Fidel, 1926–. 2. Castro Ruz, Raul, 1931–. 3. Cuba—Politics and government—1959–. 4. Heads of state—Succession—Cuba. 5. Brothers—Family relationships. 6. Brothers—Cuba—Biography. I. Title.

F1788.22.C3L38 2005
972.9106'4'092—dc22   2005048857
[B]

A catalogue record for this book is available from the British Library.

Design by Newgen Imaging Systems (P) Ltd., Chennai, India.

First edition: October 2005

10 9 8 7 6 5 4 3 2 1

Printed in the United States of America.

This book is for Jill

Contents

"Pity the country that has no hero. Pity the country that needs a hero."
—Bertolt Brecht, *Galileo*

"For a leader to emerge, the only thing needed is the need for a leader."
—Fidel Castro, 1985

Acknowledgments

To the extent readers find Fidel and Raul Castro vital in these pages, I am indebted to their many family members, former friends and schoolmates, teachers, associates, and acquaintances who agreed to be interviewed. Ernesto Betancourt was the first and most frequently consulted. Fidel's daughter Alina Fernandez and his sister Juana Castro have been especially generous. I am also indebted to Luis Aguilar, Domingo Amuchastegui, Bernardo Benes, Luis Conte Aguero, Norberto Fuentes, Barbara Gordon, Juan Grau, Alcibiades Hidalgo, Huber Matos, Ramon Mestre, Lucas Moran Arce, Fidel Pino Martinez, Jose Ignacio Rasco, Manuel Romeu, and Fathers Armando Llorente, Quevedo, and Feliz. Others who knew the Castro brothers in Havana and Oriente, but wish to remain anonymous, have also assisted in critical ways.

Many friends, former students, and colleagues old and new have generously aided my efforts. They include Ignacio Alvarez, Jose Alvarez, Carlos and Rosa Batlle, Adriana Bosch, Peter Corsell, Hans de Salas-del Valle, Sergio Diaz-Briquets, Luis Fortuño, Georgie Anne Geyer, Andy Gomez, Eduardo Gomez, John Hamre, Meaghan Marshall, Timothy Naftali, Jorge Perez Lopez, Alexei Porfirenko, Natasha Porfirenko, Dr. Jerrold Post, William Ratliff, Sally Roessler, Henry Rowen, Juan T. Sanchez, Thomas Sanderson, Harry Shukman, Jaime Suchlicki, Juan Tamayo, Maria Urizar, Marc Wachtenheim, Kevin Whitaker, Betty Whitehurst, Abby Yochelson, and Luis Zuñiga.

Special thanks to Maria Werlau for the many essential ways in which she helped and to Raul F. Pino for his generous assistance in providing copies of documents and correspondence related to the Castro family.

Many conscientious and creative archivists and librarians at several divisions of the Library of Congress, and at the Hoover Archives at Stanford University, the Butler Library at Columbia University, the Cuban Heritage Collection at the

University of Miami, and the Lauinger Library at Georgetown University helped in ways too numerous to mention here.

Among my many mentors at the CIA in the 1960s, and at the National Intelligence Council, three must be singled out because their influence was so profound. They taught me how to write, to think critically and analytically, and to serve the national interest dispassionately. They are Archer Bush, Harold Ford, and Richard Lehman.

My agent Sterling Lord, and Robert Guinsler of Sterling Lord Literistics, never lost faith in this project. Their continuing support and encouragement is greatly appreciated. Gabriella Pearce, my editor, has offered consistently sound advice with exquisite good judgment.

But most importantly, I could not have written this book without the love and support of my wife Jill, and our sons Jerry and John. Jill provided the first commentaries on every word that follows and for many years has patiently endured my fascination with Cuba and the Castro brothers. This is her book as much as mine!

Cuban President Fidel Castro (L) and his brother, Raul. Photograph by Niurka Barroso/AFP/Getty Images.

Prologue

I began work on the CIA's Cuba desk in July 1964, up on the sixth floor of the Agency's new headquarters building in Langley, Virginia. There were five or six of us working on Cuba, at a time when there were few other leaders of such intense interest in Washington policy circles as Fidel Castro.

New CIA analysts in the 1960s learned by the seat of their pants. There was no "CIA University," with pretentious bureaucrats posing as deans or department chairs, and not much codified wisdom about analytic tradecraft. We probably learned better and faster than later generations did, but if so, it was because we were mentored by some of the best the Agency has ever produced.

My teachers were all from the founding generation of intelligence analysts. Most were wise and worn veterans of World War II, many of them scholars and old school intellectuals with broad ranges of interests. Among them were nationally recognized camellia and orchid experts, medievalists, linguists, anthropologists, former English professors, and cross-cultural psychologists. Many of them, even those who had no direct responsibility for Cuba or Latin America analysis, were keenly interested in Castro. They gave me good counsel.

"You've got to get into his shoes," several urged me. They really meant Fidel's trademark combat boots and khaki uniform. "You have to try to think like him, understand why he reacts as he does." They told me to examine his cognitive style, his emotional underpinnings, psychological dynamics, and to discover whatever was behind the artifice of his performance style.

They told me to ponder the way he makes decisions and goes about problem solving. What motivates and disturbs him? How did all of his experiences before winning power influence his outlook and personality? Unfortunately, very little of his biography was known at that time, as he did his best to obfuscate his formative years and live down his gangland past and penchant for violence.

Almost nothing about his painful, dichotomized childhood was known outside of Cuba, and there was little reliable information about his intellectual formation. Assessing his personality was a high priority precisely because he was so difficult to understand. There was a need to get under his carapace, to probe and understand his inner workings.

Remote leadership assessment enjoyed considerable legitimacy in the CIA in those days, much more so than in recent years. Nationally respected political psychologists and psychiatrists were on staff, and their work was highly valued. It was a positive legacy carried over into the Agency by veterans of the wartime Office of Strategic Services, the OSS, CIA's parent organization.

During World War II the OSS commissioned a classic psychiatric study, the first of its type ever done inside the U. S. government. A team of four distinguished professors and psychologists completed a book-length psychological analysis of Adolf Hitler. It was classified Secret, although a review of an unexpurgated copy today finds no apparent use of sensitive information.

A landmark work, it brilliantly probed Hitler's character and personality, preparing the ground for many similar studies of other foreign leaders. It was a particularly appropriate model for a young Cuba and Castro analyst. That was not because I or any of my mentors compared Castro with Hitler or rejected his revolution out of hand. There was actually a lot of sympathy for what he was trying to do in Cuba, and we appreciated that he was one of a kind.

Except for the Soviet Union, there may not have been any intelligence targets of so much concern in Washington. McGeorge Bundy, President Kennedy's National Security Adviser, is said to have kept three boxes for incoming mail on his desk at the White House. There was an In box, an Out box, and a Cuba box.

Fidel was an obsession for that administration. The Bay of Pigs fiasco in April 1961 and a number of CIA-orchestrated assassination plots against Fidel and his mysterious brother Raul were followed by the covert Operation MON-GOOSE that unleashed terrorist-type raids and sabotage attacks on the island. Cuba's strategic alliance with the Soviet Union had been solidified by the time I joined the Cuba desk. Every property on the island owned by American citizens or companies had been nationalized. The list of grievances on both sides of the Florida Straits was long and ugly.

The October 1962 missile crisis was the only time the world's two superpowers went to the brink of nuclear conflagration, all because of the strategic importance of the Castros' Cuba. American officials at that time mistakenly considered Fidel merely a pawn of the Soviet Union, and his brother Raul, the defense minister, to be Fidel's obsequious minion. By the time I got involved in Cuba analysis, the first of those assumptions had been discarded although the second endured for many more years.

The Castro regime posed many types of challenges to the United States in the 1960s. Brutal dictatorships and flagship democracies alike were targets of Cuban subversion. Fidel's speeches were broadcast by powerful Radio Havana antennas and were easily heard through much of Latin America. He had a huge, sympathetic following in the region. Young people, nationalists, intellectuals, and others in large numbers were converted by his revolutionary incantations and, with Cuban government encouragement and support, guerrilla groups took to the hills in several countries.

American intelligence concluded that some of them would probably succeed. A national intelligence estimate—the highest level of finished intelligence analysis—concluded in June 1960 that the chances were "appreciable that one or more Castro-like regimes" would seize power.[1] Through most of the decade of the 1960s, and again during the 1980s, fear that sibling revolutionary regimes would be lifted into power with Cuban assistance was a central preoccupation of American policymakers.

Working the Cuba beat as a CIA political and leadership analyst was an exciting challenge. It was a hot, front burner issue, guaranteeing that the conclusions I wrote up for Top Secret intelligence assessments would reach readers at the highest levels of government.

Latin America had been my core interest since graduate school. I had lived and studied in Spain and Mexico but had no interest in a career in overseas espionage. Analysts and operatives in the CIA have always been distant relatives. Analysis is sedentary, mostly anonymous, often tedious work, and even in the 1960s, before there was any structured congressional oversight of intelligence, there were risks in getting it wrong. Nearly all the examples of notorious intelligence failures have been errors of analysis.

Nonetheless, there was nothing I wanted to do more than to examine the entrails of the Cuban revolution as a CIA analyst. What that really meant was that I was dedicating myself to becoming a Fidel Castro specialist. He was one of the most complex, dynamic, yet inexplicable leaders of the twentieth century.

Raul, younger by five years and slated to succeed him since the earliest days of their regime, gradually rose in my thinking as an essential key to understanding Fidel. By the 1970s I had concluded that Raul was underestimated by nearly all foreign observers, an easy oversight considering his brother's titanic personality and charisma. I realized that Raul was his brother's one truly indispensable ally and that his brilliant, steady leadership of the Cuban armed forces secured the revolution. Without him it is unlikely Fidel would still be in power.

The truth, I learned, was that each of the two was his brother's keeper. Their talents, styles, and proclivities intersect and complement each other. Raul's greatest leadership strengths are Fidel's most notable weaknesses. Where Raul is deficient—in communication skills, strategic planning, and crisis management—Fidel is a grandmaster. Since the mid-1950s they have worked together hand in glove, with only a few known aggravations.

I recently discussed the brothers' relationship with an astute former Cuban intelligence officer, now living in Miami, who knew them both. He said that if the Cuban Revolution can be considered an ongoing drama, then Fidel must be thought of as its director and Raul its producer. Fidel is the visionary. He has been the creative genius of its many acts and scenes for more than four and a half decades. But almost none of them would have been possible without Raul's organizational skills.

Today, as the aging and infirm Fidel is nearing the end of his reign, Raul is assuming a larger decision-making role and waiting in the wings to assume power in his own right. What kind of leader will he be? Will he want to improve relations with the United States? If so, he will have little experience to guide him. He has spent a total of only about twenty-four hours in the United States, many years ago, and since then has expressed almost no interest in developing contacts with Americans or trying better to understand his neighbor.

Raul has frequently been described as "enigmatic." My hope is that he will emerge in ensuing chapters as a leader at least as fascinating as his better-known brother.

More Radical Than Me

Fidel Castro rampaged around the presidential suite on the eighteenth floor of Houston's ostentatious Shamrock Hilton hotel, spewing squalid invective in the spit-fire Cuban Spanish that most Latin Americans would have difficulty understanding. He was exhausted after an eleven-day whistle-stop tour of the northeastern United States and was infuriated with his younger brother Raul, the utterly unintimidated target of his wrath.

Fidel had just arrived in Texas after a stopover in Montreal, and Raul had come up earlier the same day on a Cubana Airlines flight from Havana. Both traveled with retinues of advisers and bodyguards, many of whom, like the brothers, were still sporting the wrinkled fatigue uniforms of guerrilla warriors. The Castros were resilient survivors of violent conspiracies that had begun in July 1953 and that culminated, after a two-year insurgency, in the ousting of the dictator Fulgencio Batista. Raul had subordinated himself to Fidel throughout the entire revolutionary process, and until their shouting match in Houston, they had worked together with no evident difficulties.

But at that moment in their government's infancy they had come to diverge on a number of critical matters. They had different visions and priorities, at least for Cuba's short-term future. They seemed to have contradictory loyalties and affinities. Raul was in more of a hurry, more ideologically fixed, and less cautious than Fidel. Perhaps most ominously for the brothers' partnership, their trust in each other seemed to be plummeting. Houston turned out to be a convenient midway location between Canada and Cuba where they could meet and thrash everything out. One witness remembers them at the Shamrock that night spewing profanities at each other for hours, although nothing else of what they said was intelligible.

It was late April 1959, not quite four months since they and their ragged guerrilla bands had triumphed in Cuba. On the first day of January the Castros, along with the doomed Che Guevara and processions of other hirsute guerrillas under their commands, had descended from mountain sanctuaries to be greeted with a tumultuous reception across the island. They were young, exuberant, romantic heroes like none Cuba—or perhaps any other Latin American country—had produced before. The euphoria their revolution stirred in the Cuban masses suggested they enjoyed near-universal approval as the Castros and their lieutenants were thrust, on that exciting New Year's Day, into the glare of an incredulous international media.

Fidel's trip to the United States was unofficial. He had been invited to address a meeting of newspaper editors at the National Press Club in downtown Washington, and he accepted even though President Eisenhower chose to ignore him by playing a round of golf in Georgia. Relations were already strained by then. The dignified sixty-eight-year-old president, the hero of the Normandy invasion who had put away his uniform years before, was repulsed by the prospect of sitting down with the unkempt and khaki-clad thirty-two-year-old Castro who was criticizing the United States regularly in nationalistic perorations.

If Eisenhower would have nothing to do with him, Castro thought, he would go directly to the American people to explain himself and the revolution. After wooing Washington's media elite, he extended his stay, traveling up the East Coast. He took the train to Princeton and was cheered by a large crowd of university students. The next day he continued on to New York where he told reporters mischievously that Cuba should have its own major league baseball franchise. He addressed a curious and excited crowd estimated at thirty-five thousand from a band shell in Central Park. Later, in Boston, he thrilled an audience of about ten thousand at Harvard. Newspaper and wire service reporters tracked his every move. He was interviewed on popular television programs. Fidel's strategy for winning over American public opinion was succeeding beyond his wildest expectations. Speaking halting but often charmingly lilting English, he seemed to be as popular on his American tour as he was in Cuba.

He was uncomfortable, though, with the sometimes rough give-and-take the American press demanded and grew tired of having to grin at fawning American businessmen hoping to cut profitable deals. Reporters clamored around him to ask probing questions he did not want to answer. "Premier Castro, when will Cuba have elections? Is it true your brother Raul and Che Guevara are communists? Is your government supporting violent revolutions in other Latin American countries?" In public Fidel concealed his irritation with theatrical flair, always smiling, always quick with a finely calibrated and reassuring response. But in phone conversations with Raul back in Havana, he railed.

Fidel blamed his brother for undercutting him, provoking tensions with the United States at precisely the moment he was trying to assuage them. With his principal ally Che Guevara, Raul was sponsoring revolutionary groups hoping to overthrow other Latin American governments. One such expedition had just landed on the east coast of Panama, and all but one of the intruders, it turned out, were Cubans. The first of hundreds of such entanglements by the Castros' regime in support of revolutionary causes in third world countries, the incursion generated widespread criticism in the United States and Panama and provoked American military forces in the Canal Zone to go on alert. Put on the defensive by the Panama affair, Fidel repeatedly had to deny to American questioners that his government was involved.

And to make matters worse, Raul was no longer trying to conceal that he was a communist. Only a few weeks after the guerrilla victory, and still at his command post in Cuba's second city, Santiago, he had consented to an interview with a reporter from *The Worker*, the official weekly of the American Communist Party. To an appreciative audience, Raul muttered darkly about "the yoke of imperialism" and came across as the veteran Marxist he was.[1]

He had first come to Soviet attention in early 1953 when he traveled to Vienna to participate in an international communist youth festival and then went on to visit three Eastern European communist capitals. By 1959 there was perhaps no better judge of Raul's communist principles than Nikita Khrushchev, the Soviet premier, who was impressed with him. Khrushchev would write in his memoirs that Raul was "a good communist" who had managed to keep his convictions hidden from Fidel.[2] Since then, documents from once secret Kremlin archives have confirmed that Soviet leaders believed Fidel had been deceived about his brother's true beliefs for a number of years.

They wondered if the famously mercurial Fidel was capable of the discipline required of a communist, a trait they clearly believed was one of Raul's finest qualities.[3] Wanting to protect its most powerful ally in the new Cuban regime, Moscow tried to hide the blossoming relationship with Raul, even from his own brother. In reality, however, the Soviets had almost no understanding at that time of the labyrinthine relationship between the Castro brothers, and they certainly had no idea yet how to assess Fidel.

It was during Fidel's American public relations tour that Raul clandestinely initiated Cuba's first official contacts with the Soviet Union. Ironically, his request for assistance to help consolidate the small and disorganized armed forces he commanded was approved by the Kremlin at about the same time Fidel was huddled secretly with an influential CIA official in Washington. Raul may have been aware of that three-hour meeting and that Fidel had agreed to institute regular intelligence exchanges with the Agency to keep tabs on Cuba's communists. The arrangement would never take effect, but a government minister traveling in Fidel's entourage observed that the CIA officer was in a state of euphoria after the meeting. He is said to have assured Agency superiors that Fidel was not a communist and that he could be counted on to restrict communist activities in Cuba.[4]

In Havana, Raul was becoming more alarmed that his brother's revolutionary convictions were being compromised. Fidel had been delivering speeches in which he promised to maintain good relations with the United States and to have elections in Cuba so that democracy could flourish after years of dictatorship. He had condemned the incursion against the government of Panama and promised that Cuba would not support such interventions. But Raul feared his brother was telling American audiences exactly what they wanted to hear—worse, he worried that Fidel was beginning to believe it himself.

In a candid interview with a Mexican reporter years later, Raul was uncharacteristically reflective in recalling his sentiments in those days. He said he would never have put his life at risk as a guerrilla for only "a few reforms."[5] He had fought for comprehensive socialist change, for a sweeping restructuring of Cuba's institutions and political culture. And in April 1959, already the second most powerful man in Cuba, the tough and seasoned twenty-eight-year-old Raul was not inclined to be silent or subservient. A close associate of Fidel's who traveled in his entourage wrote that while in New York, Fidel received an angry call from Raul. It was "being said" in Cuba that he had "sold out to the Americans."[6]

It was true that Fidel's meeting with Vice President Richard Nixon at the Capitol in Washington had been surprisingly cordial. Nixon viewed the young revolutionary somewhat sympathetically while also astutely taking his measure. Castro had demonstrated naiveté and assorted deficiencies, Nixon wrote in a memo for Eisenhower, but he also observed that the Cuban exuded "indefinable qualities" that would assure him an enduring leadership role in Cuba and the rest of Latin America.[7] During the overnight stop in Princeton, Fidel had remarked to Ernesto Betancourt, a Cuban official traveling with him, that the Americans he met during the visit were not like the ones he had previously known at home.[8] It was a potentially momentous discovery.

The Castro brothers had grown up near large American mining and sugar enterprises. There, Fidel objected bitterly to the comfortable lifestyles, private clubs, and neocolonial attitudes of the extended expatriate communities near the Castro family home. The United Fruit Company was the largest foreign proprietor. The daughter of the company's manager knew Fidel around the time he married a local girl in 1948. She remembers that when Fidel visited, he was often incensed that United Fruit maintained a beach for its employees that Cubans could not use.[9] Perhaps, as Raul feared, Fidel was reconsidering those anti-American impressions amid the embracing enthusiasm of the crowds he encountered everywhere from Washington to Boston.

Hugh Thomas, the first scholar to produce an ample history of the Cuban Revolution, concluded that the April 1959 visit was the "high point of Castro's democratic phase."[10] If Fidel was ever to have adopted a benign view of America's role in the world and its dominance over Cuba, it was most likely to have been then, while he was basking in the warm glow of American public approval. Many other Cuba specialists remain convinced, in contrast, that Fidel's antipathy for nearly everything American was already indelible by April 1959, and that he cynically staged the visit.

As with so many other mysteries surrounding his intentions, little hard evidence has ever come to light to resolve the matter. As a young CIA analyst I thought he had been sincerely interested in improving relations and that the Eisenhower administration had let a good opportunity pass. But later, as I learned more about Fidel and discerned duplicitous patterns in his behavior, I concluded that his main intention had been to manipulate American public opinion. Raul really had nothing to worry about.

But he believed Fidel had been away from Cuba too long. He urged him to return home in time to announce new revolutionary programs at a mass gathering in Havana on the first of May, which was to become one of the revolution's most important holidays. Fidel had been out of touch with developments on the island; tensions and political rivalries were increasing. Critical decisions were being postponed. Doubts were growing about who was in charge, and even whether Fidel—still untested as Cuba's fledgling prime minister—was really more of a dilettante than a purposeful leader.

Many years later he ruminated about the quality of his leadership in those days: "I shiver to think about my ignorance at the time the revolution triumphed," he told two American interviewers. "It amazes me."[11]

Some who knew the Castros well in those early days actually suspected that their relationship was so tortured in early 1959 that it was potentially violent. Huber Matos, one of the most effective and popular of the Cuban guerrilla commanders, believed they had a psychologically seething, even possibly murderous Cain and Abel type relationship. Matos told others Raul would some day murder Fidel.

And one of Fidel's university professors—a leading scholar and intellectual of the pre-revolutionary era, a man known for his impeccable probity—independently reached the same conclusion. He wrote after he went into exile that a foreign journalist who knew the brothers was also convinced Raul at that time was capable of murdering Fidel. The journalist is said to have questioned Fidel about it, and Fidel reportedly responded, "Yes, Raul would be capable of that."[12]

Indeed, the younger brother had a record of especially bloodthirsty behavior that began in Mexico when the Castros were preparing to launch their insurgency in Cuba. As a guerrilla commander he had insisted on executing a large number of civilians suspected of collaborating with the enemy. An American adventurer who briefly served with him recounted that Raul's patrols often captured suspected informers and brought them back to camp "and Raul would string them up."[13] Actually, firing squads were the standard revolutionary means of execution then and ever since. A hundred or more of Raul's prisoners were summarily shot in the final days of the guerrilla war at the end of 1958, and according to a regime insider, he continued mandating executions even after being directed by his brother to desist.[14] Some of the executions were remorselessly carried out by Raul himself.

Philip Bonsal, the new American ambassador in Havana, a career diplomat fluent in Spanish, was selected by the Eisenhower administration in the hope that he could find a modus vivendi with the Cuban regime. Unsuccessful, he later wrote in his memoirs that prisoners "were mowed down" at Raul's instigation and then bulldozed underground without the semblance of a trial.[15] During the first months of the new government Raul had advocated the execution of Felipe Pazos, a mild-mannered and internationally respected economist suspected of a minor disloyalty. Huber Matos, the guerrilla commander, scolded Raul and told him, "We are a government now and should avoid violence." Raul angrily responded, "No, that is romanticism."[16]

During that chaotic early stage of the revolution it was the Jacobin Raul who did the most to inflict a reign of terror on its enemies. And curiously, it was his own brother who did more than any other individual to promote Raul's early reputation as Cuba's Robespierre. After only three weeks in power—in mid-January 1959—Fidel told a large crowd gathered at the presidential palace in Havana that if he were assassinated, "behind me come others more radical than me." In the next breath he made clear that above all he meant Raul. He announced that his brother would henceforth be second-in-command of their Twenty-sixth of July Movement as well as his choice as his successor.[17]

But by April the brothers were probably more at odds over tactical issues than at any other time before or since. Above all, Raul was conniving to acceler-ate the pace and severity of revolutionary change while bringing leaders of the Cuban communist party into the government so they could help implement redistributive and revolutionary programs. With Che Guevara, he wanted to sponsor and assist young revolutionaries from other Latin American countries who were flocking to Havana, hoping to emulate Cuban guerrilla successes.

Fidel should come back immediately from his extended hegira in the United States, Raul believed, and he should speak plainly and with genuine revolutionary passion to the Cuban people on May Day. After all, he had publicly promised before he left Cuba that he would be back by then.

Perhaps because Fidel had no idea what he would say if he did preside over those festivities, he decided not to return immediately. Instead, he extended his itinerary to Buenos Aires and Montevideo while summoning Raul to confer with him in Houston. Accepting a standing invitation from the local Junior Chamber of Commerce as the public cover for the visit, Fidel arrived at Houston International Airport on April 28.

Raul, who had arrived three hours earlier, went directly into seclusion at the Shamrock and did not return to the airport to greet Fidel. Although Raul had never set foot in the United States before, he had no interest in sightseeing, no agenda except to consult with his brother. Houston, itching with the boosterism that would soon transform it into a major American metropolis, was alien territory, and Raul was in no mood to mix with American businessmen or crowds of well-wishers or to engage in charming small talk. He may have feared as well that if he did he would be viewed by his more radical revolutionary colleagues back in Cuba as toadying to the Americans. As it turned out, he went out of his way to be rude and diffident.

The ever-ebullient Fidel was tired after the long flight from Montreal, but he went straight from the tarmac into the terminal's Cloud Room, a restaurant and lounge where the elite of Houston's younger generation of capitalists held a lively luncheon for him. He was jocular and expansive as usual, but he declined to give a press conference. He reasoned that reporters repeatedly asked him the same questions, which he had already answered. Texas rice producers, oilmen, and cattle ranchers jostled to talk to him. Cuba was a lucrative market for their products, and they hoped for assurances that the revolution would uphold normal trade and economic relations with the United States.

An oilman, teamed with a prominent Hollywood producer, hoped to nail down a deal for Marlon Brando to star in an adventure movie about the Cuban Revolution. Brando, of course, would play the inimitable Fidel. The movie would be filmed entirely in Cuba, improbably with members of Raul's rebel army as extras.

Texas's oil hub turned out to be the last stop of Fidel's fourth sojourn in the United States. He had spent his honeymoon in late 1948, mostly in New York, lavishly spending his father's generous wedding allowance. In November 1955 he visited New York again from exile in Mexico where he delivered a speech at the Palm Garden on Fifty-second Street. The largely Cuban exile audience was beseeched to donate funds for his revolutionary movement. During that trip he also spoke at the Flagler Theatre in Miami. "We do not care if we have to beg for the fatherland," he said, "we do so with honor."[18]

Houston was new to Fidel, but in fact he had visited Texas once before. It is the only one of his now-numerous visits to the United States—a clandestine one—that he has never publicly acknowledged. In 1956, when the brothers were in exile in Mexico, training and preparing for the insurgency they launched at the end of that year, Fidel needed to enter the United States a second time to solicit contributions. But his visa had been canceled following protests by the Batista regime.

In an unguarded moment during a press conference in Havana in February 1959, Fidel revealed that American officials "invented a series of things, and refused the visa."[19] Undeterred, and with characteristic audacity, Fidel trekked north to the Mexican border and then swam or forded the Rio Grande. He did so alone, and probably in the dark of night. Then, after meeting a former Cuban president in a Texas border town and receiving a grant from him of $50,000 for his cause, Fidel returned covertly to Mexico the same way he had departed.

His second sojourn in Texas would be much more luxurious. The Shamrock Hilton was Houston's premiere hotel, and for several years after it opened on St. Patrick's Day in 1949, it embodied the entrepreneurial spirit of that booming city. The Shamrock was boisterously colorful, as extravagant—and perhaps as vulgar—as many of Texas's new oil millionaires. Glenn McCarthy, "the Irish Wildcatter," had built it.

Eighteen stories high, with more than one thousand rooms and an enormous swimming pool that some said could accommodate water skiers, it was a magnificent caricature of uniquely Texan hyperbole. McCarthy had all the rooms and public spaces decorated in no fewer than sixty-three shades of green. One visitor recalled that the bathroom faucet knobs were faux pineapples.

The grand opening had been heralded by the arrival of a trainload of Hollywood stars and dignitaries. About fifty-thousand gawkers came to witness the spectacle, and the lines to get in that night were so long that it took Houston's mayor two hours to poke his way through. It's said that Edna Ferber's fascination with McCarthy and the extravaganzas he regularly staged at the Shamrock inspired the central character in her novel *Giant*.

The hotel was perfectly cast as the site for the Castro brothers' confrontation. They had been born and raised in Cuba's own version of Texas, the wild and then mostly untamed easternmost province of Oriente. The Castro family was parvenu in the extreme. Neither of the parents could read very well, and Angel, the patriarch, for all his long life remained ill at ease and out of his element in Cuba's cities. The peasant Castros certainly made no appearances in the drawing rooms or country clubs of Cuba's upper classes.

But like so many hardscrabble Texas wildcatters and ranchers who struck it rich, the elder Castro was filled with ingenuity, ambition, and considerable cunning as he accumulated one of the largest fortunes in Oriente. The brothers grew up in contradictory circumstances in the 1930s and '40s, at once rich and miserably poor. Like the archetypical new oil-rich Texans of the 1950s, the brothers were paragons in their country of a brand of personal exceptionalism and bravado that the establishment classes had almost no ability to comprehend.

With their entourages they filled fifty-six rooms at the Shamrock, and as soon as Fidel and Raul were reunited in the spacious suite 18-C, the tensions that had been building for weeks erupted. They shouted reciprocating jeremiads into the pre-dawn warmth of that mid-spring Texas morning. Ernesto Betancourt, still a member of Fidel's entourage, could make out little of what they said from a nearby room but has told me of distinctly remembering each of the brothers repeatedly inciting the other with the gutter profanity—*hijo de puta*—a shameless slander of their own mother.[20] Few in nearby rooms could sleep through the turmoil. They were appalled and fascinated by this fraternal clash that seemed to threaten the sundering of the Castros' infant regime.

The next morning, the brothers appeared in public. Fidel was relaxed and serene once again. Asked by local reporters if they had "fallen out," Raul responded that that was "absurd." Fidel said, "Never! How could that be possible? Me, prime minister, and him the commander of the armed forces. We almost never have disagreements."

To further discredit reports of a rift, the two spent much of that day together. In the morning they crowded with a driver onto the front seat of a limousine to travel about sixty miles to the Bar JF Ranch near the town of Wharton. A Houston *Chronicle* photographer captured the moment as the brothers left the Shamrock. Fidel sat high in his seat, gazing straight ahead with a large cigar clutched jauntily between his teeth. The unsmiling Raul sat rigidly next to him, gazing down under hooded eyelids. Their twenty-two vehicle caravan paused along the way so they could have a hearty breakfast of steak and fried eggs at a country café. There, as at every other stop that day, they were greeted with gracious Texas hospitality. Fidel in return was engaging and loquacious, as usual.

At the ranch, he was given a gold-and-platinum pistol and a prize quarter horse colt that, he said, reminded him of one he had as a boy. He smiled broadly under a crimped-brim Stetson presented to him by an oilman, and he went out of his way to be sure these souvenirs of Texas would get back to Cuba with him.

Raul was sullen and insisted on wearing the trademark beret he favored during his years as a guerrilla commander. There were no reports in the Houston press that he was offered any mementos of the visit. Raul sulked in the background during his stay at the ranch, refusing to join in the cowboy camaraderie. The Houston *Post* commented indulgently the next morning that he had been interested mainly in hanging out in a parking area with Vilma Espin, his bride of a few months, while Fidel and his hosts regaled each other with stories.[21]

From the ranch the brothers returned directly to the Houston airport where they conferred alone one last time in a baggage office. Ernesto Betancourt, who would now return to Havana on Raul's plane, remembers that in private the brothers argued again, loudly and at length. Fidel then flew from Houston to Buenos Aires. Raul and his party left about ten minutes later. Betancourt, for many years in exile, recalls that on Raul's plane they traveled almost the entire way to Cuba in silence. He said Raul refused to acknowledge him because "he was convinced I had been persuading Fidel to improve relations with the Americans."[22]

That hastily arranged Houston summit proved to be a Rubicon of sorts for both Castros. During the ensuing decades the brothers worked together closely, virtually as one, with no public disagreements or disputes. As with any siblings, particularly such ruthless and intractable ones, there have been other conflicts and estrangements, but only hints of discord have filtered out. Although it will probably never be known what they demanded or extracted from each other in Houston, soon the most searing issues that had divided them were resolved.

Within weeks of his return home, Fidel committed to virtually all of his brother's more radical positions. In mid-May a sweeping agrarian reform was proclaimed that among other things, "proscribed" the privately owned sugar plantations that had defined Cuba's economy since the eighteenth century. Latin American revolutionaries received stepped-up Cuban support, with Fidel giving his personal blessing to a group that landed on the shores of the Dominican Republic in June, imbued with the quickly vanquished hope of overthrowing the entrenched dictator there.[23] Rapprochement with Cuba's communists progressed as relations with the United States deteriorated. The liberal ambassador Bonsal, who clung to the belief that an amicable relationship could yet be established, would have only two more substantive meetings with Fidel. By October he had given up all "hope for rational relations."[24]

The shift leftward provoked opposition on many fronts—including in the United States, where the seeds of the Bay of Pigs invasion two years later would soon begin to germinate. Many Cubans opposed to Castro were going underground or into the hills where they hoped to topple the regime that increasingly resembled the dictatorship it had replaced. There were a number of defections and purges of moderates and anticommunists, with Raul and Che Guevara typically passing judgment on them. Novice military forces that Raul was developing began to track down guerrillas who were receiving covert support from the CIA.[25]

As threats multiplied, the impulsive and disorganized Fidel knew that his brother's managerial and military skills, network of loyal lieutenants and aides, and penchant for employing brutal force would be indispensable if his enemies were to be eliminated. Fidel inspired and mobilized others to do his bidding while Raul methodically built the structures through which they could be successful.

And brother or not, Raul was objectively the outstanding candidate to lead Cuba's military services. The other guerrilla commanders were either hopelessly disorganized romantics or obsequious followers with scant education or imagination. Unlike them, Raul had exhibited exceptional organizational and leadership qualities during the year he commanded his own guerrilla front in the Sierra Cristal mountains in northern Oriente. He had matured and gained confidence, demonstrated skills few suspected he possessed, and succeeded in ways that exceeded even Fidel's accomplishments as a guerrilla commander.

The areas that Raul brought under his control were more extensive than those Fidel dominated, and within them he created an elaborate revolutionary administration that in many ways would be the model for the new regime in Havana. Raul kept a diary during his guerrilla days. It shows that he started out with fifty-three men, a nucleus that within approximately nine months burgeoned into an effective force of more than one thousand fighters.[26] He promoted men from within his ranks up to the rank of lieutenant, and organized his own local intelligence service as well as factories, schools, hospitals, and administrative bodies throughout the zone he controlled.

A number of diary entries reflect his interest in organizing peasant committees to indoctrinate the local populace and to induce them to provide support. In a notation inscribed within days of the launching of his Second Front, on March 10, 1958, he wrote, "I began the organization of the Majaguabo zone." Overall, the most impressive theme of the bland diary is Raul's obsession with organization.

He had excelled as the most tenacious and versatile of Fidel's guerrilla chieftains. Even then, in his mid-twenties, five years younger than Fidel, he was creative at identifying and encouraging the talents of men who could usefully serve the revolution. While training in Mexico City in 1955, it was he who first noticed the Argentine Che Guevara and arranged for him to meet Fidel. In the mountains of Cuba Raul recruited and then developed the military and leadership skills of many other young men, some uneducated, who enthusiastically joined his ranks. Several of them are now ranking generals. Others who worked loyally under him for years have retired or taken influential civilian positions. These so-called *raulistas* are scattered across the top levels of military and civilian power.

Raul has a knack for preserving the loyalty and friendship of subordinates over extended periods of time. That is because unlike his brother, he readily delegates responsibility, solicits opinions, treats his men as intellectual equals, and maintains close personal relationships with them and their families. He invests emotionally in others, developing ties based on trust and frank interaction. He is also patient, exercising a paternal influence by encouraging and rewarding promising younger men. Fidel is notoriously incapable of any such empathy in his relationships.

Fidel has never admitted any weaknesses in his leadership capabilities, probably not even to Raul. Nonetheless, by 1959 there was ample evidence that he had blundered badly and repeatedly as a military tactician and organizer. The attack of July 26, 1953, on the Moncada army garrison in Santiago was the opening sortie of the revolution that followed. It was a disaster, so badly planned and executed that it proved suicidal for most of the participants.

Many years later I interviewed one of the survivors in Miami who recalled Fidel's confusion as they met stiff resistance. "He ran around screaming orders hysterically. The orders made no sense."[27] Fidel was captured a few days later—because of carelessness that he has said was one of the worst mistakes he has ever made—and after a trial and imprisonment he began to regroup in Mexico.

There was considerable confusion there too as Fidel trained and organized for the voyage in November 1956 aboard the sixty foot *Granma*, the yacht he had purchased with some of the money he received in his clandestine visit to Texas. The *Granma* stratagem was nearly as calamitous as the Moncada attack, and just as disorganized. Fidel himself has admitted "there was no medicine" on board.[28] There was barely enough food for the eighty-two men and water and fuel were running out just as they reached the Cuban coast. Fidel had no navigational aids and no experience as a seaman.

He unwisely gave the order to set sail from the small Mexican port of Tuxpan just as gale force winds started blowing in from the Gulf of Mexico. Not surprisingly, they went wildly off course and when, days later, they finally came within sight of land, they were not sure if it was Cuba or Jamaica. Fidel did not think to bring maps of the Cuban coast where they would land to launch the insurgency.[29] What little equipment he had brought on board was lost in the confusion of the disastrous landing. "We were all wearing new boots," Che Guevara recalled, and soon "everyone was suffering from blisters and foot sores."[30]

Fidel's talents as a political strategist and propagandist would soon compensate for his organizational and management deficiencies, and his exceptionally good luck would help get him through many more close calls. Yet he was gradually realizing without ever acknowledging it that his principal weaknesses as a leader ironically were his brother's greatest strengths. A subordinate later wrote that Raul was promoted to captain while aboard the *Granma*. "Raul climbed up on the roof of the boat with pencil and paper in hand. 'I've just been promoted to captain, and I am making a list of those I've selected for my platoon.'"[31] It was the beginning of his first real command responsibilities.

Notably, until then he had not been consulted by his brother, who insisted on controlling every detail of his movement's activities and plans. Fidel had no chief of staff, no deputy then to help structure military operations, and he had very little experience himself. It seems likely in retrospect that had he recognized Raul's talents earlier—or been willing to delegate more responsibility to another qualified subordinate—some of the disastrous errors of those early days might have been mitigated or avoided altogether. Possibly, too, the lives of many colleagues who bravely took risks under Fidel's bizarre orders might have been saved.

It is in this context that after Houston the brothers worked out a successful division of labor that has remained in force ever since. Raul was given control of the military and considerable freedom to operate autonomously, more than any other Cuban leader has ever been granted. Under his direction, the military soon became the only true meritocracy in Cuba, despite Fidel's enduring fear that any strong institution under capable leadership might be turned against him. Raul would be the single exception. So in October 1959 he was named Minister of the Revolutionary Armed Forces, the position he has retained to this day.

In that capacity, many years ago he became the world's longest-serving defense minister, and one of its ablest as well. With the exception of Israel, no other small country has tallied as many stunning battlefield victories as Cuba has. Not even the Israeli military has ever exhibited the long-range force projection capabilities that Cuba's did in the 1970s, when tens of thousands of troops were dispatched first to Angola and later to Ethiopia, both many thousands of miles from Cuban shores.

It was Fidel to be sure who was the grand strategist of those interventions and who astutely calculated the geopolitical benefits and risks. Most of the glory for those feats was reaped by Fidel, who, always loath to share the spotlight, has never explicitly acknowledged his brother's essential role. But without the years Raul spent systemically organizing and training Cuba's armed forces, those successes would have been impossible.

Raul is also the linchpin in Fidel's succession strategy. Other than in the world's small number of surviving monarchies, there have been few countries in the last half century or more where political succession possibilities have been so definitively frozen. Obviously, this has been a crucial factor in preserving the stability of the Castros' regime. As first in the line of succession in the government, state, and communist party, Raul has had no rivals.

He has been so feared—and respected, too, by most government officials— that no one dares to undermine or even contemplate trying to eclipse him for Fidel's favor. Through successive generations of Cuban leaders it has been understood that any challenge to one brother would immediately threaten and mobilize both into action. As one former high level official who worked closely with the Castros told me over dinner in Miami's Little Havana, "Each of them is very dangerous, but the combination is terrible to contemplate."[32]

Today they maintain adjoining offices in the Palace of the Revolution in Havana, with a connecting private corridor that is off limits to all but their closest aides.[33] There is no question that these remarkable brothers consult regularly, discussing policy options and priorities. Their disagreements and debates are now conducted in private and protected spaces, in secret chambers, usually with no witnesses who might gossip or defect some day. As with any such cloistered activity, the secrecy surrounding their deliberations and relationship has given rise to enduring mysteries and misunderstandings, especially about the normally self-effacing Raul.

The principal result is that Fidel almost always receives the credit for every new revolutionary initiative, every policy and pronouncement. He is Cuba's colossus: all power and revolutionary principle emanate from him. Fidel has persistently promoted this perception of himself. It burnishes the image of his invincibility that he appears not to depend on anyone. In a long interview with a trusted Marxist confidante in 1992 he spoke favorably of Raul when asked, but as in so many similar situations, he also could not repress a certain meanness and jealousy. "I don't know how much he has been harmed by being my brother, because when there is a tall tree, it always casts a little shade on the others."[34]

Working diligently in that shade since the Houston summit, Raul has allowed himself to be perceived as an insignificant subaltern, a dull factotum who stiffly salutes Fidel and carries out his orders. Raul has been ridiculed from the beginning because physically he compares so unfavorably to his robust brother. The historian Hugh Thomas described him as "mysterious, physically almost child-like."[35] A full head shorter than Fidel, he struggled as a guerrilla to sprout a wispy beard as the other *barbudos,* or bearded ones, cultivated thick, black growths that for a long time were a revolutionary trademark. Raul has been mocked and misrepresented in many other ways as well, underestimated by most outside observers. One result is that almost nothing of weight has been written about him. At least a dozen biographies of Fidel have been published; not even a decent biographical sketch of Raul has appeared.

Yet the truth is that if the depths of the brothers' relationship could ever be understood, the secrets—the innermost workings of the Cuban Revolution through its entire history—would become transparent. Each brother demonstrates unique leadership qualities, personalities, and character traits that seamlessly complement the other's. They fit perfectly, like the stone walls built by the Inca civilization in Peru hundreds of years ago. The rocks were chiseled so finely, so precisely, that when placed together, one on top of the other, no mortar or filler was required. The joints are barely visible. Together, the Castros, like those Inca walls, have stood solid and imposing, in their case for more than four and a half decades. That is a longer run in power than all but one or two modern world leaders and longer than all but one in the entire history of the Western Hemisphere since earliest colonial times.

It is highly unlikely that Fidel could have held power so long without Raul's steady control of the armed forces. In what other Latin American country over the last four or five decades could it be said that no general or colonel was ever known to conspire against the president? Where else have the troops stayed obediently in their barracks without stirring politically? Raul has been the guarantor of that political stability in Cuba.

But Fidel has often seemed to resent the only truly essential man in his regime. When they were together in the mountains, in the earliest days of the guerrilla campaign, Fidel was enraged one day by some tactical mistake he said Raul had made. A witness recalls Fidel screaming at Raul. "You *hijo de puta.* If it were not for me, you'd be working at a warehouse in Biran."[36]

CHAPTER ONE

A Peasant from Biran

Pacing with restless energy at his home in Mayaguez, a verdant university town on Puerto Rico's southwestern coast, Fidel Pino Martinez reminisced with me about the Castro clan. Bougainvillea trees flashed their iridescent magenta blooms that mild winter morning, the last day of February 1986. I had taken a year-long sabbatical from the CIA to do research on Cuba and Mexico at Stanford University. I sought out people who had known the Castro brothers, wanting to learn more about their dynamic relationship.

Pino was seventy-eight, retired from a construction business he had operated with his son. Tall and taciturn, he spoke of Cuba only when coaxed, but he was not an angry or bitter exile. He was content living in Puerto Rico, the nearby island that the Cuban poet and patriot Jose Marti had memorably paired with Cuba as "two wings of the same bird." Its green hills and sugar cane fields, and especially its vibrant, garrulous people, reminded Pino of the homeland he had forever left behind a quarter of a century earlier. All of his family—his wife, siblings and their spouses and every one of the twenty-eight children they had among them—also chose exile. Many of them retained vivid memories of the Castros because the two families had been so closely linked in Oriente and Havana across the span of three generations.

Fidel Pino's youngest brother, Raul Pino Martinez—after whom Raul Castro was named—served during the late 1940s and 1950s in Santiago as attorney for the Castro brothers' parents, first for their father Angel, and later for his widow Lina Ruz and some of the Castro siblings. Raul Pino Martinez's son, also named Raul, has generously shared with me copies of intimate documents and correspondence related to the Castro family that were originally in the possession of his father and are now preserved in the Pino family collection.

In Mayaguez, Fidel Pino had vivid memories of the Castros. His knowledge of the immigrant patriarch Angel, his sons, and Biran, the remote community where the brothers grew up on a sprawling plantation, was fortified by the trick of fate that connected him to Fidel Castro. Both men were named after Pino's father, Fidel Pino Santos. The elder Pino, born in 1884, would be a lifelong friend of Angel Castro. The two had started out dirt poor in the early years of the twentieth century in the municipalities surrounding the Bay of Nipe on Cuba's northeastern coast.

Mayari, where Biran is one of fifteen *barrios*, or districts, and the neighboring municipalities of Banes and Antilla were at the cusp of spectacular economic and demographic expansion, as workers from all over Cuba sought opportunities in the booming local economy. American sugar and fruit interests were building large mills while clearing vast tracts for sugar cane plantations. Bananas were grown for a while, and later, valuable nickel deposits would be developed. A few towns in the area, notably Banes, became comfortable expatriate centers where American workers and managers enjoyed nearly all the amenities of home.

During the first three decades of the century, Mayari alone burgeoned from about twenty-one thousand to nearly one hundred thousand people. For industrious, shrewd, strong, and eager young men like Angel Castro and Fidel Pino Santos, fortunes could be made. There was enough cheap land so that they could assemble large tracts of their own and then profitably sell cane to the American mills close by.

With each man helping the other, the emerging potentates would become two of the richest entrepreneurs in eastern Cuba. They collaborated on many deals, Angel frequently borrowing money from the wealthier and politically more influential Pino Santos. In Mayaguez, the latter's son, Fidel Pino, told me of a huge diamond—four or five carats, he thought—that Angel had once given to his father as collateral on a loan. The diamond resided for a long time in a small vault in the Pino family home in Havana.

Outsiders, certainly the few who came from the cities to visit Biran would not easily forget the frontier settlement the Castro compound dominated. One found it barbaric "beyond belief," like "something out of Dostoevski." It was rough and isolated when Fidel and Raul were young. Outlaws roamed the hills, and it was wise to always have firearms close at hand and to know how to use them swiftly.[1]

As many as a thousand people, nearly all of them somehow indentured to the Castros, were drawn to this rustic melting pot. They came from all over the island, from Haiti and Spain, and probably other countries as well, seeking work and little plots of their own where they could throw together a simple hut, maybe grow some sugar cane, and stake out a claim. Sexual mores were casual, unencumbered. Documented marriages were a luxury few bothered with, just as government authority of any kind rarely intruded.

Disputes were generally settled on the spot, often with sudden lunges and slashes of the ubiquitous machete. Eye-for-an-eye forms of justice and retribution were meted out. To be weak was not just disgraceful on the Cuban frontier, but dangerous. None of Angel's children has ever reported witnessing maimings or other bloody confrontations at Biran. But there can be little doubt that they occurred, most predictably when the rum flowed and the game cocks fought.

Children at Biran did not remain innocent very long. Fidel and Raul's sangfroid in later years—when ordering or presiding over executions and engaging in many forms of lethal violence—was ingrained at an early age. Most of their Cuban contemporaries, raised in more refined settings, would never be able to understand this. The brothers may even have learned to rationalize murder by observing their father Angel, who was rumored to have coldly killed men himself.[2]

The busiest time was during the sugar harvesting season, the *zafra*, when Biran throbbed with frenetic labor as the merciless heat of the late spring and summer descended. Brigades of *macheteros*, cane cutters, sweating in long-sleeved garments and rhythmically swinging their machetes, sliced their way through the fields. First the leaves had to be stripped, then the stalks cut close to the ground, *donde canta el sapo*—where the toad sings—so that the best juices nearest the roots could be captured. The most skillful *macheteros* fairly danced through the cane rows, gracefully arching their backs, smoothly reaching high and low. There was a constant crisp metallic echo as the men sharpened their cutting blades.

The harvest began just after dawn as the morning dew mingled with the cane sap, a strong, pungent aroma of the virgin sucrose hanging heavy in the air. Creaking oxcarts, stacked high with cane stalks, groaned across dirt tracks toward a rail siding that connected to a sugar mill. During the *zafra* the mills churned six days a week and all through the night.[3] Not surprisingly, it was sometimes called the "dance of the millions."

The cockfighting ring was a short distance from the Castro house. Every Sunday during the *zafra*, and on holidays, crowds—including children—gathered for the noisy spectacles. There was a great deal of gambling, raucous cheering and rooting, and wanton drinking of the local rum. It was Raul's favorite sport, and as a young man living at Biran he kept his own fighting cocks.

There was no church in the village, and a priest ventured out there only about once a year, to perform baptisms and other sacraments. Instead, superstitions from many cultures intersected. The song of the owl—a strident screech heard overhead during the night—or the unanswered crowing of a rooster at dawn were sure signs of bad luck. *Santeria*, Afro-Cuban rituals with secret rites and animal sacrifices, mixed with Haitian voodoo, had a strong hold on many, including some of the Castros' kin.

Angel Castro imported workers from Haiti through an arrangement with that country's consul in Santiago. As boys, Fidel and his brothers enjoyed visiting the Haitians in their hovels, eating roasted corn with them, playing with the children. Fidel's daughter Alina Fernandez, in exile in Miami, has written that her extravagant uncle Pedro Emilio, Angel's eldest son, once regaled her with a family secret: Pedro Emilio's half brother Ramon—as a thirteen-year old—had maintained a passionate relationship with a Haitian woman there.[4]

Biran was such a dangerous and uninhibited place that Fidel Pino would never allow his daughter, a contemporary and friend of Raul's, to go there. A girlhood friend of Mirta Diaz Balart—the beautiful young woman from Banes whom Fidel married in 1948—told me when I met her at her home in

Washington's Georgetown neighborhood that, before her marriage, even Mirta never visited Biran. Few friends of any of the Castro children were invited.[5]

Altogether Biran resembled, perhaps, an extravagant town from one of the magical realist novels made popular by Fidel's friend, the Nobel Prize laureate, Gabriel Garcia Marquez. The community's core was the family *finca*, the farm or plantation they called Manacas, where Castro, Ruz, Gonzalez, and Argota relatives of several generations mingled. The lively and wily Lina Ruz Gonzalez, Fidel and Raul's mother, was the daughter of itinerant laborers. As a teenage maid in Angel's house she began bearing his children, eventually seven.

The main house was a large, ramshackle wooden contraption built on pilings sunk deep in the hard red soil. Shade from an enormous tamarind tree helped cool one side; comfort could be had while lazing on the wide plantation-style porch. The house was a larger, tropical version of peasant-built shacks in Angel's native Spain. Furnishings, mostly hand-made of local woods, were sparse. There were few adornments other than life-size statues of saints, with little decoration or family memorabilia. Almost no culture—literature, art, or music—mediated the crude realities of the household.[6]

Malodorous livestock huddled beneath the floorboards, including the family dairy cows that were milked there, and all manner of other domestic animals—pigs, chickens, turkeys, geese, and other fowl. There was a narrow second story, the "lookout," that included bedrooms. Most of the house was "in a state of chaotic untidiness," according to Leycester Coltman, Fidel's most recent English-language biographer and formerly British ambassador to Havana. Chickens hopscotched about, mostly undisturbed, even, according to the ambassador, "roosting" in several rooms.[7]

Kitchen and bathroom facilities were rudimentary at best. There was no electricity, no motor vehicles when the Castro brothers were young. To reach the farm, Fidel told Frei Betto, a Brazilian friar of the Dominican order, in a twenty-three-hour autobiographical interview in 1985, "you had to take a train and then a horse."[8]

There was a dairy, a bakery, a slaughterhouse, mechanical shops, a rickety little primary school, postal and telegraph facilities, and a store the Castros operated. Fidel worked there grudgingly one summer during school vacation, and Raul was behind the counter for longer periods. Angel paid police to man a small rural guard station. He ran a locomotive that looked like a streetcar with a large cattle scoop in front, on a narrow-gauge track from his property to a nearby sugar mill. On its flat front large letters proclaimed: "Angel Castro and Sons."[9]

Gradually, Biran expanded into an alternately alluring and menacing outpost, oppressively primitive but exhilarating too. Fidel and Raul have retained fond memories of growing up there. Uncharacteristically, Fidel grew nostalgic when reminiscing about it in the interview with Betto, telling of when he was ten or twelve, riding on horseback to picturesque pine forests—the *Pinares de Mayari*—where Angel leased land on a high, cool plateau.

"The horses had to struggle, climbing up the steep hillsides, but once they got there, they'd stop sweating and be dry in a matter of minutes. It was marvelously cool up there, because a breeze was always blowing through the tall, dense pine trees, whose tops met, forming a kind of roof," Fidel recalled. "The water in the many brooks was ice cold, pure and delicious."[10] Cuban geographers have said that the area around Biran and the *Pinares de Mayari* is perhaps the most beautiful anywhere on the island.

Fidel relished the freedom to roam Angel's ever-expanding realm, to hunt assorted game with a slingshot, bow and arrow, and a little later with firearms (he became a very good shot), and to swim in the numerous streams. A family photograph taken when he was seventeen shows him in the countryside, posed somewhat self-consciously as if he were on safari. He's alone, on one knee, wearing a pith helmet and boots, confidently holding a rifle. He has a nearly foot-long dagger in a scabbard tucked in his cartridge belt. A handsome hunting dog is at his side. He looks every bit the pampered favorite son of a prosperous gentleman landowner, not the scion of a rough peasant living in a huge chicken-infested shanty. Such contradictions abounded in the younger generation of Castros.

Raul seems to have felt an even greater affinity for Biran and has always been more proud of his heritage than Fidel. He often went home for replenishment when living in Havana, the big, alien city where, as a young man, he was never comfortable, unable to find a niche or purpose of his own. He had fled toward Biran on foot after the disastrous attack on the Moncada garrison in 1953. And he promptly returned when he and Fidel were released from prison on the Isle of Pines after serving almost two years following Moncada.

Their sister Juanita, who fled Cuba in 1964 and has lived in Miami ever since, spoke to me about her brothers in a lengthy conversation in 1986. Seated in the small office behind the pharmacy she has owned for many years, she recalled that Raul lingered at Biran after his release from prison.[11] Fidel, however, went immediately to Havana to begin rebuilding his revolutionary movement. Juanita and others who have known the brothers often comment on Raul's sentimental nature, his need for family and friends that contrasts so strikingly with Fidel's insistence on preserving absolute personal autonomy. She is convinced that Raul became hard and unscrupulous in his twenties while under Fidel's influence.

Angel Castro was born in the rocky, northern Spanish province of Galicia, and thus, not disparagingly, referred to as a *gallego*. He was sent to Cuba in uniform at the time of the Spanish-American War, but never spoke to his family of his role in it.

That is understandable because he is believed to have fought against the Cuban *mambises*, the guerrillas who were struggling for independence and who provided the heroic models for his two sons as they waged their own campaigns to overthrow Batista. Fidel deplored his father for many reasons, but Angel's wartime role and his refusal to renounce it or to learn much about Cuban history were surely among the most profound. Angel did not become a Cuban citizen until 1941, when he was sixty-six years old.

Juanita told me he kept a gun "but no artifacts, relics, or other things to remind him of military service." She does not recall his ever expressing anti-American views. Fidel and Raul, with greater motive to assert that their father was anti-American, have never said so publicly either. All the evidence indicates, to the contrary, that Angel respected and enjoyed working with Americans—in no small part, to be sure, because his prosperity was so closely linked to his business dealings with them. Juanita is convinced that if her father had survived to live under the revolution, he would have been "Fidel's enemy."

After the war Angel started out at an uncle's tile factory in Santa Clara, in the middle of the island, but, according to Juanita, soon migrated east toward greater opportunity. Settling in northern Oriente he began to acquire teams of oxen and organize groups of workers to provide hauling and other services for the American companies. They cleared forest lands that would become United Fruit cane fields and sold firewood to fuel the mills. The company also employed him as a warehouse man before he began to acquire lands of his own. In all of this enterprise Angel demonstrated exceptional leadership qualities—just as Fidel and Raul later would—that put him in charge of a steadily growing force of unskilled laborers.

Fidel Pino told me during our discussions in Mayaguez that his father and Angel were like brothers. Nine years older than the elder Pino, Castro nevertheless deferred to his more sophisticated and better educated friend, who was a mentor of sorts. Pino Santos had been born in Cuba, so he could help the immigrant Angel understand its Creole and tropical peculiarities. The two men trusted each other and collaborated for many years, even as their social paths inevitably diverged. Pino Santos wanted to advance socially and politically as he had financially. He and his son Mario would become politically prominent in Santiago and later win seats in the national congress. For the uneducated and barely literate Angel, however, the microcosm he created at Biran would always suffice.

It was probably more than he had ever hoped to acquire. He had no interest in owning city houses, as Pino Santos did, or in melding into society circles where he would have no idea what to say or do. He was unassuming, thoroughly and contentedly a rustic. Fidel told the Brazilian priest Betto that his parents had no social life, maintaining relations only with people like themselves. "They worked all the time." Visitors rarely came.[12] Fidel Pino recalled that during the elder Castro's few visits to Santiago—and even rarer ones to Havana—he would stay with the Pino family where he was at ease.

The patriarch had little time for his sons, and no affection was shared. Armando Llorente, a Spanish Jesuit who was Fidel's favorite teacher at Belen, the elite Havana preparatory school he attended as a teenager, told me he never met Angel. Nor could the priest, whom I interviewed at a retreat house in Miami, remember either of Fidel's parents attending his graduation.

"I would often say, Fidel, let me meet your father. We are both Spaniards. I am from Leon and he is a *gallego*. But he would always change the subject."[13]

Jose Ignacio Rasco, Fidel's classmate at Belen and the University of Havana, had a similar recollection. Rasco told me in Miami that Fidel "rarely spoke" of his father, "but unfavorably when he did."[14]

Fidel portrayed Angel in generally favorable terms during the 1985 interview with Betto. But twenty years earlier, during extended conversations with the American photo-journalist Lee Lockwood, he was mordant. He criticized Angel "in a curiously detached voice," Lockwood wrote: "He had been a latifundista, a wealthy landowner who exploited the peasants. He had paid no taxes on his land or income. He had 'played politics for money,'" Fidel told the American reporter.

Raul was present for parts of the interview, and he sought to reminisce about Biran and the family, and no doubt to reflect more pleasantly on Angel, but he and Fidel argued heatedly in front of Lockwood before Raul, as always by then, deferred.[15] All the evidence suggests that as Fidel matured and became known in national political circles, he was ashamed of his roots, avoiding discussion of his parents and their humble circumstances.

In more recent years he has occasionally admitted that his father remained a peasant—a *guajiro* in the Cuban vernacular—all his life. Angel perpetually wore work boots with no socks, and crude work clothes. The few times he was seen in Havana he wore a *guayabera*, the long, embroidered cotton shirt favored by men in many tropical countries. It is easy to imagine his hands, leathery and calloused, as he proudly performed hard physical labor almost to the day he died. Fidel may actually have had his father in mind—if only subconsciously—when he told Lockwood that, until the revolution, "when he went to the city, the peasant felt very timid and inhibited."[16]

Like Fidel and Raul, Angel has been the subject of extraordinary, possibly slanderous tales. One, repeated for decades, is that when he was starting out at Biran, he labored quietly on moonless nights moving fences to expand the lands he would claim. A source for Fidel's biographer Georgie Anne Geyer reported that Angel had a way of "acquiring" United Fruit Company tractors and then painting them different colors. He was apparently also a tough taskmaster. A former revolutionary who knew the Castro family told me during an interview in San Juan, Puerto Rico that Angel "worked the Haitians and local *guajiros* very hard. He worked them to the point of exhaustion."[17]

However, his treatment of his workers was not something Fidel deplored when growing up at Biran, or later when he was studying in Havana. Credible accounts indicate that he also treated the *guajiros* cruelly, and perhaps, unlike his father, imperiously as well. During our meeting in Miami, Juanita Castro told of how, as a boy and young man, Fidel took no interest at all in the plight of the family's workers. "There were a lot of employees working on the farm and serving at the house. Fidel never took care of these people," she said. "On the contrary, I remember he criticized my father for being too generous with them."

She distinctly remembered an incident involving a *guajiro* at Biran named Aracelio Peña who arrived unexpectedly at the Castro house one evening when the family was eating a holiday dinner. "He was a worker who climbed the palm trees to get coconuts to feed to the pigs. The farm was closed down for the holidays," Juanita recalled. "When he came into the house Fidel grabbed him by the collar and lifted him up from the floor. Fidel pushed and pulled him to the door in an angry way and then threw him down the stairs at the front of the house. He was angry that Aracelio had interrupted our dinner." Members of the Pino family have similar memories of Fidel, as a young adult living in Havana, urging his father to bear down harder on his workers.

Fidel was always the most headstrong and spoiled of the children. Angel, in his early fifties when Fidel was born, probably recognized very early that it was in his third and most audacious son that many of his own qualities resided. From childhood Fidel was driven by the certainty that he would rise above his origins to fulfill some important destiny, on an even grander scale than what Angel had accomplished.

None of his siblings was so generously supported or indulged. His father paid for his charge account at the Ultra department store in Havana and, judging from the splendid wardrobes he sported during the pre-revolutionary years, he spent extravagantly. Angel bought him new automobiles on different occasions. His first was purchased in 1945 despite the wartime shortage of new cars in Cuba, as he was preparing to enroll at the University of Havana.

Raul, the youngest and the runt among the Castro boys, got considerably less than Fidel. He is not known to have received expensive gifts, let alone a department store charge account or a new car. As a young man, his tastes and ambitions were considerably more modest than Fidel's, yet the difference in how the brothers were subsidized is striking. In early 1953, traveling in Europe during his youthful Marxist apprenticeship, Raul ran out of money in Paris. He wired for help, but Angel refused to send him a peso. Juanita says that it was she who eventually bailed him out so that he could buy a steamer ticket home.[18]

Although Fidel had always been Angel's favorite son, in the discourse with Betto, he said he could not remember when his father had died. It was in October 1956 when the brothers were making their final preparations to sail on the *Granma* from Mexico with their expeditionary force to instigate their insurgency. News of Angel's death was brought to them by Rafael del Pino, one of Fidel's longtime rebel colleagues.

Del Pino, who was later accused of betrayal and who either committed suicide or was murdered in one of the Castros' prisons, told another colleague that Fidel barely reacted. With no emotion at all, he muttered, "What a shame." He then changed the subject, demanding that del Pino inform him of the latest political news from Cuba. Raul, in contrast, is said to have gone into a bathroom and cried for a long time.[19]

Angel was tough and single-minded in the pursuit of his goals, and when he decided he wanted something—whether a tract of good land, a choice team of oxen, or a woman—he was sure to get it. His first wife, Maria Luisa Argota, was a provincial schoolteacher with whom he had two children, Lidia and Pedro Emilio, who survived into adulthood. But Maria did not retain Angel's affections once the teenage Lina Ruz Gonzalez was hired as a housekeeper. Lina's large family—nine brothers and sisters—had migrated to Biran on foot and by wagon, across the breadth of the country from Pinar del Rio at the western end of the island. Fidel referred to some of his mother's Ruz forebears in 1966, when he expressed pride that "part of my blood is Arab."[20]

His daughter Alina, raised by her mother without Fidel's involvement, was named after her grandmother and has written admiringly of her. "She overflowed with an exuberant, rebellious energy, quite unlike the submissive and defeated country girls" whom Angel "had gotten pregnant" and who "bore him many children."[21] Alina says that when her grandmother came into the Castro household, she was about the same age as Angel's daughter Lidia, probably about fifteen.

Lina was "a vulgar person," according to Fidel Pino, "very hard working." She swore like a *machetero*, was uneducated and minimally literate. Fidel does not remember her ever saying anything about attending school, but she taught herself basic reading and writing skills. Lina was shrewd and ambitious and grasped every opportunity to advance herself.

Soon she was bearing Angel's children. An apparently indeterminate period followed when the two families coexisted—no doubt precariously—under the same roof, or at least in close proximity, until Lina prevailed, succeeding her rival as the undisputed mistress of Biran. She impressed Angel with her organizational and business sense, helping to manage the store, monitor the finances, and run the farm.

The lands Angel owned or leased extended for miles in all directions, a vast holding even by Cuban standards of the day. Fertile sugar cane fields were the mainstay, but the old *gallego* diversified. He once had a hundred thousand cedar trees planted to support his lumber business. There was a productive orange grove, which was apparently Lina's pride. She once caught thieves stealing oranges and, accosting them, demanded that they pay for every one. They may very well have complied. She is said to have commonly patrolled the family holdings on horseback, leaving the house at dawn with a revolver strapped to her side.

Fidel Pino told me she drove all the tractors and farm equipment at Biran wearing *ropa fuerte*, rough peasant attire.

Over time, she became more socially self-confident than Angel and, with the help of her four daughters, learned to dress up and use cosmetics. Fidel's friend Teresa Casuso described her as tall, thin, angular, with dyed black hair, when they met in Mexico in late 1957.[22] Lina visited Casuso and other supporters of her sons' movement when Fidel and Raul were fighting in the Sierra Maestra and threatening to destroy sugar crops to undermine Cuba's economy and thus the Batista dictatorship.

"I have come to see you people about the burning of my cane fields. I want you to arrange to have them left alone."

Casuso was no admirer of the Castro matriarch, who by then had been widowed. She was offended by Lina's remark that Cuban army officers, including a local commander, were in the habit of visiting her at Biran and sharing coffee. But it was no secret that Lina sympathized with her sons' enemies. Early in the insurgency she was quoted in the Cuban press lamenting how mothers of government soldiers were suffering because of the conflict. After Fidel and Raul won power and nationalized her properties, Fidel Pino remembered her denouncing Fidel as *mi hijo sin verguenza*, "my shameless son."

In contrast to the way he was treated by Angel, and perhaps to compensate, Raul by all accounts was Lina's favorite son. Even as a child he was more tranquil and affectionate than his brothers, less rebellious, more content to ponder patiently the idiosyncrasies he saw everywhere at Biran. She appreciated the genuine care he always demonstrated for his extended family and his mischievous sense of humor. Juanita recalled that her mother gave Raul the nickname "Muso." It seems to have had no meaning other than as a term of endearment, probably the result of family baby talk. The humorless Fidel, however, was never given a family nickname.

Lina's affection for Raul was evident when they arranged a reunion at his mountain redoubt toward the end of the guerrilla conflict. They had not seen each other since his visit to Biran after being released from prison. Fidel, in contrast, had no interest in seeing his mother while he was preoccupied with waging the guerrilla war. He told Betto that Lina had no contact with him while he was in the mountains because "she was under constant surveillance."[23] Perhaps he didn't recall the photos of Lina, safely at Raul's guerrilla headquarters, that had been published years before.

From Lina's personal collection, the photographs show how readily she adapted to the guerrilla experience. In one she is cradling a pistol with two of Raul's guerrilla comrades, each armed to the teeth, posed next to her, a lone palm tree in the background. In another, she is wearing a beret, readying to aim and fire a rifle. She looks rugged and ready for anything. More genteel women who remembered her from those days said she seemed *de pelo en techo*, like a hairy-chested man.

Much as she regularly did when monitoring goings on at Biran, she appears in another photo comfortably bearing a sidearm, a holstered pistol on her right hip, secured on a thick belt with a shiny metal buckle.[24] There is no record outside of Cuba about how long she spent with Raul and his toughened guerrillas in the hills, or what agenda other than seeing him she may have had. There is a good likelihood, however, that she pleaded with him to intercede with Fidel so that her cane fields would not be burned. She knew that Raul could be reasoned with, but once Fidel had made up his mind, no one—other than perhaps his brother—would be able to budge him.

When her mother, Dominga Gonzalez, died in June 1963 at Biran just two months before Lina herself, it was Raul, not Fidel, who attended the funeral. Soon after, when Lina was dying at Juanita's house in Havana, Raul spent a great deal of time with her. Fidel Pino remembered that he slept in the same room, stroked his mother's head, and cared for her. Twenty-three years later, Juanita Castro told me that Raul cried at Lina's wake but that Fidel "came in strutting, ordering us all around."

Raul's commitment to the extended Castro clan has continued throughout his life. For years, long after she decamped from Biran with her two children, Raul even stayed close to Angel's first wife. When I interviewed Fidel's daughter Alina, in Miami, she told me that in contrast to her father, Raul "has always been a nice person with me."[25] He has also acted as an intermediary arranging visits between Fidel's first wife, whom he divorced after just a few years, and their son Fidelito, who has remained in Cuba.

Today, as he has since the beginning of the revolution, it is Raul who plays the role of Castro paterfamilias. He reportedly hosts regular family gatherings at his home in Havana. Raul has been married to Vilma Espin since early 1959. They have four children, including a rebellious daughter named Mariela, and grandchildren.[26]

Biran was an exhilarating, sometimes dangerous, but also a lonely and isolated place for young boys growing up. Fidel and Raul had cousins there from Lina's side of the family, but Juanita says it was Raul who formed friendships, not Fidel. "Fidel never had any friends," she said, only slightly exaggerating the truth.

Among the multitude of *guajiro* and Haitian boys who lived in the area, none was so privileged or indulged as Fidel. Such playmates would have been wary of him, seeing him as the nearest thing to the crown prince of Angel's domain. Fidel threw tantrums when he did not get his way, was an angry loser at almost any game he played, and bullied other children. Juanita recalled a childhood baseball game.

"His team was losing so he stopped the game and took all the equipment. He hated so much to lose."

All through his life these boyhood traits have persisted. He has never enjoyed close friendships with men who could interact with him more or less as equals. Even Che Guevara—who, years later, may have come closer to him than any other male associate—invariably deferred to Fidel. Since he won power, his "friends" have all been loyal and obsequious followers, Sancho Panzas to his Quixote.

He had little in common with his two older brothers. Pedro Emilio became a writer and a poet, though not of any particular distinction, and was said to be somewhat unstable, working fruitlessly on a novel.[27] Juanita believes that Fidel despised his half-brother because of conflicts over money. That aside, it is difficult to imagine the effete Pedro Emilio and Fidel having any common interests.

Ramon, the eldest of Angel's sons with Lina, has contrasted with Fidel in other ways. He was content to follow in Angel's footsteps as a farmer and country paramour. He had scant interest in school and later was unwilling to join his brothers in their revolutionary and political pursuits. On a small scale he helped to get supplies to them in the sierra. Once, however, expecting a shipment of arms or ammunition from Ramon, Fidel complained that his brother had merely sent him an expensive watch he had no need for. After the revolution, Ramon's lifelong interest in farming was indulged, and since the mid-1980s he has intermittently appeared in ceremonial roles in Cuba and abroad.

Raul was always less athletic and brazen and did not try to participate or compete with Fidel in physically demanding activities. He was more Juanita's confidante, more inclined to stay close to home. Juanita told a Havana newspaper shortly after her brothers won power that they had been very close as children, though she was probably telling the fawning press what it wanted to hear.[28] The best indication of this is that in all of his public remarks, whether in speeches or interviews, Fidel has never spoken of Raul as a boyhood playmate or as anything resembling a friend in adulthood.

Fidel was pressed once by two American visitors. "Do you have many close friends?"

His response was evasive: "I don't really have what you might call a circle of close friends."

He then rambled defensively, commenting on the many *foreign* friends he has, about close associates who might be considered his friends, and employees, including his cooks and chauffeurs and other subordinates he takes fishing with him. He seemed oblivious to the reality that nearly every one of the men he mentioned must obey him, pay him obeisance. Even more telling, it never occurred to him to mention Raul as a friend.[29]

Fidel's sense of autonomy, his apartness, have always been remarkable by any standard. At a precocious age he had begun to demonstrate an extraordinary sense of self-containment. Not just independence, but an emotional ferocity that inculcated in him an unusual exceptionalism that is key to his abiding belief that he has always been destined for greatness. "I can't recall ever having had doubts or lack of confidence. I've never had them," he told interviewers in 1986.[30]

There is no reason to believe he was exaggerating a nearly lifelong determination to prevail against whatever odds, with the conviction that he would succeed and would do so by his own devices.

"I never had a mentor," he told Betto several times. He has said this so often and in so many ways that there can't be any doubt of its odd emotional authenticity. In truth, he has never needed genuine companionship or sharing relationships, although he must surround himself with people nearly all the time. On occasion he has even admitted that he hates to be alone.

"He was different," Juanita told an American author, "he didn't show his feelings easily, he was very reserved."[31] As a child, Fidel's sister recalled in another interview, with a Havana newspaper just after her brothers' victory, that Fidel was "serious and introverted, he read and thought a lot."[32]

He was determined, even as a child of five or six, to forge his own identity, to prevail over his circumstances. Certainly he was ambitious and exceptionally intelligent. As a youngster he spent a great deal of time alone, fantasizing about heroic roles he could play so that like his boyhood heroes—Napoleon, Alexander the Great, and Julius Caesar—his name would also be emblazoned in the history books.

His epic daydreams were fueled by voracious reading. He says that when he was still quite young he consumed a ten-volume history of the French Revolution. When he was ten he also became fascinated with the Spanish Civil War then raging. "A lot of Spaniards lived on my father's farm and some of them could not read. So I read to them all about the war in Spain."[33] It was then, he says, that his lifelong habit of devouring the news began.

"I read all the newspapers, all the international news, ever since the Spanish Civil War." His interest in revolutions and revolutionary heroes was indelibly fixed at an early age.

Fidel's remarkable self-confidence, even as a child, and the expectation that a glorious destiny awaited him, owed a great deal to Angel and Lina. Each of them had risen from abject poverty and obscurity, each methodically plotting advancement, brooking no opposition, and succeeding. Yet Fidel has never given them credit for demonstrating that even illiterate peasants could rise above the masses and become incredibly prosperous.

The ideal of peasant empowerment would become his regime's central tenet, regularly bruited about in speeches and rhetoric. The revolution is for Cuba's *guajiros*, the poor, the once exploited rural folk. One of Fidel's earliest and most ballyhooed government programs was the recruitment of literacy brigades that fanned out across the country to uplift and perfect the *guajiros* even in the most remote communities.

The romanticized peasants, noble and nationalistic in the revolution's credo, would also be among its principal beneficiaries, providing Fidel with his most reliable bloc of popular support. But if for him the connection between the Cuban peasantry and his parents exists at all, it must be deeply submerged in his subconscious.

Juanita has observed that "the personalities of Fidel and my father are very similar . . . very *gallego*."[34] One can search the vast record of Fidel's oratory, interviews, and press conferences, however, and probably find no more than a single reflection suggesting that he ever agreed with that assessment. The shame he felt as a boy and young man about his parents' rustic, *guajiro* simplicity never really abated in adulthood, though over time he learned to disguise it better.

There is, nevertheless, one exception on the record. In a speech Fidel delivered on March 23, 1991, to a group of Cuban secondary school students, words laden with emotional content leaped out of his mouth, as if propelled by some power of their own. The Berlin Wall had been torn down only a little more than a year before; the Soviet Union was in its death throes. He was under enormous pressure.

The opening remarks of his speech to the students were introspective. He reminisced about his own high school years, telling them how he felt when he had arrived in Havana from the countryside for the first time to begin at Belen. He was fifteen. He had never stepped foot in the capital before.

He wanted the students to understand that he could appreciate their trepidation on their first day in the big, strange city. He may even have been seeking some sympathy from them. In what was most likely an unintended confession, he linked himself to his father and all the poor peasants he had known growing up.

"I am a peasant from Biran," he exclaimed.[35]

He had never said anything like that about himself in public before and never would again. His statement was entirely and strangely out of character. It was an implicit admission of the wrenching dualities and contradictions of his childhood. Admitting that his parents were peasants was a truth he rarely cares to admit.

But volunteering that *he* was also a *guajiro* has never—except for this one slip of the tongue—been a part of the grandiose public role he created for himself and that he has performed unrelentingly for decades.

CHAPTER TWO

The Victim of Exploitation

Fidel was twelve years old when his mother Lina, sulking and fearful, composed a remarkable letter to be delivered to Fidel Pino Santos.

Angel's friend was then in his first term as a member of the Cuban congress with the Conservative Party, his political influence growing apace with his wealth. Pino Santos was Angel's most trusted confidante and had a great influence over the wary old *gallego*. Lina had no illusions about how risky her stratagem was, how easily it could backfire. But doing nothing seemed to her the greater danger, so she gambled her fortunes and those of her children that Pino Santos would help. Sent from Biran on December 8, 1938 the letter was a desperate plea for his good offices. She begged him to convince Angel to officially recognize that he was the father of her children and implicitly, to marry her.

"*Estimado Compadre*," it began, meaning both dear friend and esteemed godfather. She said her children—she referred to them as "the poor creatures"—already are learning "the pains of life." They were being tormented, and it was not their fault. Their status was precarious. The older girls were being blocked from admission to Catholic schools by conservative nuns who demanded that they first receive the sacraments. That they were all illegitimate and suffering was more important to Lina than her own uncertain status. But that too had become an issue as her physical labors and organizational talents were contributing substantially to Angel's financial success. By the late 1930s she had become a virtual full partner in Biran's enterprises, though not yet in Angel's household.

She had been bearing his children, one after another, for many years, probably assuming that with each new arrival her leverage was increasing. All seven had been born by the time she wrote Pino Santos. Angela, the eldest, was fourteen. Ramon was a year and a half younger, and then Fidel, followed by Raul, and then Juanita, and Emma. When Lina sent the letter, Augustina, the youngest, was four months old. A marriage certificate was long overdue.

If Angel was ever going to take her as his wife, give her legal standing, and bestow legitimacy on her brood in the eyes of the law, the time had come. Maria Argota had vacated the *casa grande*, the main house at Biran, but still Lina and her children were kept waiting for Angel to acknowledge them legally, to give them the right to bear the Castro name and be accepted by the Church.

She urged Pino Santos to intercede with Angel, "to inculcate in Castro the duty he has to recognize and legalize their situation." She begged him not to tell Angel that she had written. She referred to him deferentially as "Mr. Castro." The letter was typewritten, the language in places so florid that it seems likely Lina had solicited the services of some amanuensis—perhaps the accountant at the farm, who is said to have been particularly close to her—to help compose it.[1]

Most of Fidel's biographers have treated his illegitimacy cautiously, if at all. Tad Szulc concluded that Maria Argota had died after her two children were born, thus clearing the way for Lina. Robert Quirk and Leycester Coltman delicately skimmed over the matter. Others don't mention it. Georgie Anne Geyer, on the other hand, concluded that Fidel's illegitimacy imposed a substantial psychological burden. She quoted Jose Figueres, a former president of Costa Rica, who knew Fidel and said that he "could have suffered terribly from being a bastard son."[2] Those early biographers were all handicapped by the paucity of reliable information about the Castro household available when they were writing, and perhaps too by their understandable concerns not to be associated with antiquarian attitudes about illegitimacy.

However, Fidel's most recent biographer, French journalist Serge Raffy, discovered new information about the family that upholds Figueres's observation.

Fidel's illegitimacy was profoundly traumatic for him as a young boy and also seems to have influenced his outlook as an adult. Raffy found that Fidel was not legally recognized by Angel until five years after Lina wrote Pino Santos. The French author conducted interviews in Cuba and dug up revealing evidence from regional archives.[3]

Though humiliated and estranged from Angel, Maria Argota was still very much his legitimate wife. She would not fade away without a decent settlement, though that was complicated by Cuban law that, before 1940, made divorce difficult.

Under the circumstances, Pino Santos, upon receiving Lina's letter, may have urged his friend to preserve the status quo, to maintain the more respectable schoolteacher as his wife, and to sequester the love children with the servant girl somewhere out of Maria's sight.

To be sure, the cantankerous *gallego* procrastinated. An expensive divorce, marriage to the still very young, uneducated scullery maid, and acceptance of her children as his heirs, might not be in his best interests. It might be better to temporize rather than confront the dilemma head on. The result was that the children were known by Lina's surname—they were Ruz's—until years later, and for lengthy periods the three oldest were at first hidden at Biran, and then banished so Maria could save face.

Raffy discovered that Fidel and his older siblings were not welcome as young children in the main house at Biran, the one place where Maria Argota could still defiantly stand her ground. Instead, they lived in what was known as the *casa de los abuelos*, the Ruz grandparents' little house, by some accounts a hut or a shack. It was near but out of direct sight of the *casa grande*. The three older children were cared for there by their maternal grandmother as Lina toiled in the main house. Angela and Ramon were born in the little *casa*, the grandparents' shack, according to Raffy. Fidel's daughter Alina Fernandez adds that her father spent his first days there as well.[4]

Nothing more certain about Fidel's first few years is known for sure. He and his siblings have never provided a hint that some of them began life amid such uncertainty. Old family photos suggest that if indeed Fidel was born in his grandparents house, and then spent some period of time there in shameful seclusion, there were moments at least when his status seemed assured. In a black and white picture taken when he was about two years old, he is posed like Gainsborough's *Blue Boy*, standing erect in a shiny dark suit fringed with a fussy white collar and cuffs. His right arm is resting on a wicker chair. He seems unhappy, glowering at the camera with a stern and unsmiling countenance.

In that, and another photograph said to have been taken when he was three, he is dressed in finery that no family of a Cuban peasant child at that time could have reasonably hoped for.[5] But Lina was no ordinary peasant girl, and surely she used her wiles and leverage with Angel to extract favors from him for her children. Assuming it is really the young Fidel in the photos, what seems most likely is that during his first few years he was perilously suspended between the two worlds that coexisted at Biran, between Angel's vacillating indulgence and banishment to a peasant shack.

He says he was three or four when his education began in the front row at Biran's version of a little red schoolhouse. It was there where he started to read, and write, and do arithmetic. But he was incorrigible.

"I spent most of my time being fresh in school. I remember that whenever I disagreed with something the teacher said to me, or whenever I got mad, I would swear at her and immediately leave school, running as fast as I could."[6]

Schooling ended abruptly, about two years later, he says, when he and Angela and later Ramon were shunted off to Santiago, supposedly to be tutored in the impoverished home of the Haitian woman who had taught them at Biran. She lived in a dilapidated, damp little house in one of the oldest quarters of the city with her sister and their father. For Fidel that foster home represented a wrenching, shocking abandonment, though in the interview with Betto he did his best to put a good face on it.

"A teacher had led my family to believe I was a very industrious student. She made them believe I was smart and had a talent for learning. That was the real reason why they sent me to Santiago when I was around five."[7]

His formidable cognitive gifts certainly would have been evident by then, but the Haitian house was hardly a place where a bright child could be educated. There was nothing to read, for one thing, just multiplication tables and notebooks. By his own admission Fidel got very little schooling there, but his mathematical skills were awakened. He learned his multiplication and division tables so well, he once boasted, that "sometimes I calculate like a computer."[8]

He spent two and a half, maybe three years with the Haitian foster family, suffering and, he says, wasting his time. He remembers being very skinny, hungry, dirty, and unkempt with scraggly long hair because the Haitians could not afford to pay a barber.

After his brother Ramon arrived, six people—three adults and the three siblings—shared the gruel from a single small container that had to provide both lunch and dinner. It was during the Depression. The stipend Angel—or perhaps Pino Santos—sent for their sustenance was not enough, or as Fidel intimates, the children's food money was being used for other purposes because the Haitian family had almost no other source of income.

He was helpless, required to conform to what he considered the peculiar and oppressive standards of the foster family. They were refined, spoke French, and prohibited the children from using the crude language and barnyard manners learned at Biran. Fidel told Betto he was occasionally abused physically. If, as it seems, he felt great anxiety in this shamed exile, he has never admitted it explicitly or openly discussed the emotions that ate at him during those early formative years. He prefers to speak of the childhood triumphs that came a little later.

His account also indicates that there was no contact with his mother or other relatives, except for one period when the three siblings returned to Biran. He specifically remembered spending three consecutive winter holidays—January sixth, the Christmas feast day when gifts are exchanged in Cuba—at the Haitians' house. More than a half century later, he recalled bitterly that the gifts he found under his pillow each of those years were cheap trinkets, little cardboard and tin trumpets.

"Three times I was given a trumpet, I should have become a musician."

If in fact the three children did not visit Biran during those holiday seasons, their longing for home and their sense of abandonment and imprisonment would have been extreme. It seems from Fidel's account to Betto that they rarely left the dark little house. Lina and other family members seldom if ever visited, and Angel not at all. Raul was just young enough to have been spared the foster home, though he too probably spent most of his first few years at the *casa de los abuelos*, living out of Maria Argota's sight.

The three older children could not have been oblivious to their precarious situation. Fidel especially would have understood that they were in the eye of a towering, unpredictable storm that could at any moment demolish whatever standing or prospects they had at Biran and in Angel's esteem. In its aftermath they might all be relegated to a servants shack and penurious futures, possibly even to lives as subservient *guajiro* laborers. Under Cuban law they had no rights at all to anything of Angel's.

Of all the personal subjects that Fidel avoids discussing, his childhood has been the most rarefied. Most of what is known about his early years before he went to Havana and Belen derives from two interviews. The first, with Carlos Franqui, a one-time close colleague, a writer and fellow revolutionary, the first editor of the official daily newspaper, *Revolucion*, was probably not intended by Fidel for public consumption.[9] The second, the sometimes confessional session with Betto, provides tantalizing details. It is here that Fidel is the most unguarded, coaxed gracefully by the liberation-theology priest into unprecedented reminiscence.

It was no accident either that an empathetic and politically kindred priest was the only interviewer ever to extract so much autobiography from him. A devout Catholic as a youth, Fidel was susceptible to Betto's priestly blandishments. He had confessed his sins regularly to priests as a boy, and at the Dolores middle school in Santiago he attended daily mass. The adults he most admired were the Spanish Jesuits who taught him there and at Belen. Armando Llorente, the Jesuit he was closest to at Belen, remembers Fidel's open displays of religion as a teenager. So it is reasonable that he would be more amenable to conversation with Betto than he has ever been with other interviewers.

Many years after the revolution, Father Llorente reminisced with me about his favorite and certainly most memorable student. During numerous camping expeditions they talked for hours at a time.

"Fidel often spoke of family problems, of not really having a family. He rarely spoke of his parents but suffered considerably as a child. His parents never came to a single event at Belen because they would have been humiliated. The Castros were richer than most Belen families, but Fidel was nonetheless the son of *guajiros*. I gave him lots of reassurance. I counseled him about trauma."[10]

Sessions like those with the Jesuit were rare for the young Fidel, and rarer still for the adult Castro. But his dialogues with the Brazilian priest in 1985 revealed the contours of indelible childhood anxieties. He spoke to Betto with some passion about his exile at the Haitians' foster home. He felt rejected by his father and abandoned by his mother. He remembers that period as his St. Helena, his Siberia, or something worse. The experience seared him in ways he would never forget—if never fully acknowledge either.

Raffy writes that this was the cruel price Lina had to pay to preserve a measure of peace at Biran. She had to give up her children temporarily to maintain whatever leverage she had with Angel, whatever hopes she held of someday displacing Maria Argota. Fidel, the most impressionable and brightest of her children, told Betto quite plainly: "I was the victim of exploitation."[11]

It was a remarkable admission. There may be no other record of his acknowledging so explicitly experiences of personal vulnerability during any period in his life. He has occasionally discussed the nearly two years he spent in prison in the mid-1950s, when in many ways he thrived under minimum security conditions. Reading voraciously from a huge personal library, holding regular meetings with his followers, and in regular touch with the outside, he was anything but helpless or exploited during that incarceration on the Isle of Pines.

In fact, other than the childhood confinement in Santiago, there are no periods or episodes in his life when he has admitted to having felt helpless or exploited. None of his biographers or former associates has ever described such a situation. It would be supremely out of character for him to admit that as an adult he might ever have been anything less than in control.

Strength, valor, and decisiveness are the personal and performance traits he values the most. They are the qualities he demands from all those around him and he expects to encounter as well in his adversaries. If anything, his legendary courage and propensity to take risks have led him at times to wanton, even irrational behavior, but allegations of pusillanimity have never been credible. To reveal any type of weakness, vacillation, or personal dependency on others has been anathema to him. His insistence that he has never had a mentor reflects that singularity of spirit, his extraordinary sense of personal sovereignty that he admits began in his childhood. He told Carlos Franqui in the mid-1950s: "I can't have any weaknesses. No matter how small they might be today, you would never be able to count on me tomorrow."[12]

These defining attitudes probably were fixed in Fidel's psychological structure during his formative years in Santiago. His acknowledgment to Betto of being subjugated and exploited when living in the foster home seems to establish a direct link to his adult obsession with themes of exploitation and injustice. These twin evils would become the defining, inviolable keys to his entire revolutionary project. Combating exploitation and injustice would provide the enduring justifications for nearly everything that followed in Cuban domestic and foreign policies.

And consistent with his adult character, the pre-teenage Fidel did not remain a helpless, exploited victim for long. He conceived of and then launched a series of childhood rebellions of escalating ferocity that, presaging later revolutionary exploits, relieved all of the worst conditions he had endured. Through the exercise of personal fortitude, devious manipulation, and militance—including threats and acts of violence—he managed as a child to prevail in situations in which anyone less determined would have meekly given up.

He told Betto and Franqui of his ability to succeed when under pressure, to rebound psychologically by seizing the initiative, to take command of situations, and in the end to prevail over adversity and adversaries. Triumphant in ending once and for all the exploitation and injustice he had suffered in the Santiago foster home, Fidel braced himself for his adult revolutionary missions.

After about two years of desultory tutoring by the foster family, Fidel began attending La Salle, a respected Christian Brothers school within walking distance of the Haitians' house. Pino Santos had used his influence to get him admitted even though Fidel had not yet been baptized or received his first communion. He was still far from his family, but it was a liberating development that allowed him for the first time to have sustained interaction with middle- and upper-class contemporaries.

It was also then when the taunting by other boys began. He told Franqui, "I was on my guard." They goaded him as the "Jew," he said, because he was not baptized. "People used to call me a Jew . . . He's a Jew. I didn't know the meaning of the word Jew, but there was no doubt it had a negative connotation, that it was something disgraceful."[13]

He was probably not taunted, as he claims, because he was unbaptized—hardly the kind of invisible omission that would mobilize little boys to cruelty—but because he was illegitimate and a backwoods rustic. The taunt he most likely heard—the *hijo de puta* he so often snarls himself—would have been directed, of course, both at him and his mother. His unmistakable *guajiro* affect, appearance, and speech pattern would have been red flags to supercilious city boys eager to persecute him. Many years later, a close friend at the University of Havana told one of his biographers that Fidel would rather pardon a physical assault against him than endure someone's ridicule.[14]

He soon realized too, apparently for the first time, that passivity would get him nowhere, that without taking action, without precipitating events, he could damage his situation further. Years later in a letter quoted by Carlos Franqui, he said: "It is better to sin through excess than through default, which can only lead to failure."

If he aggressively seized power in the foster home, he could improve his lot now that he was enrolled at La Salle. "I was a day student, and felt I was worse off than the boarders. They were taken to the beach or out on walks on Thursdays and Sundays. My life was very dull."

He was in the first grade, six or seven years old, and it was at that impressionable age that he organized the first of his many rebellions against authority. He decided that he wanted to be a boarding student to escape the misery of living in the Haitians' house. So he launched a confrontational campaign against them. He explained his strategy to Franqui: "I made up my mind then, and proceeded to rebel and insult everyone. I told them all the things I had been wanting to tell them for a long time. I behaved so terribly that they took me straight back to school and enrolled me as a boarder. It was a great victory for me . . . From then on I definitely became my own master and took charge of all my own problems without advice from anyone."[15]

"I had acted by instinct—or rather, on intuition," he told Betto, "which was how I really functioned."

What Fidel euphemistically likes to describe as "intuition" might better be described as paranoia or prescience. Through all of his subsequent peregrinations, both before and after winning power, he has demonstrated uncanny survival skills, somehow eluding ambushes, betrayals, and numerous assassination attempts. As a university student involved in violent political gang warfare, he survived close calls on more than one occasion, including in April 1949, when he avoided a serious assassination plot.[16] Frequently in life or death situations he has gambled or guessed the best escape route, always successfully. Colleagues have told how in the Sierra Maestra, more than once, he somehow sensed that a military ambush was imminent, just in time to evade it.

Such seemingly preternatural skills have never been attributed to, or claimed by, the more linear and terrestrial Raul. Perhaps that is why he so admires his brother's ability "to smell danger like a bloodhound."

"At the personal level, among the many virtues I have often valued highly in him is his great capacity to foresee danger and sense with incredible precision enemy plans when they are still confusing or imperceptible to other comrades."[17]

A classic example of Fidel's ability to sniff out dangers dates to his first months as a guerrilla in the Sierra Maestra. Norberto Fuentes, a leading Cuban intellectual and novelist now in exile, was once close to the Castro brothers. He told me a story that Fidel himself has not yet fully revealed in public.[18]

Eutimio Guerra was one of the first peasants to join the Castro's guerillas, and with members of his family struggling to subsist in the rough Sierra Maestra mountains region, he provided provisions and intelligence on local conditions. One day, as Fidel and Eutimio, and a few others, were resting and cleaning their weapons in a secluded grove, a relaxed, seemingly innocuous conversation ensued.

"Fidel," Eutimio asked out of the blue, "what will the revolution do for me once it is victorious?"

Fidel imperceptibly drew in a deep breath. He knew with cold certainty in that instant, as if the shaft of a saber had plunged into his chest, that Eutimio had already betrayed him. His intuitive paranoid sense told him that the simple but shrewd peasant had been asking similar questions of Batista's military commanders in the area, that he was weighing his prospects, seeking the best potential deal from whichever side could help him the most. Fidel's armed band numbered no more than twenty or so at the time, and to an uneducated peasant they probably seemed more like ordinary bandits and outlaws than idealistic heroes. Eutimio really cared little for either side; he was adrift in what for him was an incomprehensible conflict.

Fidel discussed Eutimio at length in a long speech in June 1987 that was devoted entirely to betrayal and traitors, themes that recur regularly in his oratory.

"Eutimio was cynical. I will not tell anecdotes about that now. One day I will tell the whole story. . . . He even slept next to me with two grenades and a pistol and asked where the sentry was. However he had instructions to kill me. . . . Actually he did not dare . . . I went and gathered a number of very subtle details until I saw the full picture."

Fidel personally conducted the interrogation. Eutimio did not plead for his life, refusing to say anything except that he should be shot.

Raul was in charge of that. He wrote dispassionately about it, as always, in his campaign diary.

"They tied his hands and brought him to the camp. He was terrified and his eyes were bulging out of their sockets. There stood the traitor who had led the enemy to our camp on three different occasions. . . . My impression was that he was disgusted with himself and that his insistent demands to be executed were nothing but a show of cowardice, a way to get out of his predicament as soon as possible."[19]

Fidel left the camp to recline under a palm thatch shelter as the execution was arranged. This would always be his modus operandi when the coup de grace was delivered to an enemy of the revolution. There is no record of him ever participating directly in an execution, of either literally or symbolically getting blood on his hands.

Executions would always be Raul's responsibility. He was already experienced by the time he had to dispatch Eutimio. Raul had first been cast by Fidel in the role in Mexico City a few months earlier. In late November 1956, as they were making the final preparations to set sail for Cuba and begin the insurgency, Fidel ordered him to murder a young colleague he suspected of being a Batista informant. There seems to have been no incriminating evidence. Apparently it was just Fidel's paranoid intuition, his inordinate fear of betrayal. Raul is said to have murdered the man with cool detachment. Many years later Raul told close colleagues in Havana about the incident. His chief of staff at the time, Alcibiades Hidalgo, was present and, after his defection in 2002, the story for the first time was put on the public record.[20]

It was Raul's first known act of lethal violence. Fidel was probably testing how ruthless his previously impassive younger brother could be, how he would respond under duress, how he would measure up as a leader of the revolution.

Later that night, driving at high speeds on narrow, winding Mexican roads, traveling from the capital to the little Gulf coast town of Tuxpan where the *Granma* was docked and ready to set sail, Raul reportedly recorded his second kill—a hapless Mexican, probably a poor peasant walking along the shoulder of the road in the dark. Raul is said to have accidentally run down the peasant, killing him instantly. According to a former close associate who heard the story from Raul, he did not pause to investigate and never reported the incident to Mexican authorities.

So Raul was experienced as an executioner when he was again faced with that necessity as a guerrilla. Eutimio Guerra was led away. Raul noted dryly in his diary that the execution on February 17, 1957, occurred exactly one month, almost to the hour, after "we had executed Chicho Osorio, a man notorious for the crimes he had committed against the peasants."[21]

Like so many others in later years who were executed, purged, or imprisoned, Eutimio was largely oblivious to how easily one could run afoul of the Castros. He had no sense at all about the requirements of their moral code that requires an unspoken blood oath of unquestioning fealty. Others, undoubtedly like the murdered colleague in Mexico City, have been innocent of any real disloyalty though unfortunate enough to have fallen victim to Fidel's suspicions.

Over the years, the victims of many other executions would go to their graves never understanding what they had done wrong or why. Fidel has never had the slightest qualms about preemptively inflicting the ultimate penalty on anyone thought to be even contemplating disloyalty of any type. His well-tuned fear of betrayal may very well have originated in childhood.

The Castros' once trusted revolutionary colleague Norberto Fuentes adds a final important codicil to the Eutimio Guerra story. The experience also steeled Fidel in another crucial survival strategy, setting the stage for how he would govern. Fidel realized that he was the only one in his small band of guerrillas who had divined that Eutimio was a traitor. Even Raul had not understood this. Nor had Fidel's trusted bodyguard, who, more than anyone else, had a duty to be suspicious and alert.

As a result, Fidel concluded that he would need to create independent, competitive intelligence and security services so that in the future the carelessness of one might be compensated for by the diligence of another. He would need them not only to track down actual and potential Judases but to detect and eliminate all possible conspiracies even before they coalesced.[22] The result was that Raul set out immediately after their victory to start organizing the revolutionary secret services that would effectively operate as among the best in the world.

The survival skills that Fidel began to develop as a child—being on his guard, fearing betrayal and rejection, improvising solutions, seizing initiatives, trusting almost no one, threatening and committing acts of violence, and relying on his instincts rather than waiting for fate to be dealt him—have carried over through the rest of his life. Because he has applied his ruthless operating code without mercy and without exception, he has managed to survive in power virtually without any serious challenges since January 1959.

A second childhood rebellion—this time a violent one—occurred at La Salle after Fidel was repeatedly abused physically by one of his teachers, a member of the religious order of the Christian Brothers.

"He came up to me from behind and hit me on the head. This time I turned on him, right then and there, threw a piece of bread at his head and started to hit him with my fists and bite him. I don't think I hurt him much, but the daring outburst became an historic event at the school."[23]

Several years later, Ramon Mestre, a prep school contemporary of Fidel's at Belen had a similar experience. He recounted it to me in 1986 in a restaurant in Coral Gables, adjacent to Miami, after having served every day of a twenty year prison term for opposing the revolution.

"When he came to Belen," Mestre began, Fidel "looked like a crazy *guajiro.*" Mestre and others were in the habit of calling him *el loco*, the crazy one, because of his reckless behavior and demeanor.

The San Pedro family lived in a house near Belen, and Fidel, who had a crush on their daughter, was visiting her. Mestre went out in the street in front of her house and shouted at Fidel, "Come on out *loco*." Never shrinking from a fight, and in a rage over the taunting, Fidel rushed out. During their struggle, Mestre says, Fidel failed to land a single blow on him, but furiously bit him on the arm. He then ran into his dorm room to look for the pistol he kept there.

Father Llorente remembered the incident as well. He told me he intervened, saying: "Fidel, why do you have this pistol?"

"Father, I will kill him."

By the time Llorente confiscated the pistol, Fidel was already calm.

"It's all right father, I have another."[24]

When he discussed this incident with me, Llorente remembered that Fidel readily expressed rage, but never sadness or tears.

The most astonishing of Fidel's childhood rebellions is one he related to Franqui, though in his conversations with Betto he deleted the most psychologically incriminating details. His behavior was extreme, perhaps sociopathic. Without describing to the Brazilian friar exactly what he threatened to do, Fidel justified his frightening outburst in his characteristic fashion.

"I think I had very clear ideas about the matter—the result of instinct; because of some notions of justice and dignity that I was acquiring; or perhaps because, when I was still quite young, I'd begun to see incorrect, unfair things by which I was victimized."[25]

It is not clear from his accounts how old he was, though he was definitely not yet a teenager. He and his two brothers had become so unruly at La Salle that his family was told to withdraw them. Ramon was delighted with the chance to return to Biran and be free to work on the farm. Raul, much to his pleasure, was enrolled in a rigorous military school in Oriente run by a retired sergeant. A photo of the young Raul, wearing a military field cap and straddling the barrel of a small cannon, was probably taken when he attended that school. It shows Cuba's future defense minister quite happily astride the cannon, with an inscrutable smile on his face. He was seven years old.[26]

Fidel was not offered the option of military school, which surely he would have rejected. He was ambitious, still an outcast of sorts at Biran, and was appalled by the prospect of becoming an apprentice farmer there. He was brought back forcefully knowing that his chances of escaping a life of rural drudgery would all but evaporate if he was compelled to stay. He had no legal standing with the still remote Angel.

Fidel grew more and more surly, demanding that he be sent back to La Salle. "It was a decisive moment in my life."

He pleaded with Lina, telling her it wasn't fair, insisting on being allowed to return to school. At first she was adamant because she knew Angel was opposed. But Fidel, in a soaring rage, warned her that if they did not allow him to go back to La Salle as a boarding student, he would set fire to the wooden *casa grande*. He would burn it down.

"I really threatened to set the whole place on fire if I wasn't sent back to school," he told Franqui. "So they decided to send me back."[27]

At that time he must have hated that off-limits house where only Angel's legitimate family had free reign, where he was a pariah. It was a tinderbox to be sure, and his threat was so powerful, so credible that Lina was able to persuade Angel to yield to Fidel's indomitable will. There is no way of knowing for certain, but this standoff may well have been one of those melodramatic turning points in his evolving relationship with Angel. The tough old *gallego* may actually have admired his young son's courage and ferocity. The credible threat of calamitous violence had proved a success.

A number of years later, toward the end of summer in 1954, the *casa grande* did burn to the ground. Fidel and Raul were in prison on the Isle of Pines at the time, and the fire was not the result of arson. Angel was at home alone, resting after lunch. At about two in the afternoon he lit a cigar while still in bed, and soon got up to turn on the radio. He forgot the smoldering cigar he had left at the edge of the wooden table at his bedside.

It was during the dry season, and there was almost no one around to help quench the fire because it occurred during the "dead time" after the sugar *zafra* was finished and workers had dispersed. The rambling wooden structure was quickly engulfed in flames, reduced to ashes and rubble in only about twenty minutes. Angel, about 79 at the time, managed to scramble out, apparently unhurt. Fidel mentioned the blaze, somewhat ruefully, in a letter from prison. Years later a slightly idealized reproduction of the house was constructed on the site as a tourist attraction.[28]

Fidel was not christened until after he was eight, a disgrace he says that imposed a terrible stigma on him. The sacrament normally is performed on newborns in the sacristies or near the side altars of Catholic churches. Inherited sins are washed away by the baptismal waters. Babies are welcomed into the faith, their souls cleansed so that by the time they are five or six they can receive the Church's second childhood sacrament, holy communion. Baptism was rarely waived as a requirement for admission into Catholic schools, and it bestowed a certain social standing.

Godparents are essential accessories in the ceremony. In theory, at least, they assume responsibilities for the child second only to those of the parents. For an upwardly mobile, ambitious Cuban boy such as Fidel, the choice of a godfather was a matter of considerable import. A wisely chosen one could act as a mentor, a spiritual and intellectual guide, and could enhance one's social standing or even lubricate a political career. In all respects Fidel's namesake and intended godfather, the wealthy and prominent Fidel Pino Santos, was a propitious choice. But for reasons that remain unclear, he never fulfilled that role.

To Fidel's lifelong dismay, his godfather turned out instead to be Louis Hipolyte Hibbert, the Haitian consul in Santiago, Angel's canny cohort in the trafficking of Haitian farm workers, the abusive foster father. Fidel remembers walking with Hibbert to the cathedral in Santiago where he was sprinkled with holy water and baptized.

"The consul of the poorest country in Latin America," he caustically told Betto, somehow became his godfather.

Angel was not present, though the more religious Lina was. For several years—until he took matters into his own hands—Fidel's middle name would be the un-Cuban, unpronounceable, and for him humiliating Hipolyte or Hipólito.[29]

Pino Santos had committed to be his young namesake's godfather, but according to Fidel, year after year he was unable to be present for the ceremony. He said the problem was merely that the annual visit of the lone priest from Mayari would have to coincide with Pino Santos's presence at Biran. The long delay was his namesake's fault, by his account, and it was therefore because of him that Fidel was taunted by the other boys in Santiago.

Fifty years later he still remembered the christening imbroglio with resentment. But the self-serving account he shared with Betto was largely a contrivance. By blaming Pino Santos for his belated baptism, Fidel was trying to conceal the real reasons for his childhood sufferings. Regardless, his criticism of Fidel Pino Santos ranged from the petty to the damning.

"He did not give me many gifts, none, in fact that I can remember."

On other occasions he has denounced Pino Santos as a "usurer" and corrupt establishment politician.

"I don't remember a single instance when Don Fidel solved any of my father's problems."[30]

Pino family members say that their patriarch always considered himself Fidel's godfather. Fidel maintained close and dependant relationships with several members of the family for many years prior to the Moncada attack. While he lived in Havana, he received a regular allowance bankrolled by Angel through Pino Santos. From the mid-1940s until the early 1950s, a large number of checks in amounts typically of 100 or 200 pesos (the Cuban peso was worth about a dollar at the time) were signed by Pino Santos and made out to Fidel. Many of these checks were intended for Fidel's tuition or expenses at Belen and were cashed by the school. The rest Fidel endorsed himself.[31]

He was often at the Pino family house in Havana. Fidel Pino Santos was living in the late 1940s and early 1950s in Santiago while Fidel, Raul, and some of the other Castro children were in Havana. So as a result it was Pino Santos's son, Fidel Pino, and his wife who assumed the responsibility for doling out the allowances from Angel's trust. In the early 1950s Fidel was a regular visitor at the Pino home near his apartment so he could collect his stipends. The lavishly embellished Italianate mansion was enormous, three stories high with a tile roofed bell tower above.

Fidel flirted with Pino's daughter and charmed the cooks and household staff. With his legendary appetite flaring, he would typically come into the house, and ask, "What's cooking?" He bought a dog, a Doberman pinscher, but soon realized he could not keep it in his own small apartment. The Pinos had a dog of their own so they agreed to board Fidel's to keep theirs company. The dogs were named Whiskey and Soda. Family members recall too that Fidel visited Pino Santos frequently when the old man was gravely ill in Havana and showed his respects by attending his funeral. They conclude that Fidel's account of his christening is self-serving, intended to conceal childhood demons.

Ironically, it surely rankles Fidel too that the stout and solemn Pino Santos did manage to find time to assume the honors at Raul's christening—and officially to become *his* godfather. That this reversal of fortunes involving the

Castro brothers and their respective godfathers has been a sensitive subject between them is suggested by Raul's avoidance of any known discussion of the matter either on or off the record.

Typically too, Raul's fond memories of the Pino Santos clan contrasted with Fidel's. The first January after the triumph of the revolution, back in Havana for the first time since the summer of 1955, Raul made a stop at the imposing Pino house on Seventeenth Street in the Vedado neighborhood. He reminisced for a couple of hours with family members, telling tales of his experiences as a guerrilla leader, and he was charming, as he can be when it matters to him.

Raul had earlier also received checks signed by Fidel Pino Santos, though always in smaller amounts than his brother's stipend. And unlike Fidel, Raul did not forget old friends and their favors. Usually intrepid in enforcing revolutionary edicts, he was lenient with a Pino family member. A grandson of Fidel Pino Santos, also named Fidel, who had been a friend of Raul's in the early 1950s, was allowed to go into exile with some valuable possessions that normally would have been confiscated by the revolutionary government.

Some of the tensions related to the children's illegitimacy began to ease when Maria Argota finally agreed to leave Angel's house. It seems to have been in January 1936. Fidel was nine and a half years old. It was only then that he and Lina's other children were allowed regular access to the *casa grande*. It is not yet known how the divorce was accomplished, but Pino Santos seems to have helped engineer the solution for his friend. Maria Argota moved with her two children temporarily to Mayari, and soon after to the first floor of Pino Santos's house at 357 Corona Street, in the old quarter of Santiago. Later they resettled again, in Havana.

Fidel was not legally acknowledged by Angel until December 11, 1943. Angel traveled from Biran to the magistrate's office, the *ayuntamiento*, in the picturesque little town of Cueto, near Biran, where doctor Amador Ramirez Sigas, the municipal judge in charge of civil records, signed a notarized document that recognized Fidel Alejandro Castro Ruz as Angel and Lina's son. He was seventeen years old, a student at Belen. Raul and the other children were legitimized at the same time.[32]

Schoolmates and teachers in Havana had always known him as Fidel Castro, so in the unlikely event that the middle name Hipolyte or Hipólito still clung to him, it had been well concealed, probably simply ignored. The confusion about Fidel's middle names is compounded by the existence of a Cuban government secondary school diploma issued in September 1945 in the name of Fidel Casiano Castro Ruz. Raffy, the French biographer, says that Fidel took the initiative when he was legitimized to replace the imposed middle names with his new one, Alejandro. Alexander the Great had been among his childhood heroes and role models.[33]

By taking the Macedonian prince and warrior's name, he forged a permanent link with his fantasy world of historical heroes. Alejandro would be Fidel's *nom de plume* when he wrote for underground publications in the early 1950s. Later it also served as his *nom de guerre*. In three different variations—Alejandro, Alexis, and Alex—he would obsessively give his middle name to sons by his second marriage. Raul's only son is yet another Alejandro.

The legal action at the Cueto town hall acknowledged once and for all the paternity that Angel had apparently conceded at some earlier time. It is not known exactly when that occurred, though clearly it was sometime in the aftermath of what turned out to be the decisive December 1938 letter Lina had sent requesting Fidel Pino Santos's intervention.

Angel completed a last will and testament in August 1956, just a few months before he died. He left one third of his sizeable estate to Lina who was also named executor. The remaining two thirds was divided equally among his nine acknowledged children.[34]

We Will All Be Heroes

Belen was the largest and most prestigious collegiate prep school on the island, probably in all of the Caribbean, a stepping stone for the sons of the wealthiest and most influential Cuban families. The royal charter that established it in 1854, originally in the center of Havana, was signed by Spanish Queen Isabella II. By the time Fidel and Raul enrolled in the 1940s, the elite institution sprawled across more than sixty acres in what was then a Havana suburb, near the Tropicana nightclub. Perhaps to contrast the school with that infamous fleshpot, the Jesuits advertised it as the "Palace of Education."

Many of the most important differences in the characters, personalities, and styles of the Castro brothers were first apparent when they were boarding students there. Fidel thrived while Raul crashed. For Raul it was a brief and humiliating experience, and the only time he talked about it on the record, about forty-five years later, he was still bitter. Fidel remembers his time at Belen fondly and many times has spoken favorably about his Jesuit instructors and even about his religious training.

Fidel had lobbied his family persistently to be transferred from the small and provincial Dolores. He wanted to be in the capital. He sought greater challenges, a more strategically located launching platform for his ambitions, and he no doubt wanted to leave behind the unpleasant memories associated with

Santiago. His years at Belen, beginning in 1941, were the happiest in his life until then, and in retrospect they were easily the most carefree he has ever had.

Characteristically, he made the best of the splendid opportunities Belen provided. Many of his rough edges, but not his undaunted spirit, were smoothed over. Intellectually he began to blossom under the doting guidance of the Spanish priests who formed the majority of the faculty. He was an outstanding athlete, admired especially for his incredible tenacity. Distinctive adult character traits and habits began to be shaped and expressed. In short, as the administrators of elite male prep schools have always been prone to claim, they received a boy at Belen and graduated a sturdy young man.

One classmate recalled that when Fidel arrived, "he looked like a *guajirito*. His speech pattern was rough and his crude eating style was that of a country boy."[1] Initial shyness gave way as he became comfortable with his more sophisticated classmates, but he was never especially sociable and did not confide in others. "He was a little difficult, not very open," another schoolmate remembered.[2]

Nonetheless, the time at Belen was probably the only chapter in his long life in which he was not despised by large numbers of his peers and contemporaries. He distinguished himself in numerous ways, succeeding at almost everything Belen offered, especially in debate and oratory, competitive sports, and mountaineering.

Raul followed in his overachieving brother's footsteps, arriving at Belen later in the same year that Fidel had left. By his own account he went reluctantly. He had rebelled against the religious rigors of Dolores in Santiago, preferring the small military school he transferred to later. It was difficult, especially for shy and insecure boys, as Raul certainly was, to be boarders at Belen; the weekends were especially lonely. When Raul was there he probably almost never saw Fidel, who lived nearby but was absorbed in political life at the University of Havana.

The Jesuits found Raul apathetic and disinterested. After Fidel's intensity and promise, he was a great disappointment and was expelled not long after he began. His version, however, is that he went "on strike." Lacking in confidence and fearing he could not match his brother's accomplishments, he did not even try. No student at Belen at the time has any memory of Raul's presence there.

The recollections of Jesuits who knew him then suggest that he was withdrawn and suffered from a sense of inferiority. Everything Fidel had done brilliantly before him, he did badly. He was not athletic, did not excel in hiking or camping, demonstrated none of the leadership qualities the Jesuits encouraged, and was a terrible student. His disinterest probably stemmed from acute homesickness as well.

Father Llorente recalled that Raul attended Belen for less than a year. "He had none of Fidel's qualities, and seemed very limited intellectually."

Father Feliz, the principal, with whom I talked in San Juan, Puerto Rico, thought Raul did not stay even that long, only about three months, he recalled. Raul was so rebellious that he was asked to leave.

Another Jesuit, Father Quevedo, had the most colorful, if also the harshest, recollections. Raul performed at Belen about as well as "a sack of potatoes," he told me without any rancor when I interviewed him at the quaint Catholic retreat house in the picturesque mountain village of Aibonito in central Puerto Rico, where he had retired. He said the family was urged to come to Havana and retrieve Raul because he could not manage at Belen and would never be able to. The experience for Raul was a humiliating calamity from which he did not recover for quite a few years. His failure there became one of the many burdens he bears stoically.

Later, after he became Cuba's defense minister, he presided over the school's extinction, at least as it had been known for more than a century in Cuba. He shut Belen down, transforming its facilities into a military training center, the Gomez Brothers Technical Institute, named after two cooks at the school when Fidel was there and who later joined his rebel movement.

By 1960 the Jesuits and most of their young charges, along with their families, were going into exile. A brand new Belen, with some of its same faculty and students, was relocated to Miami in 1961. At its commodious new campus it has carried forth the Jesuit traditions of its distinguished Havana parent. I taught a number of Belen graduates at Georgetown University.

The Jesuits remembered Fidel much more vividly than they did Raul. They had taken a special interest in him, working to encourage and sharpen his natural leadership qualities and to inspire in him a solid religious faith. They did not consider Fidel promising material for a religious vocation, but their next most important mission was to train Cuba's future political leaders. He was an apt and eager candidate for those attentions: a star athlete always striving to excel, the adventurous captain of the school's explorers club, and one of the most proficient at rhetoric and public speaking.

He grew accustomed to being told he would be a great leader some day. Father Quevedo remembered how "thrilled and proud" Fidel was to hear that. Father Llorente affectionately considered him "an original, truly unique. I encouraged him to do great things."

But Father Feliz, who years later would act as a trusted messenger between Fidel in the Sierra Maestra and one of Batista's generals, was not impressed. "He was a great liar. I wasn't able to influence him much." And Father Quevedo, who was Fidel's spiritual adviser, told me that he "never came to see me once for this purpose . . . he was without scruples." They all agreed, however, that he possessed an extraordinary intelligence.[3]

Fidel was inducted into the elite Avellaneda literary academy, really a forensics club, and although one of his classmates recalls how shy and nervous he was at first, it was there he learned declamation and debate. His diction and enunciation improved; rural colloquialisms in his speech were expunged one by one; he learned how to modulate and inflect when speaking and to gesticulate with broad reaches and stabbing thrusts. Under the Jesuits' tutelage, his bearing became ramrod erect, shoulders arched back and jaw thrust forward—the oratorical stance Cubans and the world would later come to know so well.

He practiced trilling his r's, a classic linguistic flourish in Spanish-speaking countries. This would later become a hypnotically mesmerizing performance device. "It is the duty of revolutionaries to make revolutions," he would intone in militant speeches in the 1960s, verbally caressing and protracting the r's so that he all but chanted the word *revolucionario* in an almost liturgical cadence. Some of the Jesuits, filled with religious fervor when preaching from the altar, were his unacknowledged role models for future revolutionary sermons.

They taught him how to formulate arguments, to speak at length about one or two concepts, and then to debate them pro and con until absolutely nothing new could be wrung out of a topic. Father Feliz told me Fidel "learned to speak for hours about only two or three different ideas." A requirement for admission to the Avellaneda society was to be able to deliver a ten minute speech without notes and without knowing the topic until an hour before. Fidel had difficulty at first but soon was able to meet those standards. He became one of the best debaters, aided by his photographic memory.

Jose Ignacio Rasco, Fidel's prep school and university classmate, remembered his memorization abilities as "pathological." Just before tests for which he had not bothered to study because he was disorganized and more interested in sports, Fidel would rip pages from books, memorize them, and then tear them to shreds.[4]

Sixty years after they were classmates at Belen, Juan Grau also vividly remembered Fidel's gifts for memorization. Nearly everyone who has had contact with Fidel concedes that his cognitive abilities are extraordinary, but Grau considers his memory even more remarkable than his intelligence.

"He could remember books page by page, everything he read . . . I've never known anyone with a memory like that," Grau told me from his home in Mexico City.

The five- and six-hour extemporaneous speeches Fidel started delivering once he won power in 1959, almost never with more than just a few jottings in front of him at the podium, had been well rehearsed when he was a teenager.

All through his life he has reveled in showing off his photographic memory. In meetings and interviews with foreign reporters or dignitaries, he has enjoyed rattling off mind-numbing statistics, complicated historical sagas, and trivia from the distant past. At an international conference on the Cuban Missile Crisis held in Havana in 1992, he delivered long monologues, some lasting thirty and forty minutes, with details and obscure facts about the nuclear showdown between the United States and the Soviet Union that had occurred thirty years earlier. He is so much in command of details that no one—interviewers or subordinates—dares to challenge or correct him.

It is not just the printed page that is seared in his memory. Going up into the Sierra Maestra mountains to begin the insurgency at the end of 1956 after the *Granma* landing, he found himself in unknown territory. He knew the highland terrain near Biran like the back of his hand, but he had never spent any time in the more rugged range where he established his guerrilla headquarters.

Guillermo Garcia was the first peasant to join Castro's forces there. He was amazed at how quickly Fidel memorized the contours of every knoll and crevice in the areas he traversed in those mountains. In 1965, Garcia was asked about Fidel by an American reporter.

"In six months he knew the whole Sierra Maestra better than any *guajiro* who was born here. He never forgot a place where he went. He remembered everything—the soil, the trees, who lived in each house. I used to go all over those mountains. But in six months Fidel knew the Sierra Maestra better than I did, and I was born and raised here."[5]

Fidel's memory has served him well as both sword and shield politically, but it also has a blunt downside. He often uses it, intentionally and not, in ways that intimidate Cuban officials who cannot possibly know what esoteric portion of their brief Fidel may have memorized and therefore understands better than they do. Naturally, they live in dread of being challenged at any time and found lacking. To be sure, he is impatient, even contemptuous of those who can't or won't keep track of minutiae.

When he was in the Sierra Maestra he monitored every detail. From day to day he knew precisely how many unspent cartridges each of his men had and on occasion challenged some who could not account for a single bullet gone astray.

Forty-seven years later, discussing this obsession during a press conference, he said he was proud of those unusual skills. He was oblivious, however, to how his subordinates and associates all through the years have been cowed into silence or fear by the way he wields them.

"I knew the bullets that each type of rifle required, how many we had in reserve and everything . . . look, I do not hold people in high regard if they do not take care of details or need about ten advisers to tell them this and that."[6]

The Belen years coincided with World War II when Cuba was a reliable American ally and Fidel was in the mainstream. Three of his classmates once ran away from school, trying to reach the U.S. naval base at Guantanamo. They planned to enlist in the American armed forces so they could join the war against the Axis powers, as many young Cubans were doing. He had planned to go with them, according to Father Llorente, but had a last-minute change of heart.

It is not surprising that he has never spoken of that episode. Such a life-altering adventure would have been in character, but going into military training and possibly war as a lowly enlisted man would not. He has always coveted leadership roles, avoiding situations where he would be a subordinate, vulnerable to the will of others. Perhaps he decided not to go with the other boys because he knew so little then about the United States or perhaps because he did not fully sympathize with the Allied cause.

Fidel did not acquire coherent anti-American attitudes while at Belen, but there were undercurrents tugging him in that direction. A letter he had earlier sent to President Roosevelt, in November 1940—"My Good Friend Roosevelt," it began in stilted but readily understandable English is preserved at the National Archives in Washington. Fidel wrote it when he was a student at Dolores. The letter was an attention-getting stunt—he asked the president to send him a ten-dollar bill—rather than a reflection of any sincere interest in American political life.

The White House's formulaic response was posted on a school bulletin board, and Fidel, as he had hoped, was instantly the center of attention. The incident points up an interesting facet of the young Fidel, and the revolutionary adult he became, which has been neglected by his chroniclers. Franklin Roosevelt, the consummate politician and public communicator, and his sweeping New Deal reform program, seem to have been of virtually no interest to Fidel.[7]

The larger truth is that he has never been attracted to political reformers of any kind or their programs. Later in life this teenage perspective would be elevated to a critical strategic stance: reform is the most insidious enemy of revolution. Successful reformers preempt revolutionary sentiment by implementing changes that assuage radical urges in a society. As the New Deal did in the United States during the Depression, reform programs turn down the heat of popular unrest and dissatisfaction. They deter cleansing revolutionary change.

Although the teenage Fidel was not yet anti-American, he seems to have had no particular empathy or attraction for the Anglo-Saxon world either. Juan Rovira, a Belen schoolmate, remembers that "we didn't speak much about World War II."[8] Though the hostilities in the European and Pacific theaters of war were making daily headlines through most of the world, and Fidel was a voracious reader, American and British participation in the war made scarcely an impression on him. In public remarks in later years he has dwelled on Soviet military performance in World War II, hardly ever mentioning the Western allies.

Neither Belen's curriculum nor the conservative Spanish Jesuits on the faculty encouraged interest in the Allied democracies, scarcely touching on

American or British history or literature. The Jesuits did not know much themselves about the English-speaking world, and most harbored lingering resentments because of the humiliations that had been inflicted on Spain in the past by the Anglo-Saxon countries. Some were openly sympathetic to the fascist Franco regime in Madrid.

And furthermore, England and the United States had also subjugated Cuba, occupying it in different eras. British and American acts of imperialism may not have been drilled into them, but Belen boys heard plenty about the subsequent injustices Cubans had endured. The emphasis in the teaching of the social sciences was on Cuban and Latin American experience and culture, and on world history, focused on Spain and the classics of Spanish literature.

The Jesuits also touted the magnetic qualities of Jose Antonio Primo de Rivera, the founder of the Spanish falangist or fascist movement. Always known by his first names, Jose Antonio was an advocate of Spanish and broader Hispanic revival. In speeches and writings he urged his followers to be "ardent and aggressive," strenuous leadership qualities that intrigued and appealed to the young Fidel.

Fidel was attracted to Francisco Franco, Jose Antonio's falangist successor who ruled Spain with an iron fist for decades. Franco, like Angel Castro, was a *gallego* and almost certainly was spoken of admiringly by Spanish workers at Biran. Father Llorente, a conservative Spaniard himself, told me that at Belen Fidel "was more of a Francoist than I was." Later, in public life, Fidel has always been careful to distance himself from those teenage infatuations with the fascist right, to the extent in the early 1960s of engineering brief diplomatic confrontations with Franco's Spain.

In Belen's Hispanic-centric curriculum American and English leaders and authors were of little interest to Fidel and would not be in later years either, when he read mostly Russian, French, Cuban, and Spanish writers. His interest in oratory and public speakers, from the classical to the contemporary, never included the great wartime orators of the English-speaking world, Winston Churchill and Roosevelt. Certainly they were not his role models. Revolutionaries, warriors, and conquerors, not leaders of democracies, were his heroes. In a letter from prison in 1954 he summarized his view of historical turning points that had most fascinated him.

"I love the magnificent spectacle offered by the great revolutions in history."[9]

It is interesting that he seems never to have counted the eighteenth-century American Revolution among those "magnificent spectacles." Neither Washington or Jefferson, the Declaration of Independence, the long struggle of the American colonies for independence—or for that matter, the violent Cromwellian revolution in seventeenth-century England—interested him. After he publicly adopted Marxism–Leninism in 1961, Fidel would argue that the Anglo-Saxon revolutions had not torn apart old class structures, sufficiently penalized exploiters, or remedied historical injustices.

As a child and young adult he was poorly tutored in American and English history, and, for the most part, disinterested. That would change completely later. As he began his quest for power in Cuba, of necessity he became a tireless, relentless student of American political dynamics. He realized it was inevitable he would duel with the superpower to the north one day, so he had better understand it as well as he could.

So in exile in Mexico and in the Sierra Maestra during the second half of the 1950s he studied and observed, ultimately becoming exceptionally skilled at influencing and manipulating American public opinion. By the mid-1960s, every morning—sometimes twice a day—he pored over lengthy intelligence and diplomatic briefings, all heavily focused on news from the United States.

During one period in 1965 when he was staying in a remote rural area, a military helicopter flew from Havana twice a day to deliver briefings to him. With the exception of a succession of Israeli leaders, there is probably no other political figure anywhere in the world who has been more knowledgeable in assessing American politics and accurate in predicting American gyrations.

As a youth, Fidel was also ambivalent about American culture and its overwhelming impact on Cuban life before being uprooted by his revolution. That too seems to have been instilled at an early age, at Belen and even before. Luis Aguilar, a schoolmate at Dolores and the university, recalled that Fidel was the only boy at the school who hated American Western movies, and especially those that starred John Wayne. Perhaps Fidel's own experiences with exploitation as a child actually did engender a precocious social consciousness, as he claims, fueling his rage at the celluloid cowboys he saw as violent exploiters of deracinated Indians.[10]

Perhaps the boy who was so enamored of Alexander the Great, Napoleon, Hannibal, and Julius Caesar simply considered John Wayne's characters too ridiculous to be taken seriously as heroic figures. Fidel often went to the movies on weekends with Belen classmates, and the films inevitably were Hollywood releases, but as an adult revolutionary he has rarely spoken of American cinema, and only critically when pressed to do so. He told an Italian interviewer in 1987 that he preferred Latin American films with social content.

"Frankly, I appreciate them more than European and U.S. cinema, with excesses of violence, the Mafia, sex, car chases and all that."[11]

Ultimately, Fidel is best remembered by his Belen teachers and schoolmates for his energy and unrelenting determination, his "mystique," as Father Llorente described it. When he graduated he was still called "*el loco* Fidel." But by then many of his schoolmates were calling him this affectionately, out of fascination and even with grudging admiration rather than contempt. When he and his classmates received their diplomas at graduation ceremonies in 1945, he received some of the loudest and most prolonged applause.

Enjoying nothing more than being the center of attention, he was one of a kind. Father Quevedo remembered him once ostentatiously tearing up a large-denomination bill just for effect. "He always had lots of money."

On a five-peso dare he crashed a bicycle into a wall before a large audience of incredulous schoolmates with such force that he wound up spending a few days in the school infirmary. His schoolmate Jose Ignacio Rasco, who remembers the incident, concluded years later that the mad daring of that escapade presaged the zealotry of the Moncada attack. It is one of the escapades that Fidel has tried to obscure from his biographers and Cuban audiences. In a speech to secondary school students in Havana in March 1991, he recalled the incident but gave it his own twist. He said that he had never been on a bicycle until that day and was unsure riding it. When he indeed crashed into a wall, it had been an accident.[12]

Some of Fidel's most exceptional leadership qualities were first exhibited at Belen. Juan Grau, who fled Cuba, unable to live under the Castros' revolution, nevertheless still remembers Fidel with reluctant respect. "He was brilliant, likable, convincing," Grau told me. He said Fidel had three especially distinguishing characteristics: "his phenomenal memory, his persistence, and his powers of persuasion." He tells a revealing story about Fidel's remarkable persuasiveness.

Father Llorente usually led the boys on excursions into rural and mountainous areas, and Fidel was his adjutant. Fidel was determined to climb the tallest peak in western Cuba—the Pan de Guajaibon—in Pinar del Rio province, west of Havana, and to do so without supervision and with no contingent of his schoolmates along.

The Pan, as it was known, was a pygmy compared to Pico Turquino in the Sierra Maestra that Fidel often climbed as an adult, sometimes leading exhausted groups of foreign visitors. Turquino is Cuba's tallest peak, but at 692 meters, the steep and rugged Pan de Guajaibon was a challenging ascent, especially for inexperienced boys. More importantly, no one from Belen or its rival academies had ever been known to reach the summit. It was western Cuba's Everest, by Fidel's heroic reckoning. He was determined to do it, to be the first, but he had to have at least one witness, one other boy to go with him who could testify to the feat.

He persuaded a classmate named Mario Pampa to join him, but the priests did all they could to dissuade them. It was too dangerous, too far from Havana for a day trip, too ambitious for teenage boys to climb on their own. Father Llorente could not persuade Fidel to wait for a larger expedition to be organized. He then went to Grau and another boy, Diego Rubio, imploring them to find Fidel and persuade him to abandon the adventure.

Those boys were the closest Fidel had to real friends at Belen. Grau and Rubio met with Fidel with the intent of dissuading him. But almost immediately Fidel took charge. He drowned them in an articulate and absolutely convincing flow of words. He was warm and personable; he grasped their arms, spoke to them with profound conviction and an evangelical certainty.

"Join me," he insisted, "climb the Pan with me, and we will all be heroes."

Like so many others, from many countries in the decades since, they were overwhelmed. As strongly as they had at first agreed with the Jesuits that the feat was a dangerous, reckless one, they were quickly convinced by Fidel that the chance to be heroes in the eyes of the other boys made it worth taking the risk.

They were recruited to Fidel's cause, and soon the four boys climbed the Pan de Guajaibon together. They got lost along the way because, disorganized, Fidel had not remembered to bring a good map or directions, and it took several days before they returned to school as fears for their safety were mounting. But they were triumphant, welcomed back to Belen as heroes.[13]

That was the first time Fidel employed his powers of persuasion to enlist others in one of his schemes. It presaged the Moncada and *Granma* missions in the 1950s, both of which were suicidal for the majority of the recruited. But his followers stayed with him even though his badly conceived and organized attack plans were most unlikely to succeed. He allayed their doubts and fears by marshaling his extraordinary powers of persuasion.

Not only boys and callow youths rallied to Fidel's causes through his powers of persuasion. Older, seasoned military veterans, worldly men with considerable experience, have also been persuaded, often against their better judgment at first, to join him. When Fidel was in Mexico, organizing and training the *Granma* expeditionaries, he recruited a Cuban veteran of the Korean War to serve as a military instructor.

Still not satisfied, he went to the Mexico City home of sixty-five-year-old Alberto Bayo, a grizzled veteran of brutal guerrilla and conventional warfare during the Spanish Civil War.[14] Bayo resisted as Fidel launched into his pitch, trying to persuade the reluctant old general to train his recruits. Bayo found Fidel unusually charming and eloquent: "His demands were irrefutable. He ordered, he dominated."

Besieged by Fidel's arguments, Bayo finally agreed to give Fidel's men three hours of daily military training.

"All of your time for us, all of your time," Fidel demanded.

Bayo recalled that Fidel said this in tones so authoritative, so domineering that he was unable to refuse.[15]

Fidel would use the same techniques from the 1960s through the 1980s to motivate insurgents in as many as a dozen Latin American countries, usually urging them into all but hopeless life-and-death struggles, in the name of some glory that he passionately described.

Cuban volunteers, most filled with quixotic visions that Fidel inspired, joined a number of those guerrilla movements as expert advisers. Many died that way, in forlorn, faraway places on at least three continents. A few, notably Raul's longtime close military associate, Albelardo Colome Ibarra, still occupy top positions in Cuba's military and security services.

For decade after decade, Fidel has succeeded in inspiring fanatical, sometimes suicidal zealotry in his followers, both Cuban and other nationalities as well. In every instance when he was personally engaged in recruitment, the driving forces have been the same: his indomitable will, persistence, and powers of persuasion. What he always promises is a share of the imagined glories ahead.

Unlike his brother, Raul had been to Havana at least once as a young child, long before he enrolled as a teenager at Belen. When he was about six he was fitted with a replica of the uniforms worn by the Cuban Rural Guard and boarded the train to Havana with Felipe Miraval, the commander of the small guard post at Biran. Raul was one of a few hundred boys selected from across the island, all decked out as miniature guardsmen in ceremonies celebrating the anniversary of Fulgencio Batista's first coup in 1933.[16]

Since that trip, Miraval—known widely as *el Chino*, the Chinaman—has been thought by many Cubans to be Raul's biological father. Several of Fidel's biographers have recounted the rumors that are widely taken as true, although there is no solid evidence to confirm them, and there probably never will be.

The story is based on Raul's physical appearance. His two older brothers are tall and broad shouldered, and at different stages in their lives they have consistently resembled each other. Raul looks strikingly different. He is slight, a head shorter than Fidel and Ramon, and his facial features are conspicuously unlike theirs. Some are also convinced that he bears no resemblance to Angel Castro.

As a guerrilla leader, and during much of 1959, Raul sported a long pony-tail, similar to a Chinese queue. Unlike his bearded guerrilla comrades, he was never able to grow more than a wispy mustache and goatee. Photographs of him from those days typically show him squinting into the camera, his eyes narrow and hooded. Behind his back, Raul himself was called *el Chino* by leaders of the Nicaraguan revolution who knew him well in the 1970s and 1980s.[17]

Others like to point out that Miraval, then a guard captain, was spared the firing squad in early 1959 when many of his military colleagues were being led to their deaths by the new revolutionary leadership. If that was the case, it is highly unlikely that anyone other than Fidel or Raul could have given the order that allowed Miraval to survive, though confined to a prison cell.

In his biography of Fidel, Leycester Coltman observed that Miraval "gave encouraging winks and nods when fellow prisoners questioned him about the rumors."[18] Georgie Anne Geyer told a parallel story in her biography of Fidel. Miraval always became "oddly cold and quiet" whenever the subject of Raul came up while he was in prison. She adds that friends of the Castro family have always given some credence to the rumors.[19] In my conversation with Fidel's daughter Alina, she did not dismiss the rumors about Raul either. Some of his close associates in more recent years acknowledge that they may be true, although unsurprisingly, they never heard Raul allude to the subject.

One additional obscure and previously unnoticed fragment of information I discovered might bear directly on the subject. During the early months of his operations in the Sierra Cristal in the spring of 1958, Raul kept a diary that also served as a running progress report that he shared, by way of messengers, with Fidel. In one entry Raul describes his group of guerrillas passing through a coffee-growing region of Oriente and tells Fidel of happening upon a small mine operated by Ramon Castro.

Curiously, however, Raul refers to Ramon as *"tu hermano Ramon"—your* brother Ramon. The text of this portion of the diary was printed in late January 1959 in the new official daily newspaper of the revolution. In the original Spanish it is very unlikely that the reference, specifically the pronoun *your*, was a transcription or typographical error.

Raul is rarely given to irony or sarcasm, but it is possible of course that this was one such instance. Alternatively, the reference to *your* rather than *our* brother could have been an expression of contempt for this sibling who was sitting out the insurgency and helping his brothers in only trivial ways.

On balance, however, it seems as likely that Raul meant it quite literally, exactly as he expressed it, recognizing that Ramon is indeed Fidel's brother but his own half brother.[20] Raul's diary writing is invariably dry and bloodless, precise and unadorned in its descriptions. There is an absence of humor, wit, or introspection. Those portions of his notes from the guerrilla days that were serialized over a four day period in late January 1959 in the newspaper *Revolucion* are devoid of errors that might suggest the reference to *your* brother was unintentional.

Raul's use of the phrase could help explain why Angel generally treated Lina's youngest son with indifference and why he did not buy him new cars or provide a generous monthly allowance as he did for Fidel. On the other hand, it would be understandable if Angel was reluctant to bestow financial favors on this disappointing son who languished without any goals for so long.

And yet, still more rumors contribute to this mystery. Gossip of Lina's infidelity was repeated even within the Castro clan. Fidel's half brother Pedro Emilio, the son of Angel's first wife, believed stoutly that Lina had borne at least one other child not fathered by Angel. Pedro Emilio told Fidel's daughter Alina of a woman in Santiago who claimed to be Lina's child.

This woman, he said, was known about the city as *La Bella de Santiago*, the Santiago Beauty. She had written to Pedro Emilio informing him out of the blue that they were brother and sister. He said he wrote her back, apparently relishing the absurdity of it all, to tell her that was impossible, because Lina was not his mother.[21]

Perhaps in the end, the enduring and unanswerable question of Raul's paternity can be considered relevant for just one reason. Those interested in predicting how he will govern Cuba when he gets to do so will continue looking for clues in the myriad of differences between him and Fidel.

As mentioned before, no biography, full or fragmentary, has ever been published of Raul, not even in *Verde Olivo*, the monthly journal of the Cuban armed forces that he has overseen since the early 1960s. In his carefully prepared speeches, he never speaks of himself. He has rarely granted more than passing interviews—fewer than a dozen times since 1959—and in all of them he has avoided any extended personal reminiscences or reflections.

He has uttered only a few dozen words on the record about his life and background before the revolution. He has only once or twice referred to the youthful years of lassitude—perhaps dissipation—he spent at Biran after being expelled from high school. There is no record that he transferred to another high school. The one time he spoke of this, he said he went back as a teenager to the comforts and seclusion of Biran, and to an angry Angel.

"... [H]is reaction was to send me to work in the fields. I first picked potatoes, then worked in a warehouse, and in a store, all belonging to my father. Finally I was put to work in an office where I was paid sixty pesos, which was quite a bit then."[22]

Some who have known Raul as an adult believe that it was then, in his mid- and late-teenage years, that he began drinking excessively and spending too much time at the cockfighting ring. Resentments and insecurities were surely growing as he loitered and as news of Fidel's rising political star in Havana was reaching home in the late 1940s.

For Raul it was an unproductive, wasted interlude. He was not developing any serious interests or skills. He had no thoughts about a profession or career. There was no intellectual stimulus at Biran; he did not read much. To this day that has changed little. As Cuba's defense minister, he relies on his staff to brief him or to boil long reports down into cursory ones that he can quickly peruse.

Juanita Castro, in testimony before a congressional committee in 1965, said that Raul "entered the University of Havana to study administration for which a high school diploma was not required."[23] She did not say exactly when that was, though others who knew him remember that he returned to Havana in 1948 or 1949. He took non-academic courses for a time without finishing a program of studies or earning a degree. Raul has never spoken of the time he spent at the university, but it may be reasonable to assume that he acquired some fundamental skills in administration and management from courses he took there. Those are the areas in which he later excelled.

A few of the people he knew in Havana during the period from the late 1940s until 1953 have provided a smattering of observations about the young Raul, who turned twenty on June 3, 1951. He was introverted and a bad soccer player, one university student who knew him remembered, though he was self-effacing and more relaxed and likable than Fidel.

Another contemporary remembered him as a "nice, quiet guy, who never spoke."[24] A young woman living in Havana who went to the movies with him remembers him as entirely unremarkable. She confessed to having had a crush on Fidel but emphatically not on Raul at that time.

He apparently had not developed any serious interests, no profession or skills, no job or work experience other than the work at Biran before he joined Fidel's movement in the summer of 1953 shortly before the Moncada attack. He made no lasting or even memorable mark in anything he did until he was arrested on his return to Havana from a communist youth conference in Vienna and travels in Eastern European communist countries in 1953.

Raul's formal education hardly went beyond primary school. He has admitted to attending school for only about eight years. His cognitive and intellectual capacities appear to pale in comparison to Fidel's. In short, Raul had not achieved anything on his own until he was given command of his own guerrilla forces in March 1958, unless the execution he carried out in Mexico City can be counted.

CHAPTER FOUR

My True Destiny

Fidel arrived at the University of Havana in the fall of 1945 in buoyant spirits and high style, driving the new shiny black Ford V-8 that Angel had been persuaded to purchase for him. He matriculated in the law school, settled in an apartment near the campus on L Street with one or two of his sisters, and set out immediately to launch a political career.

His goal was to become president of the university student federation, a stepping stone to national politics. There was no doubting his priorities, or his determination. He was seething with restless energy, anxious to perform on the university's larger stage where approximately twenty-five thousand students, Cuba's best and brightest, were enrolled. It would be Fidel's first window on the wider worlds that he wanted to conquer, though for what purpose greater than his own ambitions he had no idea as yet.

The issues he would champion, the causes he would pursue could be grafted on later as opportunities might allow. Had there been a credible right wing political party or movement in Cuba, he could as easily have moved in that direction. In political terms he was a tabula rasa. Twenty years later he admitted as much.

"I had been a political illiterate. I had brought nothing more than a rebellious temperament and the uprightness, the severe character they had inculcated in me in the Jesuit school."[1]

What he did know for sure was that he wanted to vault into a leadership position, make a name for himself. He was aware by then that he was endowed with exceptional personal and leadership qualities that were propelling him to achieve great things. The Jesuits had reinforced his childhood fascination with heroes, conquerors, and colorful revolutionaries. After the calm, contemplative summer he had spent at Biran following graduation from Belen, Fidel had utter confidence in his own mystical aura and destiny.

Alfredo Esquivel, known by the fairly common nickname *el Chino*, met Fidel on their first day of classes and instantly was drawn to him. Fidel was relaxing outside the law school, leaning against a wall. He struck up a conversation with Esquivel almost immediately and asked him if he was interested in university politics.

Fidel had set out on his very first day at the university to begin recruiting a political following, enlisting allies and backers. The immediate goal was to take his first step on the Cuban political ladder by getting elected as his class representative to the law school council. *El Chino* Esquivel agreed to help, and thus became the first *fidelista*.[2]

Esquivel's two initial impressions of Fidel were that he was somewhat "scatterbrained" and that he had extraordinary leadership qualities. Esquivel concluded, as most would, that those abilities were innate, bred in Fidel, fixed in his genes.

"He was born with it," Esquivel observed many years later from exile in Miami. Although he disagreed with most of what Fidel had done since winning power, he was still in awe of his former friend.

Like many others who had been close to Fidel at different times in his life, Esquivel insisted that the young man he had befriended at the university was an entirely different person than the one he became, that early on he was likable and loyal. Esquivel felt that Fidel was more decisive, ingenious, audacious, persuasive, and intelligent than anyone else he knew.

Characteristics of a political prodigy began to emerge as Fidel campaigned for the law school office. Students were issued wallet-size identification cards with their names, addresses, and photographs. Fidel somehow was able to gain access to the originals—whether through duplicity or charm, it is not clear. With that information about his classmates soon committed to memory, he was able to approach them individually, address them by name, and make personalized small talk.

His tactic did not always succeed, however. Some classmates were put off, considering him a shameless grandstander. His biographer Robert Quirk tells of Fidel self-righteously approaching some fellow students in the school cafeteria. They were unimpressed when he told them that all the Catholic students should band together. He came across as a right-winger. "He was obnoxious, monopolizing the conversation."[3]

Esquivel remembers how Fidel operated when he was trying to recruit or persuade a classmate to support him. He has used the same approach ever since, first adopting it at Belen with Juan Grau and those other boys. The recruitment begins with a lot of physical contact as Fidel starts to present his argument, with gestures and extravagant body language well beyond the usual. While pulling on his target's shirt, Fidel touches, pokes, holds, and squeezes the recruit's arm, talking in a ceaseless flow, raising and lowering his voice with ingratiating charm. Fidel's pauses are strategically timed. Esquivel remembers Fidel's tone as "whining," but so persistent and persuasive that when he was working on an individual man, he was usually successful in whatever it was he was trying to achieve.

"You became a *fidelista*," Esquivel observed. "You sympathized with him because he was born with that."

El Chino came to realize fairly early in their friendship that Fidel was quite aware of his leadership gifts and special qualities. He was as close to Fidel as anyone was allowed to get in those days, remaining his ally and follower in all manner of political intrigues for several years. After the guerrilla victory, Fidel offered him the highly desirable position of Cuban ambassador to Mexico City, which he declined. They spent a lot of time together, Esquivel becoming an astute observer of his contemporary.

He knew Fidel so well that when the news broke in Havana that the Moncada barracks in Santiago had erupted in violence, and many believed that fighting had broken out between different factions of Batista's troops, Esquivel realized instantly, though he had no prior knowledge of the planning, that Fidel had led an attack.

Esquivel also tells a revealing story about Fidel's precocious sense of destiny. They were studying one night and around midnight took a break to have a cup of coffee in a café nearby. They sat with some other students who began in the quiet of the night to share with each other their dreams and aspirations for their futures after finishing law school. One said he wanted to become a poet. Another hoped to turn out to be a really good lawyer. Esquivel says that he then turned to Fidel, using a nickname that he, and few others could get away with. "*Guajiro*, what about you?" Fidel responded reflexively, without pausing.

"I want to win glory and fame!"

There was still no framework, no motivating sensibility, no intellectual or ideological foundation for those heroic aspirations. There was no plan for carving himself a place in Cuban history. But in its clarity and singularity Fidel's vision of his own exceptionalism went far beyond the casual maunderings of most youths his age. He knew in his first year at the university, Esquivel emphasizes, that he had extraordinary talents, and he was determined to use them to win recognition, acclaim, and above all influence.

When deciphered through the lens of his long record in office, what he really had meant by "glory and fame" was *power* and political greatness. He had no interest in becoming a prominent lawyer, intellectual, or businessman. Certainly he had no desire to join the Cuban military. Yet by Esquivel's account and those of others, in that first year of law school Fidel had no altruistic thoughts whatsoever about who might benefit from his anticipated political success, other than himself.

He was nineteen years old.* He had grown to be physically imposing, over six feet tall and about 190 pounds. His thick, wavy black hair was cut short when Esquivel first met him. He had the profile of a Roman nobleman or centurion, and he liked to thrust his chin out in ways that accentuated his

---

* In a January 1970 interview with an American visitor, Fidel said he was *eighteen* when he began at the university. In fact, there is good reason to believe he is a year younger than the official age he and his regime have always upheld. His biographer Leycester Coltman wrote that in order for Fidel to meet the minimum age requirement for admission to Belen, Angel "paid a bribe to get a new birth certificate" that gave his year of birth as 1926 rather than 1927. On different occasions in the late 1950s, Lina and three of Fidel's sisters publicly confirmed the later birth date. Fidel has only been pressed about this once on the record, telling Barbara Walters that: "I take the less favorable date." Therefore, throughout this book, Fidel's official age is used. Saul Landau, "Exclusive Interview With Fidel," *Eyewitness* (an *International Newsletter*), No. 1, January 1970; Leycester Coltman, *The Real Fidel Castro*, Yale University Press, 2003, p. 9; Gerardo Rodriguez Morejon, *Fidel Castro: Biografia*, P. Fernandez y Cia, Havana, 1959, p.1; Emma and Lidia Castro, "Historia de la Vida de Fidel Castro," *El Diario de Nueva York*, April 22, 1957, p. 10; and Castro-Walters Interview, *Bohemia*, July 1, 1977, translation by Cuban government Department of Stenographic Records, Havana.

aquiline nose. He was aware that his size and physical strength had worked to his advantage since childhood and had no qualms about asserting them. The strong religious faith he had found comfort in when he was younger was evaporating now as he confronted the harsher world of university politics.

He was a mosaic of contradictions, as unsure of himself emotionally as he was confident in his transactional and cognitive skills. Still prone to erratic and extreme behavior that was sometimes calculated to attract attention, on some occasions he wreaked havoc in order to advance some improbable political goal.

After the protected years under Jesuit tutelage he was immature compared with most of his contemporaries. He had no ability at all to confide in others or enter into any kind of genuinely cooperative relationship. He feared any kind of dependency that might make him vulnerable again to exploitation. What he told Betto, the Brazilian friar, about not having had a mentor or inspirational older guide when he was a boy and teenager remained true at the university.

There were no professors he looked up to, no role models or men he sought out for counsel. There was no one he respected enough to submit himself to in any way. Emotionally, it was impossible for him to become anyone's disciple, and he would live the rest of his life without ever doing so. There would never again be a sympathetic figure like Father Llorente who would try to crack the hard crust of his psyche, to offer him counsel.

Fidel was surprisingly unsocial for one so politically gifted. He did not smoke and rarely drank. He dated very little and was awkward and unsure of himself with young women. Several contemporaries from that time recall that he was referred to behind his back with a caustic play on words as *el casto*, the chaste. He had no interest—then or ever—in dancing, despite the encouragement of Cuba's Hispanic-African culture and energizing music.

To this day he does not sing—not even in the shower, he admitted once to an interviewer. Then he avoided going to parties, though it was not because he was spending much time studying. He bothered very little with academic matters, attending classes only intermittently but, as in Belen, passing tests after intense bouts of last-minute memorization. He did spend a lot of time in cafés, endlessly talking politics with whoever would listen.

Fidel still had not shed all of his rural, *guajiro* characteristics either, often appearing in soiled, wrinkled clothing. He acquired unflattering nicknames: "greaseball" and "dirtball" were the most common, and they stuck to him for a number of years. *El Chino* Esquivel remembers Fidel's utter indifference to his attire. He would wear mismatched shoes and socks, strange color combinations. He would pull a pair of pants off a hook to wear no matter what color they were. He was viewed by many of his schoolmates as an unsophisticated hick. Trying to put a more positive spin on that impression, he told Carlos Franqui once that he had been a "bohemian."

Fidel's female relatives helped maintain some semblance of order in his chaotic domestic life. In later years, both before and after he won power, his sisters were replaced by other doting women—especially his aide Celia Sanchez—who looked after him. At least two of his biographers have written that one or another of his sisters was routinely available to arrange his clothes, shine his shoes, and even to cut his fingernails. His daughter Alina has written that much later he demanded manicures when he came to visit her.[4]

A number of interviewers over the years have remarked on the incongruity of his fine hands, with long, slender fingers that have always been uncalloused, certainly unlike his father's. Fidel was already vain, spoiled, and narcissistic at the university. He expected to be tended to like the dauphin of some exotic principality, so that he would have more time to spend on more important matters.[5]

In September 1995, fifty years after he had enrolled in the law school, Fidel went back to deliver a long, self-indulgent speech to a new generation of students. He appeared in the Aula Magna, the university's great hall, to reminisce at length about his own experiences there. He wanted the students to have some sense of what he was like as a young man, some perspectives that were not available to them in any published form in Cuba. It is characteristic, especially in his advanced stage in life, to be neither modest nor self-effacing.

"Relatively speaking," he told the students of his law school days, "I had already started to stand out."[6]

The two-hundred-year-old University of Havana, prominent on a hill in the Vedado neighborhood, was distinguished by handsome if somewhat mottled and faded buildings in the classical style. Most had marble facades lined with Greek columns, impressive pediments, and adornments.

The imposing *Escalinata*, an outdoor tiered esplanade of 163 wide stone steps served as the school's formal main entry, its cynosure. Students met and mingled there, staging events of all kinds, including numerous demonstrations during the five years Fidel was in the law school. Beginning in his second year he organized many of them, leading processions of shouting protestors down the *Escalinata* onto San Lazaro Street and from there to some government building or public plaza.

In his first year he had not thrived politically as planned. With *El Chino's* help, he had been elected his class's delegate but was permanently blocked from progressing any higher in the student federation because of the opposition of those who had come to despise and mistrust him. He wanted to control everthing including the spotlight. His tenacious ambitions were just too transparent; he needed to camouflage them better. He also realized he had to identify with popular political positions, and move beyond university politics—down the *Escalinata* and into the streets of the city toward more propitious arenas.

Failure was hard to swallow, but as he would for the rest of his life, Fidel blamed others and moved on. He claimed it was corrupt politics and the dishonesty of rival student leaders that had stymied him. Regardless of how he rationalized disappointment, he rebounded as he always has after painful failures, starting afresh. He pragmatically reassessed his situation and set a new course while seeking different allies more appropriate to his new objectives. That too would become his standard operating style after setbacks. New teams of officials would perennially replace ones that he professed had not served him or the revolution adequately.

While attending the university, he made three critical choices. The easiest one was to assume a leadership role in confronting the corrupt government of Ramon Grau San Martin. Fidel was well cast in the role of strident opposition organizer, and he soon was playing that part to the hilt. His decision in July 1947 to affiliate with a new reformist political party, the *Ortodoxos*, was another matter, however. The charismatic Eduardo Chibas founded the Orthodox Party but never trusted Fidel, not believing he could ever subordinate his own ambitions and outsize personality within a hierarchical political structure. Even more damaging for Fidel's political ambitions was his 1946 involvement in the nefarious activities of violent campus mafias that were euphemistically called "action groups."

The Grau San Martin administration was a legitimate target for angry university studenjts and reform-minded Cubans of all persuasions. A former professor and reform politician himself, the president had been elected in one of Cuba's few relatively fair presidential elections and was inaugurated in October 1944 for a four-year term. Despite the high hopes surrounding his surprise victory, he betrayed the popular trust and was soon presiding over an egregiously venal administration.

Graft was condoned everywhere elected or appointed officials operated, extending from the president and his cronies down to the lowest government bureaucrats, many of them grasping for an illegal take. Grau San Martin encouraged mafia-style gangs, politicized the police, and condoned savage violence by his supporters. By one account, sixty-four political assassinations were carried out during his term.[7]

It was in this noxious mix that Fidel found his first political cause, an agenda to fight those abuses. As usual, he pushed his commitment to extremes. The government had so violated the popular trust that it had to be taken down. It was illegitimate. And by Fidel's reasoning, it was not just Grau San Martin and his henchmen who were at fault but the whole rotten political system. Fidel finally had a popular issue he could brandish while simultaneously advancing his own ambitions.

In November 1946 he delivered his first national speech, attracting newspaper coverage. He vilified Grau San Martin, attacked official corruption and violence, and for the first time took up a social cause, decrying how corrupt politicians were stealing the lifeblood of Cuba's poor.

Fidel had prepared thoroughly for that powerful, course-setting performance. *Chino* Esquivel says that as a young man Fidel drafted some speeches by hand and then memorized them "from beginning to end." Fidel also invested considerable effort in practicing just the right physical poses and gestures and their timing. He was still developing his oratorical style, Esquivel said, adding how much it struck him at the time that Fidel "was enchanted with public speaking."

He was moving tentatively to the left, in the same direction as the strongest political currents, but he was still not sure that hardline right-wing methods might not better suit him and Cuba. Jose Pardo Llada, one of Fidel's closest associates at the university and in later years—he was a groomsman at Fidel's marriage in October 1948—remembered that Fidel kept a twelve-volume Spanish-language edition of the writings and speeches of Benito Mussolini. Jose Ignacio Rasco also remembers that Fidel read Hitler with interest at the university. Their recollections are consistent with other credible testimonies.[8]

But ideology or doctrine was still secondary for Fidel; he was a man of action and had no need to tie himself down to any single creed. What really mattered was to get more attention as a leading voice of the opposition to the government. He organized demonstrations whenever an opportunity arose and at the same time began thinking in violently conspiratorial terms.

When the government announced an increase in public bus fares, he led protesting students, carrying a huge Cuban flag down the *Escalinata* and into the city where they were attacked by police. He was struck on the head, though not wounded as badly as the length of white gauze bandage wrapped around his scalp would suggest.

One of Fidel's most bizarre escapades followed. Hoping to quell the unrest, Grau San Martin invited four students, including Fidel and *Chino* Esquivel, to meet with him at the presidential palace. In 1976 Jose Pardo Llada wrote about the scheme Fidel hatched after the sixty-three-year-old president invited the students to wait for him on his balcony, to enjoy the fresh air, and discuss the increase in bus fares. As they stood there alone, Fidel whispered to the others.

"I have the formula to take power and once and for all to get rid of this old crook."

The others were dumbfounded as he persisted.

"When the old man comes back, let's the four of us pick him up and throw him off the balcony. Once he's dead we'll proclaim the triumph of the student revolution . . . it's a great opportunity for us to seize power."

Pardo Llada wrote that *Chino* Esquivel grabbed Fidel's shoulder and shouted, "Come on, *guajiro*, you're crazy."

As Fidel insisted on his macabre plan, Enrique Ovares demanded he stop. "We have come here for a lowering of bus fares, not to commit an assassination."[9]

As Machiavellian as the improvised plot seemed to the others, it was just one of several that Fidel devised between the late 1940s and early 1950s. They had in common a sudden shocking act of violence that would ignite popular rioting and disturbances, like the storming of the Bastille in Paris in 1789, and would topple the *ancien régime* and bring revolutionaries to power.

Another of these escapades occurred in November 1947 when Fidel originated a brilliantly pernicious scheme to discredit the Grau San Martin administration. It involved sequestering one of the most important symbols of Cuba's nineteenth-century independence struggle, the Bell of Demajagua, the equivalent of the American Liberty Bell in Philadelphia.

The Cuban bell was kept in a place of honor in Manzanillo, a provincial town in Oriente. Fidel's idea was to bring it secretly to the university, where it would be rung clamorously amid ceremonies and nationalistic speeches, and provoke crowds to rush to the presidential palace demanding the president's resignation.

Lionel Martin, a sympathetic biographer who was allowed access to senior Cuban officials, wrote "Fidel had dreamed of sparking a massive movement . . . that would shake the government to its foundations."[10] Unlike the balcony caper, this idea attracted the support of most other student leaders, though it could never be implemented as conceived.

Fidel's strategic thinking behind the Moncada and *Granma* attacks derived from this same conspiratorial approach, except his earlier plans were not executed. For the youthful Fidel, revolutionary ends justified almost any means. Less clear when he was at the university, however, was his own motivation. Did he calculate nihilistic acts of violence primarily to bring fame and glory to himself, or did his hatred of establishment politicians provide the compelling impetus?

Many years later, perhaps with those moments on Grau San Martin's balcony cemented in his mind, Fidel commented to an interviewer that he did not like to use the balcony outside *his* office in the building where he relocated the presidency after winning power.

"I almost never stand here on this balcony to look at the city."[11]

Soon Fidel was always armed. He once straddled a chair in the law school cafeteria where some other students were seated and promptly intimidated them by twirling an automatic pistol on the table top. He became a menacing figure in this new role, associating with truly bloodthirsty murderers and criminals in the mafia action groups. He was a dangerous *noir* character, a dark figure like the hit men in the Hollywood gangster movies of the 1930s and 1940s.

He was actually implicated in two murder cases, one of a prominent rival student leader and the other of a campus policeman. He was a prime suspect and was charged in one case and briefly held, but he was released due to either insufficient evidence or string pulling by political allies. There is no doubt, however, that he did take the lead in an earlier attack, a cold-blooded murder attempt in December 1946 against another aspiring student leader.

Though Lionel Gomez was still in preparatory school, he had declared his intent to make his mark the following term in university politics. He was ambitious, astute, and charismatic, a genuine rival on Fidel's horizon and from a mold much like his own. Gomez was affiliated with a rival mafia gang. It was the perfect formula for provoking all of Fidel's worst instincts.

Beginning with this young upstart, Fidel has never hesitated in the six decades since 1946 to take whatever actions he might consider necessary, including lethal ones, to preempt an opponent and prevent him from becoming a full-fledged threat at some future time.

Chino Esquivel was with Fidel one evening outside the university sports stadium when they saw Gomez leaving. Always armed and ready to seize an opportunity, Fidel took cover behind a stone wall and fired at the youth without warning. By some accounts, the bullet entered through Gomez's back and lodged in a lung. He was able to flee on foot, seriously wounded. A second person was shot in the leg.[12]

That incident reflected innate character traits that Fidel's Jesuit teachers never imagined were there. This was the behavior of a sociopath, someone with no ability or inclination to distinguish between right and wrong. As early as the age of twenty, Fidel considered murder and mayhem justifiable and acceptable means to advance his personal interests. In classical Freudian terms this behavior was the product of a psyche entirely lacking in superego or conscience.

All of the religious instruction Fidel had been exposed to had been discarded. The attempted murder of Lionel Gomez has never been described as an act of self-defense by any of its witnesses. The young student was not a party—at least not yet—to a conspiracy that threatened Fidel. He was not a corrupt politician in Cuba's pseudo-democracy who had wantonly violated public trusts. And Fidel was not a freedom fighter, a combatant in a "just war," situations in which moralists and theologians generally condone the taking of another life. The young Gomez was nothing more than an unrealized future threat to Fidel.

Campus conflicts became so heated that Fidel in turn was also targeted for assassination and had to go into hiding. His extended honeymoon in New York City at the end of 1948, where for a few months he and his bride lived in the Bronx while he studied English, provided just such an opportunity.

Fidel has talked about this grotesque gangland chapter in his life on a few occasions and has tried to put a noble and heroic face on it. In 1995, when he spoke at the University of Havana, he was characteristically belligerent.

"If there is one thing I learned through those years when I had to look death in the face, unarmed, on many occasions, it is that the enemy respects those who do not fear him, those who challenge him. The action I took of doing my duty . . . won their respect."[13]

Other facets of his character and world-view that would come to characterize his entire political career were also taking shape during these years. The latent anti-Americanism he had assimilated at Belen came into clear focus. Before law school he probably had only a passing acquaintance with the late-nineteenth-century Cuban hero Jose Marti. Now he became enthralled, reading almost everything Marti had written. He finally had found his missing mentor, a guide—though not a living one who could impose on him.

He started accumulating his first library, consisting entirely of Marti's works, and committed favorite articles and speeches to memory. At times he seems to have so thoroughly identified with his idol that, in a fashion, he actually impersonated Marti. Jose Pardo Llada and Jose Ignacio Rasco both remember an elaborately rehearsed speech Fidel delivered that closely mimicked one Marti had spoken years before. Pardo Llada wrote that in fact it was Marti's speech and that Fidel repeated it from memory, word for word.[14]

In a history woefully bereft of truly unifying national heroes, Marti—Cuba's "Apostle"—had it all. He was a notable turn-of-the-century orator and literary figure, a poet of real repute. He made his living as a journalist and essayist and was also a man of action, a political organizer of and fundraiser for Cuba's war for independence against Spain.

And he was a martyr. Landing at night in a small boat on the shores of southeastern Oriente in 1895 to join the guerrilla struggle that he helped organize against the Spanish army, Marti wrote lyrically in his diary: "Moon comes up red . . . We land on a rocky beach." Only a month or so later, mounted on a white stallion, a conspicuous target, he was shot dead by a Spanish colonel.

In his last scribblings Marti had penned galvanizing lines. They suggested more venomous feelings about the United States than he actually felt, but nonetheless they clearly reflected his growing fear of American imperial designs on Cuba.

"I know the monster well," he wrote about the lengths of time he had spent in New York and Florida, "because I have lived in its entrails. My weapon is only the slingshot of David."

Marti also rhetorically wondered, "Once the United States is in Cuba, who will drive them out?"

These probably are among the most influential lines Fidel ever read as his personal political philosophy was developing. Marti became his lifelong idol. The destiny he felt in him now had a north star. He would complete Marti's work. He would free Cuba from foreign domination, become its David against the American Goliath.

Fidel wrote almost precisely that in the summer of 1958, during the last months of the Sierra Maestra insurgency, in a letter to Celia Sanchez: "I have sworn that the Americans will pay dearly for what they are doing. When this war has ended, a much bigger and greater war will start for me, the war I shall launch against them. I realize that this is my true destiny."

Marti had deplored the materialism, expansionist appetite, "excessive individualism," and "reverence for wealth" of Teddy Roosevelt's robber baron America. In a typically romantic flourish, he contrasted the rapidly industrializing United States with *Nuestra America*, Our America, meaning all of the benighted Spanish-speaking nations in the Western Hemisphere, where, he believed, more modest humanistic virtues prevailed and needed to be protected. *Nuestra America* would be a phrase and slogan adopted and reiterated endlessly by Fidel's revolution.

Under Marti's spell, and with his new appreciation of Cuban history, Fidel became a fervid nationalist. Little to no nationalist sentiment had been expressed to Fidel while he was growing up in remote Biran with a Spanish father, at the Haitian foster home, or under the influence of the Spanish Jesuits.

But now he felt an acute, wounded pride in being Cuban. The positive thrust of his nationalism was mixed, however, with a sense of inherited national shame. Like many of his generation, especially at the university, Fidel became more and more preoccupied with Cuba's traumatized past, with what he believed were the injustices and exploitation it had suffered under foreign domination. He became obsessed with the Cuban people's frustrated longings for an identity independent of all great powers. Quite logically, the United States was seen as the culprit, the "monster" Marti had warned against.

It was also a stock conclusion for his generation that Marti's fellow revolutionaries and guerrillas—the *mambises*—would have won total independence for their homeland had the Americans not intervened in the Spanish–American War to fight on their side.

However wishful their thinking, Cuban nationalists believed the *mambises* would have defeated Spain by themselves. When the Spanish generals did surrender at the end of the war, it was to the Americans. American military commanders would not even permit the *mambises* to enter Santiago as victors, an historical lesson Fidel warily held close as he was preparing triumphantly to enter that city himself on January 1, 1959.

He delivered his first speech as Cuba's second "Apostle" there that night. He made clear that he and *his* revolution would not be humiliated as the *mambises* had been:

> "This time the revolution will not be thwarted. This time, fortunately for Cuba, the revolution will be consummated. It will not be like the war of 1895, when the Americans arrived and made themselves masters of the country. They intervened at the last minute and later did not even allow Calixto Garcia, who has been fighting for thirty years, to enter Santiago."

By 1948, his third full year at the university, Fidel's anti-imperialist sentiment mirrored Marti's fear of what Cubans often simply call *el Norte*, the North. Nationalists abhorred the perceived subservience of Cuban governments after the Spanish–American War, the cession of Guantanamo Bay—the best port on the island—in perpetuity to the Americans, and of course, the Platt Amendment. It gave American presidents the right to intervene in Cuba on almost any pretext, and it had been invoked several times before being abrogated in 1934 by Franklin Roosevelt. Bitter memories of the interventions were still strong a dozen years later when Fidel was being politicized at the university.

With retroactive passion, he also came to despise the big American companies, like United Fruit, that had metastasized all around the Bay of Nipe where he had grown up. American cultural and economic influence was everywhere. But like Marti, Fidel sought out opportunities to "live in the entrails of the monster," in his case so that he could better understand it and, not incidentally, to learn English.

Later, when he was fighting to overthrow Batista, Fidel deceptively concealed the true depths of his anti-Americanism. He knew that prevailing attitudes in Cuba were overwhelmingly pro-American and that he could not be victorious if he expressed his true feelings.

Following in Marti's footsteps, Fidel crossed another Rubicon, geopolitically one of the most important. "The Apostle" had considered himself not just a Cuban, but a citizen of all of Hispanic America. In this respect, his thinking ran parallel to the *hispanidad* of the Spanish falangist Jose Antonio, and in Fidel's developing world-view the two compatible currents had an easy confluence.

There were other Latin American societies besides Cuba—Puerto Rico, the Dominican Republic, Nicaragua, and Panama were the most obvious—that had also fallen under American sway. So Fidel began to look over the horizon toward those and other neighboring Spanish-speaking nations for additional challenges. His island homeland would never again be a large enough stage or provide him sufficient stimulus by itself.

Some have speculated that Fidel's political and internationalist awakening at the University of Havana bred resentments not only of foreign exploiters, but also of Cubans themselves. For centuries Cubans had slavishly endured outside domination without successfully rebelling. All other Latin American countries had fought for independence early in the nineteenth century and had extirpated Spanish rule. Cuba, known as Spain's "ever-faithful Isle," did not begin to consider independence until after the American Civil War. With Puerto

Rico, Cuba was alone in the Spanish realm in the Americas still under the colonial yoke.

By this reasoning, Fidel, the son of a *gallego*, and a *gallego* of sorts himself, looked condescendingly at his countrymen as his nationalism intensified, perhaps as he had at Biran that day when he accosted the poor peasant Aracelio Peña. The Cuban people had waited too long, endured too much colonial subjugation to be worthy of great respect. It would become his mission to awaken them, radicalize them so that, like him, they could become the masters of their own destinies. But even then, Cuba would never be a big or deserving enough platform for his Alexandrian ambitions.[15]

In 1947, at the age of twenty-one, and looking beyond Cuba's shores, he took over leadership of the university Committee for the Liberation of Puerto Rico and the separate Dominican Pro-Democracy Committee. That was perhaps the only time in his life when he worked in seemingly collegial structures, although nothing is known today about how those committees operated. Fidel has never worked effectively in situations where power or decision making is shared, and it is unlikely that those student organizations were exceptions. He has never been a team player, always loath to delegate authority, except to Raul.

Fidel's interest in the Dominican and Puerto Rican situations was in agitating, organizing student protests, and getting involved physically. He had no interest in presiding over endless discussions about the plight of those neighboring peoples or confining himself to political posturing.[16]

That summer he joined about twelve hundred young Dominicans and Cubans training at Cayo Confites, a small key off the Cuban north coast, to overthrow the Dominican dictator Rafael Leonidas Trujillo. Sweltering, he stayed nearly two months on that mosquito-infested spit of land, wearing a military uniform and training with high-caliber weapons.

He has said he joined as a rank-and-file foot soldier, and if it is true that he obeyed orders and stayed in line, the interlude—and the two years he later spent in prison—would have been the only times in his adult life that Fidel submitted to the will or command of others. It is difficult, however, to imagine that he was an obedient and reliable subordinate.

Juan Bosch, a scholar, intellectual, and later president of the Dominican Republic for a short time in 1963, was at Cayo Confites as the nominal leader

of the expedition. Years later he told Georgie Anne Geyer, one of Fidel's principal biographers, about the aggressive and heartless young Cuban he was just
then getting to know.

One of the other trainees accidentally shot himself and "his whole stomach
was hanging out," Bosch recalled. Fidel witnessed the accident from close at
hand, and Bosch said that he scrutinized his reactions carefully: "His gaze was
fixed on the face of the wounded man. Someone said, 'Put in the stomach.' And
there was terror on the face of the man. But Fidel just kept looking, very serious,
showing nothing. The man died. It was an accident. But I will always remember
that Fidel was very cold and serene. The fact was that he made no demonstration
of emotion; and he continues to be that way."[17]

Fidel has defended his involvement in the Cayo Confites adventure on different occasions, saying that Cuba owed an internationalist obligation—a "debt
of honor"—to the Dominican people. One of the top three leaders of the Cuban
guerrillas who fought against Spain, Maximo Gomez, was a Dominican. So
Fidel for many years remained determined personally to assure repayment in
kind for Gomez's sacrifices. When he initially met Bosch in Havana, Fidel had
impressed him greatly with animated grandiloquence, promising "to die for the
liberty" of the Dominican people.[18]

After the intervention was aborted, Fidel's next opportunity to support the
Dominican people came, probably not coincidentally, almost exactly a dozen
years later, in June 1959, six months after the Castro brothers had won power.
Together they supported a dead serious expedition that, on that second try, was
successful in landing Cuban-trained insurgents on the Dominican coast, and
with exactly the same goal, to overthrow the entrenched dictator.

That second expedition also failed, but not because Cuban leaders, as in
1947, had lost their nerve. Fidel told three American journalists in July 1959,
just after the second attempt, that it had been carefully planned by his government, "with three groups, well armed and the best men available." He said he
could not understand why the expeditionaries had been defeated, although
he was sure some had survived and gone up into the hills to fight against Trujillo
as guerrillas.

The discussion with the reporters was off the record and thereby unusually
candid. It was one of the few times Fidel has admitted explicitly to providing

tangible support to foreign revolutionaries. He was unguarded too when he fantasized about joining the Dominican insurgents so he could once again become personally involved in the struggle against Trujillo.

Herbert Matthews of the *New York Times*, who was trusted by Fidel and other Cuban leaders, was one of the reporters present. His notes of the meeting were kept in his private collection for many years before being released to the archives at Columbia University. He wrote that when Fidel spoke of the surviving guerrillas he presumed were still in the hills in the Dominican Republic, he brooded about joining them. He was convinced they did not have sufficiently inspiring and decisive leadership.

According to Matthews's notes of the meeting, Fidel "had no doubts that if he were able, he could go there and lead them, and said how much he wishes he could do that instead of running Cuba."[19]

Fidel's interest in toppling the brutal Trujillo, then in his third decade in power, reflected the commitment he had made as a university agitator. In one of the rare instances of its kind since the first days of the Cuban Revolution, American and Cuban policies toward a Latin American country virtually coincided where Trujillo was concerned. The Eisenhower and Kennedy administrations also targeted the dictator, covertly providing arms to Dominican dissidents who eventually succeeded in assassinating him in May 1961, when Kennedy was in office.[20]

Supporting the independence movement in Puerto Rico, however, was a much bolder undertaking for Fidel than helping romantic Dominican youths fight a grotesque dictator. The island has been an integral part of the United States since the end of the nineteenth century. Fidel took on the challenge with relish, originally as a militant student leader and later by assigning Cuba's intelligence services the high-priority responsibility of promoting Puerto Rican independence through both peaceful and violent means.

Fidel has believed since his university days that Puerto Rico is a colony of the United States and therefore must be "liberated." In his view, Puerto Ricans have suffered injustices and exploitation since the inglorious end of the Spanish–American War. They were given no choice when they came under American rule. They speak Spanish, their customs and folklore have little to do with Anglo-Saxon traditions; in short, they are a Latin American people. In a televised interview Fidel succinctly stated his view.

"The United States seized Puerto Rico and turned it into a colony."[21]

Other historical principles have also motivated this obsession. Several prominent Puerto Ricans had worked closely with Marti's Cuban Revolutionary Party, which also advocated independence for their island. Their contributions to the Cuban cause, and Marti's commitment to theirs, provided the young Fidel with moral and historical justification. He has publicly cited commonality of interests as an underlying reason for his enduring interest in Puerto Rican independence. It is another debt of internationalist gratitude he has felt obliged to repay.

His efforts to do just that started as he was assimilating Marti's works at the university and when he went on to assume the leadership of the Committee for the Liberation of Puerto Rico. He participated in pro-independence demonstrations and was bloodied in at least one of them. There were "many, large solidarity demonstrations" at the university he later recalled.[22]

"One day in front of the American consulate, in Old Havana," he remembered about thirty years later, "the police hit me a goodly number of blows because I was participating in a demonstration in support of independence for Puerto Rico."[23]

So for at least four decades, beginning in his third year at the university, one of Fidel's most cherished international objectives was the pursuit of Puerto Rican independence, no matter how that affected relations with the United States. He provided extensive support of all types—and not just political and moral help, as he claimed—to Puerto Rican independence parties and front groups, and also to terrorist cells that engaged in lethal violence on the island and in mainland American cities. Puerto Rican terrorist campaigns, assisted for decades by some of Cuba's best and most daring intelligence agents, reached their apogee in the 1970s and early 1980s.

By 1948, many of the beliefs he would hold and disseminate for the rest of his life had coalesced. His personality and character traits, leadership methods, and style were well developed by the time he reached his twenty-second birthday. The abrasively self-confident young man of action had found issues and causes that could propel his ambitions. He was unencumbered by the kinds of moral qualms that cause other men to hesitate or give quarter to real or imagined enemies. The essence of the revolutionary icon who has governed Cuba with an iron fist for more than four and a half decades had been distilled. And it was at about this time that Raul returned to Havana to come under Fidel's wing, after whiling away several years at Biran.

Fidel was not a Marxist yet, but he had begun studying the founders' theoretical works—the writings of Marx, Lenin, and Engels—and he made common cause with communist student leaders in most of his anti-government activities. But even in the unlikely event that he had wanted to join Cuba's Communist Party or its youth affiliate, neither organization would have wanted him. He was too volatile and violent, unlikely to submit to party discipline. It was suggestive of how he would evolve ideologically, however, that in those dawning days of the Cold War—1948 was the year of the Berlin airlift—he refused to identify with the anti-communist and anti-Soviet policies that were being adopted throughout the Western democracies.

He was implacably anti-American. Many other young Cubans also described themselves as anti-imperialist, harboring strong grievances against the United States. That was both fashionable and historically correct, but for nearly all of them those attitudes were largely honored in the abstract; they were issues to be parried in Cuban domestic politics, aired in café banter, but they should not be allowed to undermine good relations with the United States. For him, however, confrontation with Martí's "monster" to the north was both inevitable and desirable. It would be his destiny. It would be his surest route to fame and glory.

Philip Bonsal, the American ambassador until January 1961, bent over backwards to establish a good working relationship with the revolutionary leadership. It was not to be. And in the end, that liberal career diplomat, fluent in Spanish who worked so assiduously to prevent the rupture in bilateral relations, concluded that Fidel was determined to free Cuba of the American presence because he regarded the United States "as his major competitor." Bonsal's interpretation added a new dimension to explanations of Fidel's anti-Americanism. The ambassador wrote that in 1959 Fidel was anti-imperialist because "he sensed that the American presence was inimical to his own drive for absolute power."[24]

In retrospect it is easy to discern in Fidel, the university student, the makings of the adult adversary of the United States. It was not so easy for American observers at the time.

As he was making his way to power, Fidel was masterful in concealing and denying his true beliefs. With only a few exceptions, American journalists and government officials took him largely at his word. He professed, on many occasions and in a variety of settings, to be a democrat. He said he would schedule free and fair elections, reinstate the progressive Cuban constitution of 1940, and maintain good relations with the United States. He denied repeatedly that he had communist inclinations. The revolution was "humanist," he claimed.

There was a lot of wishful thinking by American officials, even in the CIA, that Fidel and his *barbudo* revolutionaries in the mountains were noble young romantics, determined to bring an end to a particularly odious dictatorship. By the middle of 1958 his victory seemed all but inevitable and therefore most U.S. government officials simply hoped for the best. Fidel certainly appeared to have authoritarian tendencies, but American diplomatic and intelligence specialists expected he would mature and mellow. At least there was no evidence that he was a communist, and surely he would keep the two most prominent Marxists in his entourage—Raul and Che Guevara—in check.

That wishful thinking resulted in the first of innumerable American intelligence and policy failures over Cuba. Fidel's many character flaws were overlooked or ignored. His record of revolutionary internationalist involvements was not seen as very important. Little reliable information about him had been gathered by the American embassy in Havana, the consulate in Santiago, or the CIA. His involvement in anti-imperialist activities, Puerto Rican independence, and mafia-style gangland activities were mostly ignored in the dispatches.

There would be many other intelligence failures involving assessments of Fidel. Sadly, they occurred in every decade he has been in power, and for a long time they were compounded, year after year, as the same wrongheaded mindsets about him were perpetuated. Perhaps none of them was as crucial as the original error that persisted for many years. CIA analysts and leaders insisted on believing, despite substantial evidence to the contrary, that Fidel was amenable to good relations with the United States.

CHAPTER FIVE

So We Can Seize Power

Bogotá, the somber capital of Colombia more than eight thousand feet high in the Andes, resembles no other large Latin American city. There is no tropical greenery, no palm trees or pastel colors, little surviving Spanish colonial architecture. Red brick houses and apartment buildings look vaguely Tudor, strangely out of place. The mood is formal, taciturn, wary. Shouldered on three sides by towering snow capped peaks, it is a dark, cool metropolis where even in summer it is wise to wear a coat or shawl against the chilling evening breezes.

The city was the scene of perhaps the worst single outbreak of fratricidal violence in modern Latin American history. A few thousand died there in April 1948 in convulsions of killing and looting—the *bogotazo* it was called—that erupted following the assassination of a wildly popular political leader. Jorge Eliecer Gaitan was the beloved head of the Liberal Party, the apparent presidential front runner trying to unseat the arch enemy Conservatives with promises to uplift the poor and working classes. Instead, his sudden murder at lunchtime on a street near his law office in downtown Bogotá ignited a cataclysmic outburst of violence.

Fidel was there. Just twenty-one years old, he was making his first foreign sojourn, accompanied by three other young Cubans, including his frequent comrade in violent adventure, Rafael del Pino. Fidel and del Pino had earlier collaborated in a little known murder attempt in Havana, according to a prominent historian. That one—the fourth Fidel was said to have been involved in during his university years—targeted Rolando Masferrer, the founder and head of one of the university-based mafia gangs.[1] In Bogotá, Fidel and del Pino were intent on making trouble for the United States, not participating in a revolutionary upheaval. They wound up doing both.

American Secretary of State George Marshall and the foreign ministers of the Latin American countries had gathered in the Colombian capital to hold an important pan-American conference out of which the Organization of American States emerged. Fidel was determined to disrupt and discredit the proceedings. He considered the conference the latest intrusion of American imperialism in Latin America, a menacing effort by the United States, as he once said, to "consolidate its dominance" in the region.

The Cubans, with students from Argentina and a few other countries, hosted a rival conclave that overflowed with heavy doses of anti-imperialist rhetoric, though they got little notice. Undeterred, Fidel and del Pino found a better way to attract attention and to get their anti-American messages communicated at the highest levels.

Somehow they got into the ornate Colon Theater in downtown Bogotá, where the foreign ministers were meeting. From high on a balcony they scattered thousands of leaflets on the delegates who were seated below, mingling with the cream of Colombian society. Most of the propaganda had been printed in Havana. It propounded Fidel's familiar litany of that time, demands for the independence of Puerto Rico, the return of the Panama Canal, and the end of the Trujillo dictatorship.[2]

The two Cubans were arrested and interrogated as their hotel room was searched. But Fidel says he was able to talk his way out by persuading the Colombian detectives that his intentions were idealistic and harmless, and that the conservative Colombian government was not his target. He later said he had passionately explained to the police his view of the injustices Latin American countries were suffering under American influence while making clear his noble, romantic intentions. If that part of his account can be taken at face value, as it more or less probably can, once again Fidel's gilded tongue worked its powers of persuasion. He and del Pino were soon released.

In an interview more than thirty years later with a Colombian journalist, Fidel recalled that brief detention, as well as his involvement a few days later in the *bogotazo*: "We were rather lucky in our talk with the detectives. In fact I got the impression that someone in charge even liked what we were saying. We were quite persuasive."[3]

Fidel and del Pino had met with the charismatic Gaitan just two days before he was assassinated, winning his implicit support for their rump conference. They were scheduled to meet with him again on the afternoon he was murdered. That coincidence fueled extravagant rumors, believed by many to this day, that the two Cubans shared somehow in the responsibility for the murder and the violence it ignited.

Fidel was impressed with Gaitan, a persuasive orator and organizer, the apparent front runner in the next Colombian presidential elections. He was charismatic, physically imposing. His progressive politics and energetic style resembled those of Eduardo Chibas, the leader of Cuba's new Orthodox Party, with which Fidel had affiliated the year before. Gaitan, however, was more in touch with the common people.

There was little Fidel saw in Bogotá that reminded him of Cuba. Colombia, in the Andean highlands, was like nothing he had ever seen before. Far from home, he knew no one. Colombian history and politics were largely unknown to him as well; he had almost no basis for judging why multitudes of Gaitan's supporters would soon be spilling into the streets bent on vengeance over the death of their leader. Fidel may not have known that anti-imperialist grievances were the furthest thing from their minds. The United States had never intervened in Colombia. The political situation was nothing like that in Panama or the Dominican Republic.

Like everyone else in Bogotá, Fidel was taken by surprise when the brooding city burst suddenly into unprecedented bloodshed. He did know that nothing like it had ever happened in Cuba. In fact, nothing comparable had occurred anywhere in Latin America.

The tumult erupted as soon as Gaitan's followers learned of his death. "They've killed Gaitan. They've killed Gaitan," was screamed through the streets.

"We saw an enormous procession of people–a river of people coming along a street," Fidel later remembered. "They had weapons; some had rifles. . . . It was an enormous crowd—thousands of people advancing along that street . . . I joined them. I got in the front line of that crowd."

Without much contemplation, Fidel decided to join the rioters, plunging headlong into the mayhem. It was not enough to be just an anonymous body in that roiling mass; he quickly moved up to a position in the vanguard, at the front lines of the rioters where he could more easily assert a leadership role.

He had no difficulty arming himself, at first with a tear gas gun and later with a rifle. He remained in the fray for about two days, first in the streets with the mobs, attacking and ransacking government buildings and police stations, and then overnight at a hillside redoubt, firing and being fired upon and for a period of time actually leading a squad of men ready to resist an army assault.

He had never been in a situation anything like it. Fires were burning out of control, the charred hulks of buses and cars were lying overturned in the streets, armed and raging mobs were running amok. Entirely by chance he was experiencing a popular upheaval like ones he had only read about. The storming of the Bastille by mobs of frenzied French revolutionaries was on his mind.

He thought it must be the first, chaotic stage of a revolution. He remembers being "filled with revolutionary fervor, trying to get as many people as possible to join the revolutionary movement." Later, on the first afternoon of the violence, armed with the rifle he stole, he leapt onto a bench in front of the war ministry building in the chaotic downtown of the city.

He says that he "harangued the military men who were there, trying to get them to join the revolution."

That and his other responses to the situation reflect the unique character traits he has exhibited in dangerous and stressful situations ever since. Few other foreigners caught in the maelstrom reacted as he did. Nearly all fled or hid. Del Pino was with him for part of the time in the streets, but the other two Cubans remained safely behind in their lodgings. One of them was a leader of the young communists at the university, and later Fidel would never let him forget that he timorously sat out the turbulence.

To have participated in the violence would have been insane by almost any-one's standards, especially for one who had no stake in Colombian politics. Fidel did not give it a second thought. His decision to join the rioters and the subsequent choices he made to stay and fight with them were entirely consistent with his mindset, convictions, personality framework, and proclivity for violence. His response was completely in character.

His accounts of why he decided to stay, offered much later, are exculpatory and self-serving. As always, his retrospective version of events reflected the shrewd eye he fixes on how he will be remembered in history. He asserted that his decisions derived only from internationalist convictions, that his purposes were honorable and selfless. There is nothing in his explanations to suggest the larger truth, that his actions sprung more from sanguinary compulsions than noble promptings.

Above all Fidel sensed an opportunity to win fame and glory. He lusted for action and perhaps also for danger. The *bogotazo* was a means to learn first hand how to make the best of a revolutionary situation, so that one day he could apply the lessons learned there at home in Cuba. And he should also be taken at his word that he eventually felt an internationalist obligation to help Gaitan's rioting followers. But that, by his own accounts, came later, well after he had hurled himself into the streets with the rioters.

He says it was not until the early morning hours of the second day of the unrest that he began seriously to contemplate what he was doing, and "I was overcome by an internationalist sentiment. I thought, well, the people here are the same as the people in Cuba. These people are oppressed and exploited . . . I may die here, but I am staying."

It did not turn out to be Colombia's Bastille. Gaitan's followers did not bring about a revolution; the fever of the violence abated almost as quickly as it had flared. Order was restored after leaders of the Liberal and Conservative political parties concluded a cease fire, wanting above all to end the killing as quickly as possible. Fidel later characterized that solution as a betrayal of the interests of all those—including himself—who had taken to the streets.

When it was over, as he was preparing to go back to his hotel, he realized that his personal arsenal had grown from the rifle he began with to a sword and a cutlass. He had managed to acquire a policeman's vest and a cap, which he wore as a beret. Along the way he had attempted to steal a pair of boots from a terrified policeman, but they did not fit. He had made himself as ready as he could for combat.

Fidel's usually precise memory failed him, however, when, in three different accounts of his activities during interviews in three different decades, he had diverging recollections about how many bullets he had left when the violence ended.[4]

In a taped interview in the 1960s, he told Carlos Franqui he had fired four of the sixteen bullets he acquired. In two subsequent accounts, he recalled he had either nine or fourteen bullets left at the end. The most interesting discrepancy is that he admitted only to Franqui that he had actually fired his rifle four times.

By 1948 Fidel was an expert marksman. He did not tell Franqui if any of the shots he fired struck their targets, but clearly he was choosing his shots carefully and, as always, not wasting ammunition. If he thought he had killed or injured Colombian military personnel who remained loyal to the government that night, he would not have wanted it known. He avoided the subject entirely in his three extended public accountings and has never been questioned about it on the record.

Enrique Ovares was one of the four Cubans in the student delegation that went with Fidel to Bogotá. He recalled in an interview in Miami in 1967 that Fidel was still carrying the purloined rifle when they caught up with each other. "I asked him what he was doing. Fidel only responded that it was his duty."[5]

Fidel has admitted he was fascinated by the terrible violence he witnessed, but has never said he was also appalled or repelled by it. Each time he has described his participation, he failed to express remorse for the thousands of dead and wounded, the widespread property damage in the city, or the years of savage internecine conflict the *bogotazo* sparked in the Colombian countryside. His sentiments then—and every time he spoke of those events since—were cold, detached, and bloodless. He has repeatedly insisted too that he was proud of what he did: "I acted in accord with my moral principles, with dignity and honor, with discipline and with incredible selflessness."[6]

In August 1993, Fidel returned for the first time to Colombia since those events in 1948, ironically to attend a conference not too unlike the foreign ministers meeting in Bogotá he had disrupted. He went to Cartagena, a colonial city on Colombia's Caribbean coast, for a meeting of Latin American and Iberian heads of government. He was asked during a news conference at the VIP guest house where he stayed if the decades-old rumors were true and if he had personally instigated the *bogotazo*. He denied that he had, of course, cloaking his involvement in internationalist virtue: "It was one of the most disinterested and altruistic moments of my life."[7] Enrique Ovares remembered it quite differently. "It was an hysteric, ambitious, and uncontrollable Fidel who acted in those events."[8]

Alfredo Guevara, president of the University of Havana student federation, and the communist who had stayed in his hotel room, was the fourth Cuban in Bogotá. He was also horrified by how Fidel and del Pino had behaved. Del Pino had looted jewelry stores during the rioting, and although Fidel has never been charged with that, he was considered guilty by association. He was viewed as even more disreputable after the *bogotazo* than he had been before.

Safely back at the University of Havana, Fidel found his notoriety soaring. "The Cubans," as he and del Pino were being referred to in the Colombian press, had attracted considerable attention. The conservative government was looking for convenient foreign scapegoats, even for accomplices they could try to implicate in Gaitan's assassination. An international conspiracy was a politically more palatable explanation for the violence than the truth, which was that a large sector of the population was aggrieved.

All sorts of rumors were flying, some of which continue to be believed by many today. Respected American diplomats who attended the inter-American conference later claimed to have heard Fidel, in a raging radio broadcast in Bogotá at the height of the violence, proclaim that a socialist revolution had begun.

He and del Pino reportedly were observed by Colombian intelligence agents conspiring with radical labor leaders. It was said that Gaitan's assassin had been seen that morning in a downtown Bogotá café conferring with del Pino as Fidel monitored them nearby.[9] Other, even wilder stories proliferated. None of these reports has ever been substantiated, and some have been definitively refuted. Whatever the truth of these more incendiary tales, Fidel's legend for extraordinary behavior was taking hold, and not just in Cuba.

As an adjunct professor at Georgetown University for twenty-five years, teaching courses on the Cuban Revolution, I always emphasized the importance of the *bogotazo*. Fidel emerged from it with his revolutionary character almost fully formed. I always polled my students, asking what they would have done if they had found themselves stranded in a strange foreign city as it exploded into savage violence. I never had one who said he or she would have joined the rioters.

Fidel's participation in the violence was of enduring significance for him and Cuba. The *bogotazo* instilled a number of lessons—strategic, doctrinal, tactical, and personal.

He later said he had been impressed with "the phenomenon of how an oppressed people could erupt. . . . The April ninth uprising influenced me greatly in my later revolutionary life."

Most immediately, it illuminated the path to his victory in Cuba. It gave flesh-and-blood relevance to his childhood and adolescent musings about the storming of the Bastille and other decisive revolutionary moments in history. It demonstrated in particular, that an unexpected, shocking act of violence— whether planned or not—could ignite a revolutionary upheaval. Bogotá in 1948 was therefore the precursor of the Moncada assault that launched him on his trajectory to power.

A second strategic lesson of more enduring significance for Cuba and many other countries was that Fidel's internationalist vision was cemented in Bogotá. Cayo Confites had been a dress rehearsal; Bogotá was the real thing. The commitments he made to fight for another people were fixed with certainty and finality.

That awakening happened in the streets of the city, and, by his telling, most poignantly on the slopes of the nearly ten-thousand-foot tall Monserrate mountain, on the first night of the violence as he waited for the Colombian army to attack his position with tanks. The danger seemed to be acute, but he says he decided to stay and fight with Gaitan's beleaguered followers. The way he tells it, his decision was an electrifying, life-altering event.

Through the rest of his career, he would always expect his subordinates and followers to perform in dangerous situations as he did. On two or three occasions, he says, he narrowly escaped death in Bogotá, implying that Colombians around him during one of those skirmishes were killed under military fire. He recalled that at some point he decided to lead an attack on a divisional police headquarters to obtain more weapons. It seemed "suicidal," though, as it turned out, the policemen there had joined the rioters and did not resist. For him those most dangerous moments, when he was pumped up with adrenalin, were high points, tests of his valor.

However self-serving his recollections may be, he has always expected other revolutionaries to emulate his behaviour. Zealotry in the pursuit of his revolutionary causes would be the fundamental requirement. He believes true revolutionaries must plunge willingly, heroically into action without getting bogged down in needless contemplation or theorizing. He came to expect fanaticism from those charged with defending the revolution at home and in pursuing revolutionary internationalist causes abroad. In Fidel's mind, at least, the decision to stay and fight on Bogotá's Monserrate mountain provided the model for all future revolutionary internationalists.

Once in power, with the capability to assist peoples whom he considered oppressed or exploited, he would never waver in performing internationalist duties. Internationalism would remain his and Cuba's sacred obligation as he provided clandestine and propaganda support, and on some momentous occasions massive military backing, for guerrillas and revolutionaries in about two dozen countries on three continents.

In particular, he never gave up hope that Colombian revolutionaries would one day complete the task that had been thwarted in April 1948. With Cuban government assistance, Marxist guerrillas first took up arms in remote regions of the Andean foothills in the early 1960s, inspired by the Cuban Revolution and Fidel's constant calls for revolutionary action. More than forty years later two of those movements are still waging bloody guerrilla warfare in large areas of the Colombian countryside. No other nation has for so many years been the object of his revolutionary entanglements.

The People's Liberation Army and the Colombian Revolutionary Armed Forces are no longer mistaken for virtuous, romantic advocates of Gaitán's legacy. Today they enjoy the support of no more than 3 or 4 percent of the Colombian populace, and even that small number has declined as their acts of urban terrorism have turned especially savage and their dependence on narcotics trafficking has increased.

Both groups have been certified by the U.S. Department of State as international terrorist organizations. The larger Revolutionary Armed Forces have kidnapped and killed Americans, conducting brutal campaigns in Bogotá and other large cities that have targeted innocent civilians. The People's Liberation Army, historically the closer of the two movements to the Cuban government, has specialized in bombing remote petroleum pipelines and facilities as well as kidnappings. Both groups have stubbornly refused to lay down their arms and participate in the Colombian democratic process despite the many peace initiatives and internationally assisted negotiating processes that have been mounted.

K. S. Karol, a Polish–French Marxist intellectual who spent extended periods of time in Cuba in the 1960s in the thrall of the revolution, wrote of a third critically important lesson Fidel derived from the *bogotazo*. It would prove to be the most consequential of all.

Karol traveled around the island with Fidel and was, until their later bitter falling out, an influential Paris-based supporter. He concluded that Fidel was so galvanized by his Bogotá experiences that he was impelled for the first time to begin developing a real social philosophy. By Karol's informed analysis, Fidel's reflections led to his initial attraction to Marxist–Leninist doctrine. Fidel concluded that what he had seen in Bogotá was class warfare in the raw.

Karol believed that by witnessing "the extraordinary violence smoldering just beneath the apparently peaceful surface of Latin America," Fidel returned to Cuba with an appreciation of the region's acute social problems. Gaitan's murder was what had sparked the rioting, but "desperation and hunger," in Karol's words, were its root causes.

As Karol explained it in his book, *Guerrillas in Power*, Fidel "came to realize that the fight for moral right and justice must be coupled with the fight for social improvements." Karol believed that "this discovery left a deep mark" on Fidel.[10]

Lionel Martin, who interviewed Fidel and other Cuban government officials for his biographical study, *The Early Fidel*, agreed with Karol. He wrote that ". . . it was precisely in the period following the *bogotazo* that Fidel began studying Marxism in earnest."[11]

Fidel himself has never made that connection, though his periodic musings on the subject support the view. He told Lee Lockwood that for a year or two before 1948 he had been "a kind of utopian socialist," perhaps not unlike large numbers of curious university students in almost any country during much of the twentieth century.

He says his Marxist–Leninist awakening began when he read Lenin's landmark work, *State and Revolution*, and became acquainted with the writings of Karl Marx and Freidrich Engels. He says Marx and Engels "had an almost apocalyptic influence" on him. In a speech in Chile in 1971 he recalled the discovery as an epiphany: "For me it was a revelation . . . so persuasive that I was absolutely amazed. I was converted to those ideas."[12]

He told the Brazilian priest Betto much the same, that in 1948 his discovery of Marxist thinking opened intellectual horizons for him: "It completely won me over. Just as Ulysses was ensnared by the Siren's song, I was captivated by the irrefutable truths of Marxist literature. Immediately I began to grasp it."[13]

Despite the assurance those remarks suggest, Fidel was not yet a dedicated Marxist. Over the years, he has often been inconsistent and vague about the timing of his conversion. In an interview with the sympathetic biographer Lionel Martin in 1974, he said that when he graduated from the university "I already had a Marxist–Leninist formation." That equivocation is about as close as he has ever come to claiming that by 1950 his thinking had coalesced into full-scale Marxism–Leninism.

There is no doubt, that he was keenly attracted to communist doctrine, but he was just as determined to avoid any embrace of the communist party. A ranking Cuban communist who knew Fidel well once observed that in his latter university days he liked individual communists, but not the communism of Cuba's party.[14]

Fidel was aware he could never advance politically as a member of the party. Cuban communists by and large were too cautious, even bourgeois, to support his style of confrontational militance. They had supported the Batista government during World War II; two party elders held cabinet posts in his government. The party was linked to the political establishment. Most members were café dilettantes, and Fidel knew there was no chance they would adopt a revolutionary program.

And his reservations about them were reciprocated. They were repelled by his notoriety and grandiosity and his penchant for violence. They later denounced the Moncada attack as reckless and "putschist," a term that was used to smear him as a fascist. They knew he could never function under party discipline. His more pliable brother Raul, in contrast, was a more likely prospect.

After returning from Bogotá, Fidel realized his political ambitions required him to conceal or minimize his increasingly radical thinking. In 1948, popular support for anti-imperialist causes was evaporating in Cuba. Large wheels of history were turning as global relationships were changing. The Cold War had just begun in Europe following the communist coup in Czechoslovakia, and the Berlin airlift began shortly after Fidel returned from Bogotá. Stalin's Soviet Union was aggressively challenging the West while consolidating a huge communist sphere of influence in Eastern Europe. Mao was triumphing in China.

Suddenly, there was little sympathy for anti-American rhetoric or demonstrations in favor of causes like Puerto Rican independence, which now seemed peripheral. Fidel has said that around the time he returned from Bogotá the number of anti-imperialist students at the university had dwindled to no more than thirty, including himself and the communists.[15] In terms of his own political aspirations, he understood that going back to the ramparts and brandishing anti-imperialism would not advance his political career.

He was no less an anti-imperialist but decided pragmatically to push those convictions into the background, where they would stay until some months after he won power. They were sublimated, never abandoned.

Fidel organized and led fewer anti-American demonstrations, backed off on the Puerto Rican independence issue, and got in step with the Cuba-centric programs of the Orthodox Party. Chibas and the other principal leaders of that party had no anti-American ax to grind. They were openly anti-Soviet and anti-communist.

Fidel, however, never resorted to anti-communist baiting, which is perhaps the clearest indication that he was attracted to Marxist–Leninist doctrine. With the outbreak of the Korean War in June 1950, his fundamental differences with Chibas over the Cold War became clear. The Orthodox Party leader supported the Truman administration, downplaying his earlier support for anti-imperialist bashing because now the Soviet bloc loomed as an even greater threat. Fidel never supported the war in Korea, Cuban participation, or American Cold War foreign policies in general.

He was then drafting articles for two communist youth publications reflecting his concern over the plight of Cuban workers and peasants. He signed an international petition, organized by pro-Soviet front groups, to ban nuclear weapons. He did not openly identify with Soviet or communist causes, but rejected the paranoiac anti-communism that was shaping American responses during the early years of the Cold War. Leaving himself plenty of room for future strategical maneuvering, Fidel neither condemned nor overtly supported communists or communism.

His intellectual baggage was gradually becoming more heavily weighted with the works of the communist world's leading lights. The many volumes of Marti in his library now were being nudged aside for Marxist treatises. He bought a copy of Marx's *Das Kapital* in New York during his honeymoon. He began to learn—apparently for the first time—about the Bolshevik Revolution and the rise of the Soviet Union. His friendships with communist student leaders deepened as he frequented the Communist Party bookstore in Old Havana. Intellectually and politically he may have been moving in different directions, but he sensed that someday doctrine and destiny would converge.

When Fidel completed his law studies in September 1950, he was set adrift without a course or navigating skills. His ambitions and need for political triumphs were as strong as ever, but he had no plan and poor prospects given his unsavory reputation. His biographer Robert Quirk concluded that Fidel had expected fame, but instead got notoriety: "Whatever his apologists wrote later, he never distinguished himself in any capacity during his five years at the university."[16]

He was now certified to practice law, and did not object in those days when he was referred to as "Dr. Castro," though it was soon evident he had hardly any interest in the profession. That was the latest of the disappointments he inflicted on Angel and Lina, who had hoped he would return to Oriente to represent the family's interests. Surely, however, Fidel never considered the life of a provincial lawyer as a possibility. He despised ponderous procedure, the intricacies of due process, the need to weigh evidence judiciously, and he knew that much of the legal system was corrupt.

In another society he might have thrived as a thundering prosecutor or flamboyant trial attorney. He did try his hand at least once during those wilderness years in the early 1950s at righteous legal drama. He filed an indictment against the new Cuban president for malfeasance, with no hope at all of winning but the intention of embarrassing the president while attracting attention to himself.

Fidel's only big case ironically turned out to be the self-defense he mounted at his own trial following the Moncada assault. His courtroom peroration, later rewritten and widely disseminated in pamphlet form, would be one of the most important documents ever associated with him. It outlined and endeavored to justify his revolutionary program.

The speech, *History Will Absolve Me*, is remembered by its last four words. Many scholars and Castro biographers have pointed out that Fidel's final phrase bore a stunning resemblance to the closing phrase Hitler uttered in self-defense at his trial in Munich in 1923. But Fidel's statement no doubt was also modeled on speeches by classical orators he had studied.

"Condemn me if you wish. It does not matter. Because history will absolve me."

Halfheartedly, with two working-class students who had graduated with him, he set up a tenuous practice in a walk-up on Tejadilla Street in Old Havana, advertising legal representation in "civil, criminal, and social" matters. It was the Cuban equivalent of a poverty law practice. Nearly all of the clients were poor, and usually they could not pay in cash. One defendant he managed to get acquitted—a Spanish sculptor—reimbursed him with a bust of Martí that Fidel kept in a place of honor in his library.[17]

In October 1948 Fidel had married Mirta Diaz Balart, and the following year their son Fidelito was born. The Castro family was delighted with the match; most of the conservative Diaz Balarts were horrified. Angel continued to provide an allowance. The stipends kept flowing at least into 1951, when Fidel was twenty-five years old.[18] Fidel was a married man and father, but the prospect of settling down into a conventional bourgeois lifestyle held no attraction.

By nearly all accounts he was deeply in love with his bride, although a few detractors have claimed it was a marriage of convenience because her family was so well connected to powerful political interests. He was a terrible provider, took little interest in the household, and was not often home with his wife and son. When he was there they ate mostly spaghetti. A few years later he began his affair with the equally beautiful Natalia Revuelta, who later bore him his only known daughter, Alina Fernandez.

Carlos Prio had succeeded the despised Grau San Martin as president in October 1948, campaigning on platitudes and calls for anti-communist vigilance. It proved to be the last time Cubans went to the polls in anything resembling democratic elections.

Prio was from the same political party as his predecessor and not much of an improvement. Cuban politics remained mired in corruption as gangland political violence continued to roar out of control. Nevertheless, because the economy was thriving in the postwar boom, most Cubans stoically endured their country's political scandals. Their best hope for the future was Eduardo Chibas.

Chibas had broken in disgust from the governing party in May 1947, announcing the creation of the new Orthodox Party that quickly became the principal focus of center–left opposition interests. Fidel was among the first to join its youth branch, transferring much of his passion for organizing and protesting to the party's political operations. Chibas was a mesmerizing, passionate orator who campaigned indefatigably against corruption and violence. Every Sunday night Cubans gathered in homes and cafés to listen to his radio broadsides in which he lambasted public officials with specific and sordid details of corruption. His reputation for honesty and probity set him apart from the bilious political mainstream, and his following steadily grew.

Chibas had little use for Fidel, who endeavored tirelessly to attach himself to that rising star. According to Fidel's friend Jose Pardo Llada, the Orthodox leader did not want Fidel around him. Chibas believed "he was a gangster," a notorious *pistolero* who could only hurt Chibas and the party's image.[19] It did not matter that Fidel was loosening his ties with the university-based mafia gangs by the time he joined the party. The stains of his past were not so easily expunged.

Chibas and the party chieftains thought of Fidel as unprincipled. They were aware that he was opportunistically pursuing other possibilities on the political right and the extreme left. He may even have been conniving to win a sinecure in the same Prio administration he was denouncing, and some who knew him speculate that he was receiving an illicit government stipend.

He may well have been weighing four divergent routes to a more promising political future. It was such behavior that prompted his political associate of that era, Luis Conte Aguero, who I interviewed in Coral Gables, Florida many years after he left Cuba, to suggest that Fidel had been nothing more than "a chameleon."

In early February 1950, Fidel's namesake and would-be godfather Fidel
Pino Santos, then a member of Congress, wrote to Prio's secretary of agriculture
seeking a position there for "the son of our friend Angel Castro." The minister,
Carlos Hevia, a U.S. Naval Academy graduate who had once been president of
Cuba for approximately seventy-two hours, responded courteously six days later
that he could not help. Hevia had a reputation for honesty and was a dedicated
anti-communist. He had no interest in the controversial young man whose
reputation had surely come to his attention.[20]

It was also during this period that Fidel flirted with the possibility of forg-
ing some kind of relationship with Fulgencio Batista. The one-time army
sergeant, the only Cuban ever to rise from poverty to the presidency, had ruled
for ten years in different capacities after a 1933 coup. He was fairly elected to a
four-year presidential term in 1940, proceeding to build a mixed record of progressive reforms that boosted his popularity with the working classes. But at the
same time he sanctioned targeted acts of violence against opponents. Batista
won a Senate seat in 1948, planning to be reelected as president in the 1952
elections as a right-of-center candidate.

Fidel met with his future mortal adversary at Batista's country estate,
"Kukines." Batista and Angel had known each other in Oriente, and the one-
time enlisted man who had promoted himself to general was receptive to a meeting with the intriguing upstart, Angel Castro's son. Fidel's brother-in-law Rafael
Diaz Balart, then a member of Batista's infant political party, arranged the meeting. Most of what transpired remains clouded in mystery, though it is clear that
the two men fascinated each other. Diaz Balart many years later told Georgie
Anne Geyer that they "looked at each other with admiration."[21]

They warily sized each other up but seem never to have reached any
agreement about ways in which they might collaborate while probably not fore-
closing that possibility either. Diaz Balart remembers that Fidel asked for the meeting, telling him he wanted to encourage Batista to undertake a coup. The meeting
took place in Batista's library with Diaz Balart and another Batista supporter present. The two principals toyed with each other. Fidel perused books on Batista's
library shelves and mused aloud, "Your library is very attractive, but it seems to be
missing a very important work." He paused, then added that the missing book
was an obscure old tome about techniques for conducting a military coup.[22]

With that transparent reference Fidel meant to indicate that he would support a coup by Batista. Diaz Balart recalls that everyone laughed heartily and awkwardly, too, no doubt, but the wily older man did not take the bait. Afterwards, he presciently told Diaz Balart that his friend "was very intelligent but dangerous." Fidel's Orthodox Party friend Pardo Llada, wrote that Fidel arranged subsequent meetings with Batista. He was keeping a spectrum of options open for getting ahead, whether through legitimate or revolutionary means.[23]

Fidel was still hopeful that a Bastille or *bogotazo* style event might yet provide his opening. When Chibas died of a gunshot wound, sensationally self inflicted during a live radio broadcast in August 1951, Fidel had the chance to revive his familiar anarchist notion of provoking a mass uprising. The suicide aroused an enormous outpouring of grief and concern. It had been widely assumed that Chibas would win the presidency the following year. Could the *bogotazo* be replicated in Cuba?

At the funeral, after delivering five different versions of a lengthy eulogy, Fidel approached Pardo Llada, wanting to know where the body would be taken after the ceremonies.

"To the cemetery."

Instead, Fidel insisted, they should take the remains processionally through the streets to the presidential palace. He wanted to take advantage of the large, mourning crowds that had gathered. He understood how intense the popular feeling was. "Why the palace?" Pardo Llada wanted to know.[24] "So we can seize power," Fidel retorted.

Unlike accounts of his other most incendiary proposals, Fidel boastfully confirmed this one. Speaking to a group of Latin American journalists in August 1967, he told them that Chibas's mourners had numbered around five hundred thousand. He told the reporters what he remembered saying to the Orthodox Party leaders assembled at the funeral: "Let's carry the body to the palace, and there the people will topple the government. With this multitude confronting it, the government will fall. In one hour the revolution will have triumphed."[25]

Sixteen years after Chibas's death, Fidel was proud of what he had wanted to do, convinced he might actually have sparked a revolution. Of course his wild

idea had been incredulously brushed aside, and his standing in the eyes of
Chibas's Orthodox Party successors sank even lower.

He was able, nonetheless, to bully his way, against the Orthodox Party's
wishes, into campaigning as a candidate for a seat in the lower house of
Congress. He never actually received the nomination, though he campaigned
with characteristic fervor and energy, finding ingenious ways to make himself
familiar to working-class voters in poor Havana neighborhoods. Historians
generally agree that Fidel probably would have won. He has said repeatedly,
however, that he had no intention of being a retiring back-bencher. He
described his plan in 1967: "When I was seated in the congress I would immediately present a revolutionary program to the people, four or five revolutionary bills, not so that they would be approved but to present a program for a
revolution."[26]

Just as he had no disposition for practicing law, Fidel's personality and
proclivity for violence ruled out any possibility he could ever function in a
democratic environment.

By 1952 he deplored virtually everything about democratic process in
Cuba. The country had labored through nearly its entire existence as an independent nation under dictators or corrupt strongmen masquerading as democ-
rats. Nothing in his education had led him to think positively about democracy.
Even in the large body of Marti's writings there were no ringing endorsements of
liberal democracy. By Fidel's reckoning, moreover, the nearest democracy, the
United States, was a rapacious exploiter and imperialist overlord, hardly a model
for Cuba.

Furthermore, Fidel's few personal experiences with electoral politics had all
confirmed that the Cuban system was rotten. He blamed his failures to advance
in university politics on others and on corruption, but never on his own short-
comings. He remembered as a boy helping his half brother Pedro Emilio in a
campaign to win office in Oriente. The effort failed, and again he said it was
because of corruption. In the Betto interview he deplored how his father felt it
necessary to subsidize local politicians Fidel considered venal. There was nothing
in democracy as he knew it that appealed to him. By running for Congress he
meant only to advance his revolutionary ends—to bring down the pseudo-
democratic system and to seize power.

It turned out, however, that Batista did it first. The 1952 elections, scheduled for that June, were nullified by the surprise military coup Batista staged almost bloodlessly on March 10. He did not consult with his future nemesis, of course, but the coup is all the more interesting in light of the meeting Batista had with Fidel at "Kukines."

Had Fidel in fact hoped for a military coup? If not, how can his oblique reference to a takeover of the government when he first visited Batista be explained? Was he strategically so farsighted that he could envision an unpopular right-wing dictatorship as better for his political fortunes than the alternatives? Did he give Batista even more explicit encouragement in their later off-the-record meetings?

These tantalizing questions are impossible to answer. But considered in the context of Fidel's long record of political sagacity and duplicity, it would seem there is a good chance he did yearn for a right-wing dictatorship to take power. Batista's coup was a godsend. It was the most promising turning point in Fidel's career until then. Discredited and mistrusted in Cuba's most influential political circles, he would get a new lease on life in a situation in which his audacity would be admired, in which his violent and conspiratorial methods would be considered necessary and virtuous. Rudderless after graduating from the university, he was able to set a new course toward a destiny Marti would have approved. His David versus Goliath mission would be to bring down the dictatorship. With Batista illegally in office, Fidel could *legitimately* go about trying to seize power.

The anti-dictatorial struggle would make the best of his many intellectual and leadership strengths. His oratorical and other public performance skills, his gift for recruiting and motivating followers, his indefatigability and determination would all be powerful advantages. The unflinching certainty that he was somehow meant to play a crucial historical role would no longer seem so preposterous and egotistical. Even his record since childhood of springing surprise confrontations on authority figures was perfectly suited for his new mission.

His principal character flaws—narcissism, egotism, and an obsessive need for power and control—could actually now work to his advantage. The revolutionary movement would have to be vertically structured, with strong and decisive central leadership, and a charismatic figure at the top. Fidel's need to be in control of every detail, to count every bullet, could actually be helpful. He was twenty-six and cleverly presented his youth as an asset. He and his young supporters, in what after Moncada came to be known as the July Twenty-sixth Movement, represented a generational challenge to the corrupt and failed older men who had governed Cuba for so long.

He learned to feign humility and simplicity, in the process becoming more skillful at communicating nuanced messages to sophisticated audiences. Everything about him was now primed and practiced for the challenge of taking on Batista. Everything else in his life was soon subordinated to that strategic plan. His wife and son rarely saw him. He abandoned his struggling little law practice. He ignored the family at Biran.

Planning many moves ahead on the chessboard, he knew he would need to attract broad support from diverse sectors of Cuban society. He therefore avoided his old communist friends from the university and had no interest in recruiting any of them to join him and begin military training. Years later he acknowledged that well-calculated element of his strategy. He told an interviewer that there were no communists aboard the *Granma*. He could have said the same about Moncada, except that Raul was the single exception in both cases. Any associations with communism or communists, other than those of his brother who denied them would have been detrimental.

With just as much foresight and clarity of purpose, he ceased nearly all criticism of the United States and made almost no further mention of internationalist issues. He promised free and fair elections, to reinstate Cuba's progressive 1940 Constitution that Batista had suspended, and to restore democracy. He repeated these and similar pledges whenever he had the chance. He knew he had to have the support of Cuba's urban middle classes and that he could never prevail if the American government was determined to prevent his victory.

So after the 1952 coup, when he set his course straight and clear, Fidel never again spoke critically of the United States—that is, until the first day after he won power.

CHAPTER SIX

He Is Our Father

"He is our living symbol," Raul shouted in the best basso profundo he could muster. "The most important symbol we have is named Fidel Castro."

In mid-June 1989, Raul pounded the lectern, both in anger and adulation, speaking to a large, tense assemblage of uniformed military officers in the main auditorium of the armed forces ministry in Havana. He was almost two hours into an often incoherent tirade, seemingly inebriated or on the verge of some sort of a breakdown. He growled at a hapless photographer who got between him and the television cameras.

"Are you aware, comrade journalist, that there is order in this room?"

They knew Raul to be stern, a harsh disciplinarian, but few of the younger officers had ever seen him so agitated before. One of his closest aides remembered it as the most difficult speech Raul ever had to deliver. He had desperate misgivings about what he had to say and do, but there was no doubting his loyalty in carrying out what his commander-in-chief was demanding.

"He is our father," Raul continued, bellowing now. With no prompting and no evident disagreement with that odd characterization, the generals and lower ranking officers erupted into vigorous, sustained applause. As one, they began chanting, "Fee-del! . . . Fee-del!"

"Let us be his humble children," Raul finally intoned.

It had fallen upon him to explain to Cuba's military elite, many of them skeptical and worried about what was coming next, why the country's favorite general—Arnaldo Ochoa, the hero of internationalist campaigns in a half dozen countries—had just been arrested and was about to be put on trial for treason. There was not a man in that hall who didn't understand that Raul was the messenger merely carrying out Fidel's plan. They would find out soon enough what the brothers were up to, and in the meantime there was not a thing they could do about it.

Raul's performance during that unusually stressful affair provides a valuable interpretive key to the psychological substrata of his relationship with Fidel. By referring to Fidel as his "father," Raul bared a hidden chamber of his psyche.

Rufo Lopez Fresquet, the Castro brothers' first finance minister who went into exile after serving for approximately fourteen months in the cabinet, was the first to comment on Fidel and Raul's twisted father–son relationship. He wrote, "Fidel acts rather like a father to Raul, a strict father." Lopez Fresquet recounted several incidents he witnessed in Havana in early 1959 when Fidel brutally berated and reprimanded his brother. The worst of these humiliations occurred in the presence of hundreds of officials and bureaucrats. Raul was so crushed that he cried openly as he fled the scene.[1] Other eyewitnesses have told similar stories.

Nonetheless, Raul's reference to Fidel as a father figure was unprecedented for either of the brothers. For years he had routinely extolled Fidel with worshipful paeans in public appearances, and he continues to do so, but he had never before referred to his brother in that fashion. The pressure of the moment had dredged up those emotions from the depths of his spirit. He was telling the other officers that Fidel, his "father," was also their "father," and Fidel needed all of his children to affirm their unwavering allegiance.

Raul was not exaggerating the complexity of his relationship with his brother. Beginning when they were children at Biran and in the Catholic schools they attended in Santiago, and later in the early 1950s when they were together again in Havana, Fidel sometimes acted as a surrogate father to his little brother. In the 1989 speech Raul said exactly that.

"He was always my second father when I was a student in primary school."

He meant it literally, that he had always lionized Fidel, looked up to him not just as a big brother and protector but as much more. Fidel looked after him, defended him. He was a father figure standing in for the distant and indifferent Angel, who never cared much for the family's youngest son.

The primary school Raul mentioned was La Salle, the Christian Brothers academy where it appears he was a submissive and meek little boy, probably easily bullied. Luis Conte Aguero has written that while there Raul was afflicted with the nickname *pulguita*, "the little flea," which he did not protest and seems even to have taken some self-flagellating pride in repeating. He mailed religious cards home to Biran, inscribed on the back, "To my parents with love, from *pulguita*." He used scissors to shear his hair very short, almost to the scalp. Fortunately for him, the mocking nickname, like the affectionate *Muso* his mother gave him, did not cling to him for long.[2]

Raul idolized Fidel, always his opposite in almost everything. All through his life he has strived to please him and win his approval and respect. It has never been easy. Fidel is no more tolerant of family members who displease him than he is of anyone else.

When Raul returned to Havana after his years of teenage irresolution, he had no intellectual interests and no education beyond primary school. One of his friends in the early 1950s in Havana remembered that Raul had one of the largest and most impressive collections of American comic books he had ever seen. Raul took pleasure in showing it off to his friends and registering their awed reaction. If Fidel had known of that idle interest, he would have been mercilessly disdainful.

Raul does not have Fidel's gifts of a photographic memory or loquacity and persuasiveness. As a young man, he enjoyed partying, drinking, and dating, the pastimes Fidel eschewed in order to concentrate on his career. In Havana, Raul moved into an upstairs room of the house Fidel and his bride Mirta rented, and at other times he lived with different sisters. There is no record that he ever had lodgings of his own in Havana, a job, or income other than stipends from Biran.

It is easy to imagine Raul, then, twenty or twenty-one years old, docilely following in Fidel's wake, sitting somberly on the sidelines in cafés listening to his brother hold forth brilliantly on a range of political and historical issues. He would have had little of substance to contribute, although he was absorbing his brother's lessons like a sponge. He told the publisher of *El Sol de Mexico* in 1993: "It is a privilege to be Fidel's brother. He has been my hero since childhood."[3]

The inexperienced, immature Raul was in awe of his talented, well-known older brother and surrogate father. And he was therefore impressionable raw material for Fidel's tutelage—and manipulation.

Their sister Juanita has long been convinced it was mostly the latter. She believes that once Raul moved in with his big brother, Fidel set out to twist and shape him into an obsequiously loyal follower to serve his political goals.

Testifying in Washington before a congressional committee in 1965, Juanita said that Fidel had promised Angel he would fill in for him, that he would "take care of Raul" after he returned to Havana. Her recollection was that Fidel made this promise to their father in 1951, when Fidel was campaigning for the Orthodox Party congressional seat. But Fidel was too preoccupied to fulfill that commitment.[4]

Among Juanita's most trenchant criticisms of Fidel is that either through neglect or Machiavellian cunning, he brought about Raul's change from the mild and generous boy and young man she remembered so fondly into the brutal and ruthless revolutionary he became. In her words, Raul grew "hard, even grim."

She insists that Raul's harsh public image "is not altogether accurate" because it is really Fidel who is the "tyrant." Juanita has spoken and written on a number of occasions about the two, seemingly contradictory facets of Raul's personality. On the one hand she remembers his mischievous sense of humor, love for his family and Biran, his abiding sentimentality, and loyalty to friends. She was always much closer to him than to her other brothers, and apparently, more than forty years after leaving Cuba, she still is.

But to emphasize how she believes he changed for the worse in his early twenties under Fidel's influence, she tells of the brutality and savage impulses he acquired. She remembers something Raul told her in April 1959, just before the marriage of their younger sister Emma in Havana. A big event was planned; nearly the entire Castro clan would attend the services. Raul was worried, however, about security if the wedding took place in a church, because so many Catholic priests were already opposing the revolution. His fears were greatly exaggerated, but he barked at Juanita with words that haunted her for many years: "If anything happens to Fidel there, we'll kill all the priests in Cuba."[5]

Raul's personal and ideological transformation began in 1951. It was then, under Fidel's prodding, that he undertook a precocious conversion to Marxism–Leninism. Juanita told the congressional committee that Fidel tasked Raul with receiving Communist Party members who came to the house "to offer help with his political campaign."

She said of Fidel that "at that time it was not convenient or maybe he was not interested" in meeting them himself. He knew that if he accepted communist support his prospects as an Orthodox Party candidate would have been damaged, probably fatally, and that his relations with its leadership would be further undermined. Juanita testified that "Fidel would ask Raul to receive the communists."

Fidel wanted to avoid them, but without closing the door on future cooperation. So Raul became his foil or front man, his trusted intermediary with the communists. It was an important element in the long-term, contingency planning that is so characteristic of Fidel's thinking.

Raul later confirmed much of his sister's account of the timing of his ideological conversion and of Fidel's motivating role in it. In an interview in 1975 with the Mexico City newspaper *El Dia*, he stated: "I first came into contact with Marxism around 1951." He said that until then he had been anti-communist like most Cubans—though not Fidel—at that early, tendentious stage of the Cold War. It was Fidel, he says, who gave him a copy of one of Engels's treatises on Marxism and encouraged him to read and appreciate it. He recalled that it was *The Origin of the Family, Private Property, and the State*.[6] "I read it twice. It was not a difficult book to understand," and referring to Fidel, he added, "he explained some questions to me."

In the *El Sol de Mexico* interview in 1993, Raul confirmed his earlier account. He said: "It was Fidel who influenced me into becoming a communist . . . he explained communism to me and gave me books."[7]

Raul was drawn into the radical and Marxist fold fairly quickly after those introductions. Soon he joined the editorial board of *SAETA*, a fringe publication strongly influenced by the Communist Party. Under his name it published an article in March 1951 condemning the American involvement in the Korean War, a position Fidel had refused to associate with in public because the Orthodox Party supported the war.

The extent of Fidel's influence on the composition of that article, or on those who invited Raul to sit on the *SAETA* board, is unknown, though Fidel most likely played a decisive role in both. He was also writing for *SAETA* at the time, though on much less controversial issues than the Korean War. At a minimum, Fidel probably conceptualized the arguments of Raul's article and then helped with the drafting. There is a good chance too that his role was much larger, that he was in fact the ghost author of the Korean War article.

After Batista's coup in March 1952, Raul, like so many other Cuban university students, turned his energies to anti-regime activism. He wrote later in *Verde Olivo*, the armed forces journal, that he participated in small study groups that gathered to discuss Marxist doctrine and to write and distribute anti-Batista pamphlets and newsletters. In January 1953, he worked with several young communists to organize a demonstration commemorating the death of the founder of Cuba's Communist Party. He was becoming a street-style activist, participating in demonstrations, but unlike his brother in the preceding years, he remained non-violent.[8]

It is significant that until Raul's participation in the Moncada attack in 1953 there is no record that he had engaged in violence of any kind. He had never put another human in his sights, was never implicated in a murder or attempted murder. No photographs were ever taken of him bandaged and bloodied after struggling with Havana police. No news stories ever linked him to gang violence or internationalist adventurism. And no one who knew him has ever come forward with stories like those about Fidel's bizarre capers. Innately, Raul was more measured than Fidel, disinclined to act aggressively.

For these reasons, and because of Raul's deepening ties with the communists, Fidel did not induct him into the new revolutionary movement he was organizing to confront the dictatorship violently. Raul wrote in *Verde Olivo* about the "small general staff" Fidel had created at the top of his budding organization, but he did not become one of its members. The inexperienced, physically unimposing Raul was just not fighting material. Fidel still thought of him as his mild-mannered little brother, not yet a potential revolutionary militant. According to Jesus Montane, one of the movement's original members, Raul participated only occasionally in its activities before June or July of 1953, just before the Moncada attack.[9]

In the meantime, under Fidel's watchful eye, Raul was solidifying his Marxist convictions and affiliations. In March 1953 he left Cuba for the first time, traveling to Vienna to participate in an international youth conference sponsored by the Kremlin. Afterward he also visited the capitals of three Eastern European communist countries, and returned home to Cuba enthralled with what he had seen.

Newly discovered evidence demonstrates convincingly that Fidel indeed pushed Raul down the Marxist–Leninist path. This new interpretation of one of the most critical and revealing turning points in the brothers' relationship is supported by information that I discovered in the archives at Columbia University in New York.

Herbert Matthews, the *New York Times* reporter who was close to Fidel and other Cuban leaders, interviewed a number of them in April 1966 in Havana. His unpublished notes from those conversations are among the records he donated to Columbia. Included is a brief account of Matthews's conversation with Carlos Rafael Rodriguez, then one of the highest level officials in the Castros' government and a man who rarely agreed to be interviewed by Americans.

"Old communist" Rodriguez was among the two or three most senior and best informed of the pre–Castro Cuban communists. He was an elegant, sophisticated Marxist intellectual who earned his reputation as one of the leading moderates in the Castros' government and their new *fidelista* communist party. No other "old communist" was ever so close to Fidel or as trusted by him.

Rodriguez told Matthews that Fidel had once boasted to another prominent "old communist" of his role in guiding Raul to Marxism. Rodriguez said Fidel had "deliberately made a Marxist of Raul, giving him books to read and sending him on the famous youth conference trip. . . ."[10]

A once-sensitive document in Soviet archives in Moscow confirms that Fidel bragged about this on more than one occasion. In a report to the Kremlin in November 1960, the well-connected Soviet ambassador to Havana wrote, "Fidel is convinced that he deserves credit for the formation of Raul's views."[11]

The Vienna youth conference was Raul's first immersion in international communist fellowship. More than four hundred delegates from seventy-one countries met in the ornate music society hall for six days beginning on March 22. Vladimir Semichastny, the future head of the lead Soviet intelligence agency, the KGB, addressed them in the baroque main conference hall. The event received intense coverage in the international communist media. *Pravda*, the official daily paper of the Soviet Communist Party, ran an article highlighting the courage of the Cuban delegates who had braved "the terror" of the Batista regime to attend.[12] Raul, still a neophyte Marxist and not yet a party member, was not mentioned, although Cuba and its communist party—then one of the largest and most influential in Latin America—were clearly of interest to the Soviets.

KGB officers prowled the halls and the conference floor, mingling with and gathering intelligence about the participants. They were doing counterintelligence surveillance, wanting to ferret out any CIA penetration. They were keeping an eye on their own supposedly loyal adherents, all the time mouthing the Kremlin's line. Most importantly, the KGB agents were scouting among the delegations from non-communist countries for potential agents of influence and covert recruits to spy for them.

Raul was certainly a promising prospect. By "sending" him to the conference, as Carlos Rafael Rodriguez expressed it, Fidel—wittingly or not—had dangled his little brother right under the nose of the KGB. And the KGB was attentive to the offer.

From Vienna, Raul went on to spend a month in communist Romania and to visit the capitals of communist Hungary and Czechoslovakia.

"At the congress I had an argument with a Romanian delegate on the floor," he told *Chicago Tribune* reporter Jules Dubois in late 1958, "which led the head of the delegation to invite me to his country. . . . I would travel to China if I had the chance because I enjoy it and I want to see the world, but that does not mean I am a communist."[13]

Raul later recanted the last comment, admitting he had deceived Dubois about his communist convictions. Laughing and making light of it during the interview with the *El Dia* reporter, he said that he had no choice but to lie "because of the nature of our struggle." Incongruously, he invoked the New Testament.

"Peter denied Christ three times and later was the founder of the Church. I only denied my membership twice."[14]

During the 1965 interview with Lee Lockwood, when asked if Raul had been a communist prior to 1959, Fidel for the first time acknowledged that it was true. But he did not go any further. He recognized that if he were to admit the truth of his manipulation of his brother's conversion, a harsh light would be shed on their relationship and on his own integrity. He insisted that Raul had acted independently.

"Yes, Raul, completely on his own while he was a student at the university, had joined the communist youth."[15]

Raul returned from Europe on an old Italian passenger liner, the *Andrea Gritti*. The weather-beaten ship sailed from Genoa on May 5, 1953, meaning that Raul's immersion in international communism had lasted five or six weeks. Most of the passengers were Italian immigrants traveling in steerage, but Raul and Nikolai Leonov, a young Russian about his age, traveled first class. They became good friends during that leisurely voyage, first traversing the Mediterranean, passing through the Straits of Gibraltar, and then crossing the Atlantic. According to Leonov, they "understood each other instantly, and were burning with desire to give our lives to the service of the people."[16]

The young Russian later became the KGB's top Latin America specialist and before retiring, the deputy chief of its First Chief Directorate, responsible for foreign espionage. He had booked passage on the same ship as Raul, guaranteeing considerable lengths of time spent together. Their onboard convergence brings to mind the classic chestnut endlessly repeated by suspicious intelligence officers of many nationalities: "There is no such thing as a coincidence."

It certainly did not hurt Leonov's career in Soviet intelligence to have established that early close bond with Raul or to have maintained their friendship ever since. While on board the *Andrea Gritti*, the eager Leonov practiced the Spanish he had already learned to speak fairly fluently, and Raul brimmed over with enthusiastic curiosity about life in the Soviet Union.

Leonov insists he was not yet working for Soviet intelligence in 1953, though his denials should be considered technical and deceptive. He was probably under KGB influence, if not formalized control, while responding to its taskings that included assessing and reporting on Raul and other young Latin American leftists. In *My Turbulent Years*, the book he wrote after the collapse of the Soviet Union, Leonov revealed that on that voyage with Raul in 1953 he was already acquainted with some basic intelligence tradecraft.

Back in Havana, Raul was arrested at pierside and detained for a few days by Batista's secret police. The diary he had kept during his Iron Curtain peregrinations was confiscated along with a satchel of communist propaganda and ideological tracts. He says he was beaten, and if so, surely he was further radicalized.

Jesus Montane visited him in jail and remembered most vividly that "he was very enthusiastic about his trip." Raul had been so enthralled that, with youthful bravado, he told another friend in Havana he was ready to die for the communist cause. He had been profoundly influenced by his experiences in Vienna and Eastern Europe, and his friendship with Leonov.

Not long after he was released from jail, he took up formal membership in the youth wing of Cuba's communist party. He had just celebrated his twenty-second birthday.

Raul joined Fidel's revolutionary movement at about the same time. In doing so, he was aware he was simultaneously volunteering for some kind of military action that his brother would command and in which he would be a foot soldier.

So within a matter of weeks Raul had made two life-altering decisions. In both, he committed himself to pleasing his brother. He wanted to win Fidel's respect and esteem, to impress him, like a wayward son striving for his father's approval. Raul agreed to put his life on the line in the fight to overthrow Batista and to help put Fidel on his path to fame and glory.

It was Raul's first irreversible step into a life of cold-blooded violence. Yet no one who had known him before 1953 would have thought that possible. A photo of him taken just after his capture following Moncada shows a rangy, unmuscled youth in a T-shirt and cap, staring blankly at the camera. He looked like a naive eighteen-year-old, or a Greenwich Village beatnik.[17]

As it turned out, Raul did not get the opportunity during the Moncada assault to impress Fidel with his valor. He was given a peripheral, much less dangerous mission than the main attack on the garrison. Consistent with his record until then, nothing he did on July 26, 1953, resulted in physical harm to the men on either side of the conflict that day. He and everyone on his side walked away unscathed. He did not cover himself in glory.

Nevertheless, official histories of the revolution have consistently inflated his role at Moncada. Supposedly he was the leader of a squad of men who occupied the Palace of Justice building, situated on a small hill overlooking the garrison in downtown Santiago. Their mission was to set up a sniper nest on the roof to provide cover for the main action below.

In July 1971, *Verde Olivo* published a history of the palace incident. But that officially sanctioned account inadvertently provided compelling evidence indicating that one of Fidel's early recruits, Lester Rodriguez, was actually in command of the Palace operation and that Raul went along as a subordinate. Rodriguez had been informed in advance of the mission. He then surveyed the building, checking out the entrances and access points before the attack. If Raul had really been in command, this would have been his responsibility.[18]

Their squad succeeded in seizing control of the building. In the process they neither inflicted nor suffered any casualties and appear never to have been in any danger. It is not clear that any of the attackers ever fired a shot. Once the main assault on the garrison itself had been repulsed, Raul and Lester Rodriguez simply walked away with their men. Rodriguez's family lived in Santiago, and he found his way home unimpeded.

Raul left his weapon behind and set out on foot for Biran along a railroad bed. His instinct, probably fueled by a pervading sense of failure after witnessing the bloody fiasco of his brother's plan and contributing nothing himself, was to go home. Captured along the way, he was tried and imprisoned on the Isle of Pines. His next opportunity to impress Fidel would not come until their time together in Mexico City.

Peter Bourne, one of Fidel's biographers, whose research was assisted by Cuban government officials, concluded that Raul was given credit for commanding the palace operation in order to protect Rodriguez, who had eluded capture. If it was not revealed that he had participated in the attack, Rodriguez would be able to fight on anonymously in the underground.[19] But the fundamental reason for the revised history is that once they were in power and Raul was running the armed forces, it was necessary to assert that he had played a heroic role at Moncada. The fighting that day symbolized the mythical source of the Cuban Revolution. It was the legitimizing crucible for the entire revolutionary process that followed, and the *moncadistas* ever since have been the most revered of Cuba's national heroes, comparable only to Marti and the nineteenth-century *mambises*.

It was essential to this mythmaking that Raul had performed valiantly at Moncada and in a leadership position. The Castro brothers and all the official histories have therefore faithfully maintained this deception ever since. Raul told an interviewer in 1987 that he had been in command at the palace. He seems content to take credit for a leadership role that it seems all but certain he did not assume.

Of most enduring interest, Raul's debut performance as a revolutionary fell far short of Fidel's expectations, and Raul knew it. After he slipped out of Santiago unscathed that day, he remained entirely unproven in Fidel's eyes. He had demonstrated none of the fighting qualities that had come so naturally to Fidel in Bogotá and on so many other occasions. Other tests of Raul's mettle and ability to subordinate his conscience in acts of revolutionary violence would be necessary. He would have to become tougher, more ruthless, less encumbered by sentimentality. He was not cold-blooded enough to qualify for a command position.

The Castros, along with other captured *moncadistas*, were incarcerated on the Isle of Pines, later renamed the Isle of Youth. They ate well in prison and maintained contact with their followers on the outside. Fidel set up classes and a regimented routine for his supporters. With the assistance of Raul Roa, a leftist University of Havana professor and Fidel's future foreign minister, a large library of books was accumulated. In this manner, the brothers continued to deepen their understanding of Marxist–Leninist doctrine, and for both of them the time spent behind bars provided the longest, most conducive period they ever had for serious reading and reflection.

In May 1955 they were all released, beneficiaries of a general amnesty. Because of his communist ties, Raul was soon being harassed by the police and accused, probably falsely, of having placed a bomb in a movie theater. He was therefore one of the first to flee Cuba to asylum in Mexico City. His mission there played better to his organizational strengths. He set out to find housing for the other members of the movement who began to arrive, do logistical work, acquire weapons, and recruit new members. Raul has never been able to enchant and inspire others as Fidel so naturally does, but in Mexico he was remarkably effective on his own terms.

His most spectacular success was the recruitment of the most luminous personality, other than Fidel, ever associated with Cuba's revolution. Shortly after his arrival in the Mexican capital, Raul met Ernesto "Che" Guevara, a young Marxist Argentine medical doctor, a roving incendiary always seeking new revolutionary pastures. They were immediately fast friends and ideological soulmates, meeting almost daily to discuss Marxism and how to adapt Leninist principles to win power in Cuba. Che met Fidel later, but his recruitment to the Cuban cause had been all but finalized by Raul.

Hilda Gadea, Che's new Peruvian wife, liked Raul as enthusiastically as Che did. She described Raul as fair and beardless, looking like a university student and younger than his years. But his ideas about how the revolution in Cuba should be advanced were clear and strong. He expressed them with great conviction. His "spontaneity and cheerful, easy manner opened the way into a strong friendship among us," she wrote in her memoirs. She said Raul was his brother's devout follower, a convinced Marxist who was a great admirer of the Soviet Union.[20]

Che's wife described a more mature, militant, self-confident, even articulate Raul. He had changed in prison, where his convictions both about communism and his brother's revolutionary destiny had been honed. His admiration for Fidel, if possible, was now even more fervid than before. Hilda Gadea wrote that listening to Raul expound on revolutionary views was inspiring. He was joyful, communicative, sure of himself. "He had an incredible capacity for analysis and synthesis." She added that it was for those reasons that he understood Che so well.

Her description of Raul is possibly the most effusive and complimentary of any ever given him, in stark contrast to what over the years has been said and written. She seems to have observed Raul only when he was in Che's company, enjoying himself, psychically shored up. He and Che were especially close, and they remained so when they got to Cuba. During the second year of the insurgency, when they were fighting on different fronts, they maintained a regular correspondence via courier, and they seem to have discussed ideology mostly. After victory they led a cabal that pressured Fidel to accelerate the pace of revolutionary change and confrontation with the United States.

Nikolai Leonov, Raul's Russian shipmate aboard the *Andrea Gritti*, then working at the Soviet embassy in Mexico City, supposedly as a journeyman diplomat, entered his life again. Leonov says he ran into Raul on a Mexico City street one day. With Che participating, Raul renewed the rapturous discussions about Soviet life and ideals he had shared with the young Russian.

Leonov was surprised by how much Raul's understanding of Soviet and Marxist literature had grown in the two years since he had seen him last. He was

asked to find copies in Spanish of three Soviet books that were of interest to both
Raul and Che. One was a romanticized biography—*How the Steel Was
Tempered*—about Vasily Chapaev, a legendary Red Army cavalry commander
during Russia's savage civil war in the 1920s. The other two books were also glo-
rifications of mythical heroes of the early Soviet era. Leonov managed to find
Spanish-language editions of all three for his friends.

In Mexico, Raul also maintained close ties with Lazaro Peña, one of Cuba's
most canny and senior "old communists," a labor leader from the tobacco
worker's union, and his main contact with the party back in Havana. Raul
became so close to the older man that before he departed on the *Granma*, he
entrusted Peña with what he later described as an "untitled political testament."
He said he had written it with a Cuban colleague and implied it was so radical
and revealing of his true socialist thinking that he did not want it on board the
Granma in case he was captured or killed.

He said Fidel and Che had also endorsed the "testament" before they left
Mexico. He refused to say any more about the document and was testy with the
El Dia reporter, inadvertently revealing more than Fidel probably would have
wished about the extent to which the Marxism of both brothers had developed by
the end of 1956. Raul seemed to suggest that he, Che, and Fidel were all in agreement before they left Mexico that they were fighting for a communist Cuba.

Raul rhetorically asked the Mexican reporter, "How do you think we could
have had a socialist revolution without having that clear?"[21]

Pretending to forget Raul had introduced him to Leonov in Mexico City, Fidel
once told an interviewer he had never met a Soviet before 1959. By that he
meant to emphasize that his struggle to win power had been independent of any
external leverage, as in fact it was.

Fidel is sensitive to allegations that he was recruited as a secret KGB agent in
Mexico and vigorously denied this in the Lockwood interview. On balance,
there is almost no chance that either he or Raul was ever recruited by Soviet
intelligence as a clandestine asset. No credible evidence of any sort points in that
direction, while persuasive information from sensitive Soviet files does much to
negate the possibility.

In the early 1990s, at the peak of post-Soviet openness and introspection,
two scholars were given unprecedented access to top secret Soviet era files on

Cuba, including KGB and Politburo records. Timothy Naftali and Aleksandr Fursenko, a Canadian and a Russian, found nothing in the many references to Raul in the documents they reviewed to indicate he was assigned a KGB cryptonym, or secret code name. That would have been routine had Raul been enlisted to work covertly for Soviet intelligence. The records also showed that just as he had wanted it, Fidel remained inscrutable to the Soviets until well after he won power.[22]

Raul was not recruited as a controlled agent, but by the late 1950s Soviet officials considered him to be their "man in Havana," or more precisely, their man in Fidel's inner circle, first in the sierra and later in the government. What they did not realize was that Raul was actually Fidel's penetration—his brother's access agent—in their midst. In the parlance of foreign intelligence tradecraft, it was Fidel who functioned as his brother's handler or case officer, using him as a conduit first to the Cuban communists and later to their masters in the Kremlin. Although not in the strictest sense of the term, Raul was a double agent.

Always with Fidel's approval, he maintained close ties with the "old communists." In 1958 young party members were inconspicuously welcomed into the guerrilla units that Raul and Che commanded, though Fidel continued to eschew the kind of obvious contacts with them that would belie his insistent public assertions that he had no Marxist leanings. In the expansive areas of northern Oriente that he controlled by the summer of 1958, Raul experimented with communist organizational methods.

And once the brothers were in power, while Fidel was traveling up the eastern seaboard of the United States, Raul made the first clandestine contacts with the Soviet leadership in 1959, as Fidel solemnly denied he had any interest in communism. But despite the impressions of many at the time, there is no doubt that every move Raul made in his communist capacity was coordinated with his brother.

Raul turned to Lazaro Peña, his trusted "old communist" mentor in Mexico City, then back in Havana helping to revive the newly relegitimized "old" communist party. Peña traveled secretly to Moscow as Raul's emissary and requested Soviet assistance to build up the revolution's military and intelligence capabilities. It was an early, critical step in consolidating power, and the Castros knew that Soviet assistance in those two areas would be essential as opposition to their regime continued to mount in the United States.[23]

In the Kremlin, Premier Nikita Khrushchev swiftly approved Raul's request. After that Raul participated in secret conclaves with Fidel at every crossroads on the protracted route they took together in radicalizing the Cuban Revolution, confronting the United States, and moving into the Soviet orbit. Raul played the role of Fidel's principal intermediary with Moscow for more than thirty years, until the Soviet Union dissolved.

It was for good reason that Raul was always considered the most pro-Soviet leader in Fidel's inner circle, and the most likely to defend Soviet positions, to fawn on visiting Soviet dignitaries, and to bask in the presence of senior Kremlin officials. He was enamored of Soviet culture and institutions; he secretly took extended vacations in various areas of the Soviet Union; and he filled his office in the armed forces ministry with memorabilia and souvenirs from his favorite foreign country.

Even Khrushchev, the hardened survivor of Stalin's purges and terror, would believe through the rest of his life that Raul had been *his* man in Havana. Khrushchev was convinced not only that Raul was working covertly for Soviet interests but that he had also managed to conceal much more from Fidel.

The Soviet leader, the KGB, and other informed Kremlin officials all stubbornly insisted on believing Raul was their faithful cloaked penetration at the highest level of the Cuban guerrilla movement and later of the new revolutionary government. Incredibly, Khrushchev believed, as he wrote in his memoirs, that Raul "had kept his true convictions hidden" from Fidel.

The CIA and American intelligence have made innumerable errors when assessing the Castros, but that was not one of them. If anything, the opposite tended to be the case. Raul's leadership strengths and contributions to the success and survival of the revolution were undervalued for many years. He was viewed as weak, by some as androgynous, and always as Fidel's compliant subordinate. I had never agreed with that interpretation and by the mid-1980s set out to learn more about him.

In Mexico City, Raul emerged as Fidel's reliable revolutionary partner. Although as yet he had done nothing to distinguish himself as a warrior or revolutionary, the Moncada experience and then prison and exile brought out tougher personal qualities than he had exhibited before. Above all he wanted to please Fidel, win a position of trust in his inner circle, and be able to compensate for his unimpressive performance at Moncada by earning a position in the guerrilla leadership.

He matured, growing steady and self-confident. He still idolized his brother as a surrogate father figure, but his life now had greater weight and purpose. He was becoming his own man, speaking out firmly in his own voice as his confidence in the convictions he had acquired intensified. He remained unquestioningly loyal to his brother, even to the extent now of trying to be more like Fidel than Fidel. And in one important respect that only the two brothers understood, Raul's communist beliefs and connections provided him with a strategically critical assignment all his own. It was an arena in which he did not have to compete with Fidel or follow in lockstep behind him.

Teresa Casuso, who never met Raul while he was in Mexico City, said that the brothers did not live together there and did not see each other often. Raul had enough spare time to develop an interest in bullfighting, and perhaps as a confidence-building exercise he trained for a while in the techniques of a *torero* or bullfighter. He developed close personal ties with many of the other Cubans living and training in Mexico for the insurgency and began frequently to play the role of his brother's alter ego and intermediary with them. He was developing leadership skills that had not been evident before.

His deepening friendship with Che Guevara was probably crucial to his personal and ideological development. Hilda Gadea's praises of him could not have been written by anyone before 1955 because until then he had been tentative, insecure, and vacillating in his interests. The Raul that Che's wife described embodied all of the compassionate qualities that his sister Juanita has always admired most in him. But by 1956 those traits had merged with the toughness, certitude, and political passion that have characterized his public career ever since. The seemingly contradictory duality of Raul's character—the hard and the soft, the kind and the cruel—had coalesced in a single new persona.

It was in Mexico where he first acted out the role of unforgiving advocate of the death penalty, and later, on the eve of the *Granma's* departure, that of executioner. Those two tests of ruthless revolutionary rectitude would go a long way to solidify his standing with his implacable brother.

The first case centered on Calixto Morales, a young, rural Cuban schoolteacher who left behind a home and family when he joined the Castros' revolutionary movement. He was educated, and therefore his background was unlike most of Fidel's other recruits. Virtually all of the *moncadistas* had been poor and working class, with limited education. By Fidel's calculus they would therefore be less likely to challenge his dictates or ruminate too much about the logic and fairness of the demands he placed on them. Morales made the mistakes of both ruminating and complaining.

While undergoing guerrilla training at a ranch outside of Mexico City directed by the Spanish Civil War veteran Alberto Bayo and assisted by Bayo's favorite trainee, Che Guevara, Morales defied their harsh methods. Neither instructor was a Cuban, and their demands truly were onerous. One day during a particularly grueling exercise, Morales became exhausted and fed up. There was no violence or histrionics. He simply sat down along the trail they were following and refused to go any further.[24]

Inductees into Fidel's revolutionary undertakings all through the years have been subject to draconian discipline, and Morales's actions were a cause for alarm. Che later wrote that Fidel made clear to his personnel that there were three offenses that would always be punishable by death. They were insubordination, desertion, and defeatism.[25]

When he sat down on the trail that day in training, Morales had no idea that he had come to the precipice, that he was guilty of defeatism, a capital offense in that strange world of incomprehensible revolutionary morality. He had violated one of Fidel's key tenets and would have to be made a scapegoat.

Both Castro brothers were summoned to the training camp from Mexico City to conduct a court martial. Fidel, General Bayo, and Gustavo Arcos, a *moncadista* who years later became one of the most prominent dissidents to remain in Cuba, would hear the case and decide Morales's fate.

It was decided Raul would prosecute. Perhaps he volunteered, or perhaps Fidel assigned him the task, wanting to observe him and take his measure in a stressful situation where the stakes were high. Most of the other men were horrified that it had come to this. But Raul understood what was at stake for *him*. His performance would be the test of his revolutionary fortitude.

General Bayo's word-for-word account of Raul's impassioned prosecutorial speech was reconstructed several years later from memory, possibly from notes. Bayo was one of Raul's early admirers, and therefore his published rendition of what Raul said is surely embroidered. But the old general would not have mistaken the tone, thrust, or ferocity of Raul's indictment of Morales, or forgotten some of his most dramatic words.

Bayo spoke in defense of the defendant, seeking clemency. He says that Raul interrupted him in mid-sentence, lunging verbally at Morales. Raul bolted "like an infuriated lion," Bayo wrote, and then delivered a long, angry jeremiad.[26]

Morales had disrupted military discipline, lacked proper respect for authority. He was insubordinate and oblivious to military ethics. He had stained the revolutionary uniform. Such behavior could destroy their entire noble effort. Raul shouted at Bayo, "You want to save the life of this individual? I say, 'No, a thousand times, no!' We cannot begin our history with such filthy rubbish."

Bayo was amazed. He wrote that "this was a Raul I did not know." The man he was familiar with until then was a beardless youth, he wrote. "But how he has grown right before my eyes . . . He has become a giant."

The general did not record Fidel's reaction. But it seems safe to conclude that Raul had passed the test with flying colors. What playwrights describe as an "obligatory scene," the moment when a character develops the full-throated expression of a hidden inner self, or when a developing plot line suddenly comes into focus, had occurred for Raul in that makeshift little "courtroom" in the Mexican countryside.

He demonstrated he could actually be tougher than Fidel. Bayo wrote that after watching Raul's performance, he concluded for the first time that he was "tempered steel." Through his performance Raul had risen in Fidel's esteem. By his brother's harsh standards he now had credibility as a potential commander of men. Finally, he could qualify as Fidel's Fidel.

In the end, Morales was spared the death penalty, and according to some accounts, he went to on to fight effectively in the sierra. It was Fidel, of course, who decided on clemency.

There was at least one other similar case that occurred during the training period in which the execution of a suspected Batista spy was in fact carried out. His name was never revealed, and it is not clear who delivered the coup de grace. This defendant, according to a Cuban guerrilla veteran interviewed years later by Fidel's biographer Tad Szulc, was found guilty by another ad hoc revolutionary tribunal in Mexico. The man was "shot and buried there in a field."[27]

The name of the Cuban colleague that Raul executed just before he left Mexico City in late November 1956 has never been revealed either. Ordered by Fidel and apparently conducted without any tribunal or other revolutionary due process, the execution has never been written about until now.

What seems clear is that by personally delivering the coup de grace on Fidel's orders, Raul crossed the last of his formative Rubicons. Even more decisively than his performance in the earlier Calixto Morales case, he demonstrated to his brother that he was tough enough to merit a command position. When Raul admitted to the murder years later in the company of a small group of trusted comrades, no doubt after a bout of maudlin drinking, he provided few details but did express remorse.

Raul went on to order and preside over many other executions once he got back to Cuba, both before and immediately following the guerrilla victory. One former colleague recalls that Raul and Che "competed in killings and viciousness."

An entry in Raul's campaign diary on March 25, 1958, just two weeks after he received his own guerrilla command, reveals that the first execution he ordered took place in front of the condemned man's colleagues and was carried out with "great solemnity." Others, numbering in the hundreds, were often hurried affairs.

The condemned were considered guilty of many types of crimes, in addition to the three that Che described. Some were bandits, rapists, murderers, thieves, but the great majority of the executions were politically motivated. An American journalist visiting Raul's camp in the sierra photographed him—standing stern and cool—next to a condemned murderer tied to a tree, just before the man was shot.

Some were targeted to settle old scores. Raul has spoken publicly on two occasions about the execution of a Batista military officer who a decade earlier was said to have been responsible for the death of a well-known communist labor leader. Like him, many of those killed were Batista military and intelligence officials.[28]

Fidel once admitted to a visiting American congressman that Raul's executions occurred on a very large scale: "When Raul reached the Second Front he found hundreds of people were organized by Batista, who made believe they were revolutionaries. We disarmed them and dispatched them."[29]

There is one chilling codicil to these tales of Raul's cold-bloodedness. A former high-level confidante of the Castro brothers told me in Miami of a surprising finale to all that killing. In 1966 Raul ordered the bones of all of those he had had executed in Santiago and the sierra exhumed. The remains were encased in large concrete "coffins" that were specially made. They were put on board coastal vessels and then dumped overboard off the southern coast of Oriente. The waters there are some of the deepest in the Caribbean.[30]

CHAPTER SEVEN

My Job Is To Talk

Dozens of squat, glass-sheathed office buildings have sprouted in recent years along the burgeoning high-tech corridor in Washington's Northern Virginia suburbs, many of them housing government agencies and contractor firms engaged in intelligence and security work. One of the most nondescript is the headquarters of the Foreign Broadcast Information Service, America's oldest civilian foreign intelligence organization. FBIS was founded in February 1941 and was already hard at work for nearly a year and a half when President Franklin Roosevelt established the Office of Strategic Services (OSS), the parent of today's CIA.

With a network of bureaus, most of them in cooperating foreign countries, FBIS monitors foreign radio and television broadcasts in more than sixty languages. Known to intelligence analysts as *Fibiss*, it is small, unmysterious, and operates without any covert trappings. Transcribing and translating Japanese broadcasting before Pearl Harbor, the first generation of its propaganda analysts did not anticipate the attack any better than others in the U.S. government. They did report, however, that Tokyo had become more "hostile and defiant." That was one of the important clues that went unheeded.[1]

FBIS is exceptional among American intelligence collection activities because the information it gathers every day of the year is unclassified, plucked from the world's open air waves. Its modest annual budget would probably be consumed in less than a week by any of the larger agencies. Spies, reconnaissance planes, satellites, eavesdropping and other technical systems absorb the lion's share of the approximately $40 billion spent every year on intelligence activities. But the information this unheralded little operation acquires has often been more valuable to intelligence analysts than the top secret, ultra-sensitive reporting from the bigger, more glamorous collection programs.

FBIS was never more essential than during the Cold War. The Soviet Union, its Eastern European satellite countries, and Mao's China were "hard" intelligence targets or "denied areas," where espionage and other covert collection was difficult and dangerous. Spies and eavesdropping systems can be neutralized, sensitive installations concealed from overhead reconnaissance systems, but governments in those hard target countries had to communicate openly with their own people, and they beamed large volumes of propaganda to foreign audiences they wanted to influence.

With that much to monitor, FBIS collection never flagged. Transcripts of radio programming from targeted countries reached analysts almost in real time, and in a steady flow. It was important to know what Soviet Politburo members were saying, what new communist party statements and ideological tracts portended. This open source information filled gaps about political issues, policymaking, economic, and military developments, and critical leadership dynamics in countries that were otherwise largely impervious to outside observers.

Cuba gradually became another of those denied areas after the Castro brothers' victory. With the Soviet intelligence and military assistance that Raul requested in April 1959, Cuban intelligence and counterintelligence capabilities steadily improved. Well-placed and reliable covert sources who had provided information to the CIA chose to go into exile rather than run the risk of staying on the island in the role of traitors to the revolution. It was incriminating for Cubans who stayed even to be seen with American diplomats. Intelligence reporting about the working of the new government and the thinking of its leaders became harder and harder to acquire.

Then, in January 1961, just before Eisenhower left office, his administration severed diplomatic relations with Cuba, and the American embassy in

Havana was shuttered. FBIS's role in helping to fill the widening information gaps became even more crucial as a long dry spell for American intelligence analysts concerned with Cuba began. Speeches and press conferences, statements by Cuban leaders, and government edicts and propaganda became essential as primary sources that could be sifted for valuable and otherwise hard to come by clues.

As a journeyman CIA Cuba analyst, I was impressed by the seemingly endless speeches slowly scrolling out of FBIS ticker machines in the Agency's operations center. There were nights when I stood in front of them for hours, pulling out sheet after sheet of Fidel's orations not too many minutes after he spoke them.

When Fidel came down from the Sierra Maestra to assume power on New Year's Day in 1959, FBIS—by then integrated into the CIA—was preparing to monitor his public appearances. The first was a celebratory address he delivered from a balcony overlooking Cespedes Park in Santiago, on the night of his victory. It was one of the few speeches he has ever delivered publicly that was not transcribed by FBIS though the text was published in a Havana newspaper.

Only minutes into that signal oration he made it clear to any who might still have had doubts about his intentions that Cuba would never be the same. The long guerrilla conflict was over, but a revolution, not a mere change in government or leadership, was beginning. He was not going to lead a mere reform program. The old political and economic order would be shaken to its roots. He warned the faint of heart that "a harsh and dangerous undertaking" had begun.

His outlook was dominated by unacknowledged Marxist–Leninist and anti-imperialist thinking and internationalist aspirations. But he had no precise program or timetable in mind. There was no brain trust of advisers to plan the transition, because except for Raul there was no one Fidel trusted sufficiently. Through all the campaigns to defeat Batista, Fidel had made every strategic decision himself, and he intended to continue doing so.

His leadership style had been fixed since he began organizing the Moncada attack. It was then that he began telling associates that the revolution could have only one leader. Victory convinced him that his centralized command style had been vindicated. His friend Teresa Casuso remembered him saying in Mexico City that "it was essential to inspire the people with faith in one person."[2] The once sympathetic K. S. Karol described Fidel's control obsession more critically, as a "consuming feeling of his own indispensability."

Fidel's immediate priority in those first days of power was to consolidate the gains already made. First, his small guerrilla forces—at most a few thousand individuals who were experienced and under arms—had to take control of Havana and neutralize any remaining pockets of opposition. He had to secure his personal control over a smattering of other anti-Batista groups and assert his authority over pro-democratic elements of his own movement.

Confrontation with the United States was inevitable. It was not merely the goal of "waging war" on the North Americans. It was his "true destiny." Cleansing Cuba of the large and contaminating American presence could not, of course, be discussed with the U.S. embassy, which was one reason he avoided meeting with the liberal and well-intentioned ambassador Bonsal. He knew that he could not unleash revolutionary change without antagonizing the Eisenhower administration and powerful American economic interests on the island, and so he preferred to move cautiously. Raul, in contrast, was pressing him to implement a radical program swiftly and openly embrace the communists.

The brothers agreed, however, that there were three directions that the revolution would take them. There would be conflict with the United States, support for revolutionary internationalism in Latin America, and an upheaval in Cuba to create a more just society.

It was also evident from Fidel's first oration in Santiago that he saw himself and the revolution as synonymous. He began to use the royal "we." Over the next few years the use of the first-person singular all but disappeared from his public discourse. At his insistence a law was enacted prohibiting the installation of statues of any leaders in public places, or the naming of streets, parks, or towns after them. There would be no cult of personality, as in Stalin's Soviet Union or Mao's China. But Fidel's fusion of self and revolution actually has done more to encourage a leadership cult than statues ever could have.

Many of the clues that Fidel dropped about his intentions in that first Santiago speech went unnoticed or were dismissed in Washington and at the American embassy in Havana. In the euphoria of the guerrilla victory, Cubans and Americans alike were anxious to give him the benefit of the doubt. What sounded like para-noid anti-Americanism and militant internationalism could be explained away. He was only thirty-two years old, unpracticed in diplomatic niceties and political nuance. Some thought that he was being carried away by the excitement of the ecstatic crowds when he delivered speeches. Surely, most in the U.S. government believed, he would soon settle into a more moderate and predictable mode.

In mid-February 1959, about six weeks into his reign, the American embassy cabled the State Department that there had not been "a single public speech by Castro since the triumph of the revolution in which he has not shown some feeling against the United States." But the diplomats, hoping to discern a silver lining, added there was reason to believe he was "not as anti-American as he sounds."[3] In reality, what he said in FBIS transcribed speeches was calculated and true to his thinking.

Still wary about entering Havana, Fidel moved slowly, with an ever-growing contingent of boisterous followers, westward across the island toward the capital, stopping to exhale long orations in towns and cities along the way.

When he paused on January 4 in the sugar and cattle crossroads town of Camaguey, FBIS monitors were ready. His speech, broadcast by the local radio station, was the first to be captured by FBIS. Soon, the English translation was in Washington being studied by analysts.

"A totally new era" was beginning, he exulted, not yet recognizing that he was also entering into a strange partnership with American intelligence analysts. Many thousands of his speeches and press conferences, containing billions of words, have been transcribed over the decades since then. From that first monitored appearance in Camaguey, speech transcripts have been the gold standard for all those trying to assess the Cuban Revolution.

In Camaguey, Fidel deceptively promised, as he would for several more months, to establish a "civilized, democratic system." He insisted he would restore the liberal constitution of 1940 and promised elections within "fifteen months, more or less." On January 14, after his arrival in the capital, he said "our Revolution is genuinely Cuban, genuinely democratic." When pressed, he described his personal philosophy as "humanist."

He promised "to launch an offensive against corruption, immorality, gambling, stealing, illiteracy, disease, hunger, exploitation, and injustice."

In Camaguey, and in subsequent speeches all through the years, he has dwelled on the last two matters, on his profoundly personalized concepts of exploitation and injustice. Those twin evils, broadly conceived and vaguely articulated, were, he believed, at the root of Cuba's ills. Combating them would provide the enduring justifications for nearly everything that would follow in his long revolutionary journey, not just at home in Cuba but in his many internationalist causes as well. He had begun articulating the defining themes that would henceforth undergird nearly all of his domestic and foreign policies.

Imbued with Marxist beliefs that had matured during the two years in the sierra, Fidel had come to identify more intimately with the *guajiros* and the poor, mostly landless and illiterate peasantry. His childhood at Biran and the mockery he endured because of his *guajiro* qualities drew him closer to them. He knew they would be the principal beneficiaries and symbols of the revolution. The social consciousness that he first experienced after the *bogotazo* had grown into full blown Marxist awareness of class struggle.

In those first days his message was vague but portentous. He would wage war on all those he believed exploited the poor and disadvantaged. Exploiters would be his and the revolution's mortal enemies. Perceived injustices would be rectified through revolutionary justice, redistributive programs, and a collective empowerment of the masses. No other social issues have ever had more salience in his revolutionary preachings. Themes of exploitation and injustice have consistently over the decades been the most frequently cited in his public performances.

Fidel's conversion to communism accelerated in the first weeks after victory. Raul and Che were urging him to embrace openly the "old communists," and all the immediate political imperatives he confronted were pushing him in that direction as well. Within his ragtag movement there simply were too few with the education, political skills, managerial, or organizational abilities to staff the new government. The guerrilla *barbudos* who had fought in the mountains were hardened revolutionaries but would be laughable as bureaucrats and managers.

And Fidel had no intention of relying on his movement's urban underground, the pro-democracy civilians who had been essential to fund-raising and political action but who now were expendable. Many were exactly the kind of educated and skilled professionals he desperately needed to build a government, but he considered them insufficiently revolutionary, too likely to want good relations with the Americans and to press for early elections.

He was even less inclined to listen to the technocrats and political figures from the Grau San Martin and Prio years, especially not the former Orthodox Party leaders who had disdained him. Initially, a number of men and women of that older, liberal generation were brought into the government, but nearly all would be gone within eight or nine months.

There was only one place Fidel could turn; it was to the "old communists." They comprised the most disciplined political party in the country. With about seventeen-thousand members—more than in his own movement—they were well organized across the island. They had managerial skills, bases of support in the labor sector, and considerable influence with intellectuals and other important groups. They advocated the kind of sweeping restructuring of society and the economy that Fidel also wanted but did not yet know how to carry out. The process of integrating communists into the military was already well underway, with Raul taking the lead. The next step would be to bring them into civilian administration.

Biographers and historians have disagreed about exactly when Fidel made the fateful decision to become a full-fledged communist. He first announced the socialist nature of the revolution in April 1961, and he declared himself a Marxist–Leninist that December. Some, including his sister Juanita, have said, however, he was a dedicated but secret Marxist by 1956 in Mexico, and Raul suggested that too in the 1975 interview with the Mexican paper *El Dia*.[4]

Fidel's biographer Tad Szulc concluded that the conversion occurred two years later "with finality" in the Sierra Maestra, in the late spring of 1958. Many other, wildly diverging opinions have also been offered. The nearest thing to a consensus view has been that Fidel crossed his ideological watershed sometime during the spring or summer of his first year in power.

For many years I agreed with that consensus, though more recently I have come to believe that Fidel's manipulation of his brother's outlook signaled that his own Marxist and Leninist convictions were solid by the early or mid-1950s. By then nearly everything about Fidel's character and belief system were pointing him in only one direction, that is, toward Marxism and Leninism.

Yet to a certain extent the question and the long-running debate are misleading. Fidel experienced no deciding moment to which he or anyone could date his conversion. There was no single turning point, as if a switch were thrown, after which he definitively changed. There was no incident, no act of political seduction, or inspiring tract he discovered that had made a critical difference. As with all major decisions Fidel makes, his conversion developed from overlapping layers of calculation about what would serve his ambitions best. There was no need—in fact, there were very strong disincentives—for him to openly embrace communism or the communists before he defeated Batista. It was power he wanted, not opportunities to lounge in cafés and discuss the esoteric finer points of Marxist doctrine.

Once he achieved power, however, affiliation with Soviet-led international communism was the only route that made any sense for him strategically, personally, and politically. He and Raul had probably concluded exactly that during their stay in Mexico.

Strategically, his and the revolution's entwined destinies could be advanced only in alliance with the Soviet Union. He needed the Kremlin to help protect the revolution from the inevitable American onslaught. Furthermore, allying himself and his revolution with Moscow would be the ultimate repudiation of the United States.

Personally, he was driven by his sense of destiny to exercise authoritarian control for as long as he lived. That was possible in monarchies but also in communist countries where leaders could hold on to power indefinitely and with a certain legitimacy.

Politically, he needed the skills and organizational base of the "old communists," so that he could profoundly reshape Cuban society. In a letter from prison on the Isle of Pines in April 1954 he wrote: "How pleased I would be to revolutionize this country from top to bottom."[5]

The last component in the decision to begin embracing communism openly fell into place by the end of his first month in power. Fidel enjoyed such overwhelming popular support just a few weeks after coming down from the sierra that no conceivable combination of political forces on the island could threaten him. It was then that he finally felt secure enough to adopt the "old communists" on his terms and with little fear that those wily old foxes could gain the upper hand.

Communists he knew at the university remembered his saying that he would consider becoming one only if he could be Stalin. He meant that he would never subordinate himself to the discipline of others, especially in a hierarchical party in which he would have to start out at the bottom. If he were to become a communist he would have to be in charge. He realized soon after winning power that he was in position to do precisely that.

But it was Lenin, not Marx, whose lessons and achievements most attracted Fidel. The sage "old communist" Carlos Rafael Rodriguez told Herbert Matthews that Fidel was more impressed with Lenin's writings than with Marx's. Fidel had begun reading Lenin at the university. Later, he carried one of Lenin's works with him as he recruited trainees for Moncada, apparently the same volume that was seized by Batista's police after the attack. Fidel's understanding of Lenin was perfected during the Isle of Pines confinement and in Mexico where he and Che studied the Soviet leader together.[6]

All of Fidel's political instincts since the late 1940s were essentially Leninist. Through singular, fanatical determination, often against incredible odds, Lenin had imposed Bolshevik revolutionary rule in the October Revolution. He organized the Communist Party and state, creating the Soviet Union out of the wreckage of czarist Russia. His proven methods for seizing power and then structuring it in a hegemonic political party that he alone controlled were breathtaking models for Fidel. Lenin was an autocrat who believed that Marx's concept of the dictatorship of the proletariat should be interpreted literally. The party, under his implacable control, would be the engine of the dictatorship.

For Fidel, Lenin was a flesh-and-blood revolutionary, a man of action, not a hot house intellectual like Marx. Lenin became Fidel's guide and model, the exemplar of an institutionalized personal destiny. Before the collapse of the Soviet Union, Fidel frequently delivered speeches commemorating Lenin, speaking of him like a favorite old uncle, and referring to him as the perfect role model. What he told Barbara Walters in a 1977 interview was typical: "Lenin was an extraordinary man in every way and there is not a single blemish in his life."[7]

When I was a young analyst in the 1960s, no one doubted that either of the Castro brothers was a dedicated communist. Yet, like so many of my generation in that turbulent time, I wanted to believe that they were Cuban nationalists above all.

If only the United States could devise just the right policies, I thought, Fidel might turn out to be a Titoist, a non-aligned Marxist who could deal with both superpowers as a neutral in the Cold War. The corollary in either case was that he would end or greatly curtail his economic and military alliance with the Soviet Union if given an opportunity to do so by the United States.

There were good reasons to postulate that. He was already defying the Kremlin by purging, even executing, "old communists." Nothing about him was clearer than his aggressive spirit of personal independence and nationalism. It didn't seem to make sense, therefore, that he would tear out the roots of Cuba's dependence on the United States and then plant the Kremlin in its place.

I was mistakenly seized by that logic until a number of years, and many bilateral crises later. The problem with that thinking was that it ignored or misunderstood the depths of Fidel's antipathy for the United States. For him it was a simple calculation, and it has never changed. There could not be a successful revolution while Cuba maintained good relations with Washington. His absolute personal authority would be threatened if the United States were able to exercise any influence on the island.

At least a half dozen American administrations since 1959 wanted to find a route to better relations with him, and in the 1970s presidents Ford and Carter engaged in serious, extended diplomatic efforts to do so. My view at the time was the typically naive one of my generation. I believed that Fidel placed a fairly high priority on achieving a diplomatic breakthrough, that he would see it in his interests to open up trade and get relief from the American economic embargo that outlawed almost all bilateral commerce.

I was still optimistic in 1975 when, as a more senior CIA Cuba specialist, I worked closely as the principal intelligence adviser to the top State Department officers trying to negotiate a diplomatic breakthrough with their counterparts in Havana.

But I had been making the same mistake for a long time. It was poor intelligence tradecraft to base conclusions on unfounded assumptions or wishful thinking. Learning the hard way, I subsequently came to realize that Fidel's abiding commitment to revolutionary internationalist causes, dating back to Cayo Confites and the *bogotazo*, was a much higher priority for him than improving relations with the United States. So was his alliance with Moscow. I had underestimated both, as well as the depths of his hostility toward the Goliath to the north.

In the end I came to doubt that Fidel has ever been sincere about wanting better relations with the United States—unless, of course, if he could procure them strictly on his own terms.

Fidel spoke in Havana on January 21, 1959, before a giant outdoor rally; news reports said a million ecstatic Cubans were there. He began to articulate foreign policy positions that he knew could never be compatible with those of democratic societies. Although few in the U.S. government took notice at the time, his remarks betrayed the quickening coalescence of his Marxist–Leninist orientation: "How much America and the peoples of our hemisphere need a revolution like the one that has taken place in Cuba. How much America needs an example like this in all its nations. How much it needs for the millionaires who have become rich by stealing the people's money to lose everything they have stolen."

The speech was a bludgeoning broadside aimed at the plutocrats and ruling classes of all the Latin American countries. Fidel was threatening the region's wealthiest and most powerful interests, pleading with like-minded young Latin Americans to emulate the Cuban Revolution. There was no mistaking his violent internationalist intent when he added: "How much America needs for the war criminals in the countries of our hemisphere to be shot."

He was referring indirectly to the waves of executions that Raul and Che had been carrying out. Many of the condemned Cubans had been given the hasty due process that had been extended to others in Mexico and during the insurgency. But there were grotesque abuses, circus-like show trials, and filmed executions that provoked sharp criticism in the United States, notably among some members of Congress. Fidel reacted as if the criticism had been direct American intervention.

His belligerent language was reminiscent of his anarchic outbursts on the presidential balcony and at Chibas's funeral. But now he was talking about the seizure of power by revolutionaries throughout Latin America. No American government, either of the right or the left, at that white hot stage of the Cold War could have reconciled with such subversive policies. They were theoretically compatible, however, with international communist strategy and doctrine. Marxists accepted with little questioning that world revolution was inevitable. Soviet leaders beginning with Lenin were all internationalists, dedicated to spawning new communist governments.

Fidel delivered dozens of speeches during that first year. Some lasted six or more hours as his words spoken on the record and transcribed by FBIS grew to mountainous dimensions. Most performances, extravagant and often melodramatic, generated so much excitement around the world that he was instantly a global superstar. Raul's and Che's speeches were monitored as well, but not with the same priority.

A shadow-boxing game of sorts developed between Fidel and the American intelligence analysts perusing his words for clues and indicators. Often his most attentive audience was not the gathered Cuban bureaucrats or the crowd arrayed right before him wherever he was speaking, but us, the anonymous American intelligence analysts working in distant cubicles, parsing his every sentence.

He soon understood that he was being tracked and scrutinized, but perhaps flattered by the attention or attracted to the game itself, he has only rarely been known to deliver important speeches off the record or in secure settings. Knowing we were listening imposed a seemingly welcome discipline on him.

He liked the challenge of communicating regularly with the Cuban masses while not giving away any secrets or making mistakes that could be used against him. This may help to explain his extraordinary success—with only a few really damaging exceptions through the years—at avoiding slips of the tongue and unconsidered outbursts in his public appearances.

Often he tries to confuse or entrap his distant listeners by tossing out beguiling and misleading clues about his intentions. He has also done the opposite, issuing carefully crafted warnings, roughly the equivalent of the highest level diplomatic protest notes. From the last weeks of the Eisenhower administration until September 1977, Cuba and the United States had no diplomatic missions in each others' capitals. That put Fidel in the habit of issuing warnings and threats in his broadcast speeches meant for the eyes and ears of American officials. Some of the bombast was real and some bluster, but none could be dismissed out of hand.

Fidel occasionally has also engaged in a dialogue of sorts with his American intelligence trackers. He and I have communicated with each other through the diligence of Cuban and FBIS speech transcribers. The first of our "secret" exchanges was for me, at least, the most memorable.

In February 1990, as the Soviet Union and the communist bloc were disintegrating, I was invited by the University of Miami to speak about Fidel at a large public forum. By then I was a senior CIA officer and well known to Fidel and the Cuban intelligence service. I recognized that what I said would be in his morning intelligence briefing within a day or two, probably after being taped by someone in the audience and then transcribed and translated in Havana. For years I had been a high priority target of Cuban intelligence and knew that Fidel was interested in what I said and wrote about him. My tracking of him had come full circle.

I spoke in Miami about how I thought he was reacting as international communism was disintegrating around him. It was just a few months after the Berlin Wall had fallen and as the enormous Soviet subsidies Cuba had been receiving were drying up. How could he compensate? How did he feel about the momentous decision he made years earlier to become a communist and align himself strategically with the now-dissolving Soviet empire? Did he recognize what a calamitous mistake he had made?

A speech FBIS had transcribed a few months earlier provided the hook for my talk. Fidel visited the Salvador Allende hospital in Havana, and spoke to a small audience in an outdoor courtyard. Mango trees were growing there, and as he droned on about the revolution's accomplishments in health care, he digressed. The trees somehow distracted and irritated him. The FBIS transcript had it all word for word: "Why is this mango tree here? This mango tree does not belong in this patio. It must be cut down."

It was not a typical performance. Fidel is not given to public soliloquies, and does not often digress so abruptly. The aside was a rare nugget in the billions of words he had spoken on the record that was revealing of character and personality flaws. A part of his arbitrary leadership style was in full view. I used those remarks as the centerpiece for my talk that day.

"There could be no doubt," I said, "that the mango tree was promptly cut down, despite whatever pleasures it may have provided the patients." Surely there had been no discussion about it with the hospital administrators or anyone else. The commander-in-chief said the tree must be cut down and that was all there was to it.

It was an all-too-typical example, I said, of Fidel's micromanagerial style when even the most obscure and irrelevant matters suddenly, and for no apparent reason, become important to him. It was Fidel at his autocratic worst.

It reflected pettiness, obduracy, total self-absorption, disregard for everyone. Incredibly, a mango tree had become an issue of state.

A year went by and I was still thinking about the questions I had addressed in Miami. By then, in the early 1990s, Fidel's speeches were tedious, lacking the flair and surprises of the 1960s, but I was still reading them faithfully, searching for clues and hidden meaning. Plowing through a particularly boring one he delivered in February, 1991 at a provincial assembly in Havana, I was jolted by a passage about the Salvador Allende hospital.

He was speaking again about accomplishments in medicine and health care. He boasted that the Allende hospital was "a very good institution . . . the pride of the capital."

Then, the FBIS transcribers noted, he paused. His mention of the Allende hospital had triggered the memory of my criticisms of him in Miami. In an angry outburst, he reacted, defending what he had done. I had been right. The mango tree was cut down. Except it was actually a small grove of trees that he had destroyed. As if speaking only to himself and to me, he complained: "What came out in that meeting about the Salvador Allende hospital was incredible. The fences were broken because of the construction work which, who knows how many years had been going on. There was a mango grove. That was the only time in my life that I ordered to clean, to bulldoze a mango grove.

"The mango grove was inside the hospital. The kids jumped everywhere. In fact they did not have to jump because there was no fence and they got in there to eat the mangoes. Everyone ate mangoes there. Even the patients ate the mangoes. The place was full of flies and there was a terrible lack of hygiene."

He concluded by emphasizing, "There is a beautiful park there now."

I wondered as I read on whether anyone in his audience that day, or anyone else who heard the broadcast of the speech or read the text later could have had the slightest idea of what he was talking about. He gave no explanation or context for that strange digression directed at me. I imagined dutiful Cuban bureaucrats in his audience scratching their heads in confusion. Did anyone in the Cuban leadership, other than a few of his intelligence advisers, have any idea what he was talking about?

I was surprised, especially by the intensity and candor of his response. It revealed a man with much greater sensitivity to criticism than I had imagined.

I had never thought of him as thin-skinned, but there it was, quite plainly in sight. I could think of no other examples of his being provoked into such a confessional outburst. He was defensive, even somewhat ashamed, perhaps especially because it had been a senior CIA officer who had made so much of the matter. Was the little park in the hospital courtyard that he had installed as an afterthought the penance he paid for the sin of ordering the mango grove destroyed?

I even imagined that I had been responsible for the creation of that park at the Salvador Allende hospital. I guess it was my small contribution to the work of the Cuban Revolution. Some day I plan to go and see it for myself.

When FBIS began transcribing everything Fidel said in public, no one in Washington could have imagined how long the task would last or how great the cost and commitment would be. What had started with the trickle of words in Camaguey in January 1959, followed by the steady flow in other cities on his route to Havana that first week, would soon cascade and then surge into a torrential flood of oratory unparalleled in history.

It is no exaggeration to say that he has spoken more words on the public record than any political leader in history. Probably no other human in any line of work has ever been recorded uttering such avalanches of words. The same could have been said of him hundreds of long speeches ago which could have garnered him the dubious Guinness Book of World Records-type of distinction sometime in the late 1970s or early 1980s. And now in his late seventies, he still shows no signs of wanting to retire from the speaker's platform.

Fidel's biographer Tad Szulc wrote in 1986 that the number of speeches by then had probably exceeded twenty-five hundred.[8] Szulc unsuccessfully sought a more precise count from Cuban government historians who probably did not have reliable records themselves. An extensive but incomplete electronic database of several thousand speeches and interviews, all of them transcribed by FBIS, is maintained at a University of Texas website. My own collection of English and Spanish texts of speeches, press conferences, and interviews also numbers in the thousands, and the total keeps growing. The compulsion for Fidel to speak at length and on the record is still irresistible. "As you may well know," he said in a November 1993 speech, "my job is to talk."

Standing up ramrod straight to deliver speeches has been so essential to his leadership style and imagery, perhaps even to his emotional well being, that he insists on continuing in that manner no matter how much his aura, health, and acuity have faded. It is about as unimaginable that he will ever stop delivering speeches as it is that he will cut off his beard or admit that he has made some serious mistakes.

Many of the orations, especially during his first decade in power, were incomprehensibly long, and just as tedious, lasting five, six, even eight hours. A speech delivered in January 1968 during a major political purge went on for twelve hours. About midway through it, no doubt to the shuddering relief of his captive audience, Fidel granted an intermission, though normally, even during five- and six-hour performances, no breaks or interruptions are allowed.

He still holds the record for the longest speech ever delivered at the United Nations. He opened it with an alluring but misbegotten promise: "Although we have earned a name for talking at length, do not worry. We will do all possible to be brief."

He then droned on extemporaneously, using only scraps of paper as notes, for about four and a half hours as exhausted diplomats one by one slipped out of the hall. He was openly annoyed at one point after noticing some were dozing off. Others, however, hung on his every word. Soviet premier Nikita Khrushchev and a phalanx of eastern bloc officials were present, often interrupting him with prolonged applause.

That was on September 26, 1960, in the final weeks of the American presidential campaign. The candidates had been vying with each other to promise the toughest stance against the Cuban regime, and in response Fidel was truculent. John Kennedy, he said, was "an illiterate, ignorant millionaire," quickly adding that this "does not imply that we like Nixon." He was interrupted by the president of the General Assembly and admonished to refrain from personal attacks.

In addition to the speeches, Fidel has committed millions of words to the record in interviews and press conferences, some of the former so protracted that his interlocutors were left staggering and dazed. He has been the world's most prolific monologist. All of his talks are entirely one-sided. He is always in control, cool and exceedingly articulate, grandly manipulating the occasion and later often editing his words so that the published transcripts will make him look even better.

Unlike other world leaders, he has never had a press spokesperson or adviser, but if he did there is very little he has ever said in public that would warrant a correction or elaboration. There would never have been a Cuban government press release to the effect of, "What the *comandante* really meant to say was . . ."

The billions of words he has spoken in public are on the record, preserved for posterity because for more than forty-six years one small American intelligence component has been keeping track of them. The cumulative record of speaking and transcribing, which still goes on, has been astonishing.

It is also notable that in those billions of spoken words, Fidel will not be remembered for any single galvanizing performance or sparkling passage that is uniquely his own. Unlike many great orators he has hoped to emulate, nothing he has uttered in public has reverberated over time as a defining rhetorical moment. His oratory is bereft of adornment, memorable phrases, or poignant passages. There is little subtlety, and no metaphors, aphorisms, or allusions. A majority of the speeches have been appallingly boring recitations of facts and figures, often going on self-indulgently for hours.

Fidel unquestionably must be ranked among just a few of the most charismatic world figures of the last hundred years. Yet his words, when transcribed out of their dramatic performance context, are surprisingly banal.

CHAPTER EIGHT

I Detest Solitude

Havana was a revolutionary Mecca throughout the 1960s. Leftist intellectuals, journalists, and pandering political tourists from all over the world flocked to see for themselves the presumed miracles that were being wrought. Many hoped for a meeting of some sort with Fidel, or at least a glimpse of him as he scurried around doing the utterly disorganized but noble work of the revolution. It was all spontaneous and improvised.

He was "constantly in the streets," he told a visiting American congressman.

He needed to consult directly with the people to be reassured of his popularity. It was against his nature to be sedentary, to sit in an office with tedious officials and privilege-seekers.

"I am an enemy of bureaus and bureaucrats. . . . I pay visits to the university and the centers, to the factories, and I talk to the workers," he told the congressman. "And besides all that, once in a while I get together with the government."[1]

He had no real home or office for the next fifteen years, according to his friend, Gabriel Garcia Marquez. "The seat of government was wherever he might be."[2]

Fidel's unpredictability only enhanced his charismatic appeal. Delegations of sympathetic Americans and Europeans tried somehow to lend a hand, many laboring in the sugar cane fields in the regime's *Venceremos* Brigades. Young Latin

Americans volunteered too, and some stayed on to be trained in guerrilla warfare techniques at boot camps run by the military and intelligence services. All were deadly earnest in their determination that the Cuban experiment succeed and that it be emulated in other countries. Fidel continually spoke about abolishing injustice and exploitation, and he did not mean only in Cuba.

The country's old social and economic order was being turned upside down. The wealthier and professional classes were fleeing, many under physical duress, forced to leave everything they owned behind to be seized by the state and redistributed to those who stayed or to be sold for hard currency. In 1965 the first of the surprise seaborne exoduses was spurred by Fidel, from the north coast inlet of Camarioca. Thousands of refugees boarded small boats and headed to Miami until an organized airlift was negotiated with Washington. Then, hundreds of thousands more left on the Freedom Flights. The revolution, its leaders insisted, was an enterprise of the willing and the dedicated. All the rest were denounced as *gusanos*, worms, and until they too could depart legally, they had to live on the penurious margins.

Guajiro families from all over the countryside were receiving titles to the land they worked. The agrarian reform of May 1959 abolished large holdings, including most of what Angel Castro had spent his life accumulating at Biran. Fidel was indifferent to that, but Raul made a point of paying a last sentimental visit to the homestead he loved so much before it was expropriated.[3] Urban reforms slashed rents for the poor; literacy brigades spilled into the countryside trying to reach every shanty and hovel. Hordes of country children were brought to the capital to be educated, receiving the best of everything available and boarding in the vacated Miramar mansions of the rich.

It was a time of rampant revolutionary effervescence. The heart of what came to be known as the "New Left" in the United States and in London, Paris, Frankfurt, Tokyo, and many other cities, was throbbing in Havana, of all places! Cuban leaders, and the morally superior, idealistic "new revolutionary man" they claimed to be inspiring were its icons. *Cuba, Si, Yanqui, No* became the signature mantra of that era, not just on the island, but throughout much of Latin America. And after beating back the American intervention at the Bay of Pigs, the revolution seemed invincible too. No Latin American leader had ever humiliated the United States as Fidel did.

He was the first triumphant national hero Cuba produced. In the four and a half centuries before him, no one had been so popular. He probably could have won a fair election with more than 90 percent of the vote during the first euphoric months, though he was not tempted in the least. He wore Martí's mantle but was tougher, more versatile, mysteriously anointed to fulfill a special destiny. He had survived the military conflict, taken down the dictatorship against all odds, and was confronting the Americans. The Apostle had only been able to dream of such things.

Centuries of frustrated nationalism had ended. The humiliations of colonial rule, the Platt Amendment and dependence on the United States, the feelings of inferiority and helplessness that for so long had nagged at the national ego were all lifting. Fidel instilled a sense of pride and national identity that Cubans had never before felt. For the first time since Columbus stepped foot on their island, they were truly independent, the masters of their own fate. After the alliance with the Soviet Union was cemented and Marxism was openly embraced, Fidel's popularity diminished, but he maintained a large, enthusiastic following, especially with his *guajiro* base.

He and Che Guevara—before Che was killed leading a hopeless little insurgent group in Bolivia—were the first international superstars of the tumultuous sixties. Their images were reproduced everywhere, in photographs and films, printed literature, and graffiti. There was hardly a college dorm anywhere in the United States where Che was not peering down intensely from a poster on some student's wall. Then, as always, Raul remained in the background; he was too dour, inaccessible, and mechanically pro-Soviet to be celebrated as an icon. He was first in the line of succession, but more feared or loathed than admired. As he settled into the obscure work of running the defense ministry, he was completely lacking in charisma.

Che was at the other extreme, his appeal rivaling, even exceeding Fidel's. He was more serene and broodingly complicated, a steely guerrilla leader who also wrote poetry. The American intellectual I. F. Stone rhapsodized that Che was the first man he ever met whom "I thought not just handsome but beautiful."[4]

That kind of talk was good for the revolution, but it proved to be the beginning of the end for Che. Fidel's jealousies and need to have the limelight to himself have never permitted any competition. Within a few months the

Argentine was sent off on a lengthy foreign mission, and while he was away the troops he had commanded were dispersed. That way he could not easily threaten either Castro brother.[5]

Other heroes of the guerrilla campaigns, also potential rivals to both Castros, did not even last through the first year. Huber Matos, one of the most popular, was sentenced to a twenty year prison term merely for protesting the drift toward communism. He and Raul had had a contentious, competitive relationship, and according to a regime insider, Raul demanded that Matos be executed.[6]

Camilo Cienfuegos, the third most photogenic after Fidel and Che, was a potential rival to Fidel *and* Raul. He disappeared in a mysterious plane crash in October 1959, the same time that Matos was imprisoned and Raul was taking charge of the military. Unsubstantiated rumors have flourished ever since that Raul arranged for the plane to be sabotaged or shot down. There is a good chance that he was in fact responsible, acting on his own or on orders from Fidel. When I interviewed Huber Matos in Miami several years after he was released from prison, he told me that Raul "hated Camilo for his charm."[7]

Fawning foreign visitors kept arriving in Havana. The brilliant existentialist philosopher Jean-Paul Sartre and his celebrated companion, Simone de Beauvoir, traveled the island for two days with Fidel. They wrote adoringly about what they had witnessed.

Sartre said Fidel told him he was a professional revolutionary. When asked what that meant, Fidel said, "It means I can't stand injustice."

He must have been relaxed with the philosopher, because he shared stories of his suffering as a child, telling Sartre of "the ill-treatment they had attempted to inflict on him." It was one of the few times Fidel was willing to discuss the painful years at the Haitian foster home, and in the book he wrote about his visit, Sartre noted how impressed he was with Fidel for having prevailed over those adversities. Sartre admired the qualities in the rebellious child that he saw as the makings of the successful revolutionary adult he was beginning to know. Fidel, he thought, would never be subjugated.[8]

"He never let things be, he told me, returning blow for blow."

When the distinguished Parisian visitors traveled with him, Fidel was besieged affectionately by *guajiros* in every little hamlet they visited. Sartre and de Beauvoir were among the first to be enthralled with the easy affinity Fidel had with the simple, mostly illiterate rural folk he had known so well growing up. When he was with them he used country slang, spoke informally, joked in their own vernacular.

The *guajiros* clung to him, touched his uniform, stuffed his pockets with petitions and letters. Women reached out to stroke his beard, and many pleaded for government help.

Sartre, the savant, asked Fidel, "All those who ask, no matter what they ask, have the right to obtain?"

At first Fidel did not answer.

"Is that your view?" the Frenchman insisted.

"Man's need is his fundamental right over all others," Fidel finally responded.

"And if they ask you for the moon?"

Sartre said Fidel puffed on his cigar, slowly put it down, and finally turned toward him.

"If someone asked me for the moon, it would be because someone needed it."

The philosopher was overwhelmed with emotion. He wrote that Fidel then looked over at Simone de Beauvoir and elaborated.

"Thanks to us they dare to discover their needs. They have the courage to understand their suffering, and to demand that it be ended."[9]

Such was the euphoria of the revolution and its acolytes in the early days. Fidel had thoroughly charmed his French visitors. They were enchanted with Che, too, and went back to Paris to compose glowing accounts. Of Che's musings, Sartre wrote, "Behind each sentence there are deposits of gold."

If the philosopher embellished Fidel's words, he had not exaggerated the power of the utopian dreaming that characterized those years. Many revolutionary innovations failed calamitously, and other fanciful, impractical ideas never got off the ground. One, seriously aired, was that the silent h in Spanish be abandoned. The French Revolution had created a new calendar, changing the names of the months of the year, so why shouldn't the Cuban Revolution create its own linguistic variant that might make it easier to eradicate illiteracy?

Spinning visions of utopias just over the horizon, Fidel played the role of a secular prophet. Everyone would have a house or a decent apartment. Food and government services would proliferate, reaching every little backwater.

Cuba would rapidly industrialize and no longer depend so heavily on the monoculture of sugar production. He ruminated openly about draining the huge Zapata swamplands near the Bay of Pigs to produce rice. He thought about banning money because in the ideal society that was emerging, all forms of materialism would disappear. The "new revolutionary man" would work for moral rewards, for the love of the revolution, not competitively or for tangible gain. All of the supposedly corrupting influences of capitalist market economics would disappear. Everything was possible.

The most enduring of the innovations in those early days also proved to be the most spectacularly successful. It was the new Fidel. The bearded, khaki-clad, ingenuous guerrilla—the new public persona he had adopted—was a world-class invention, entirely of his own making.

No other Cuban or Latin American leader before him had assumed such an exciting and original public identity. Fidel himself would be the prototype of Cuba's new revolutionary man. Before he reached Havana in that first week after victory, he was transforming himself into an idealized heroic figure, and with only minor variations, he has performed in that role ever since.

Had he hired a Hollywood agent, a costume director, a script-writer, and an acting coach, together they could not have devised a more memorable, inimitable character than the Fidel Castro the world has known for so long.

After I left the CIA, a former Cuban intelligence official revealed to me during long conversations in Miami that Fidel studied at an actor's studio in Mexico City while in exile there.[10] The Cuban officer and I agreed that surely Fidel had been the star pupil and could easily have won leading man parts in Mexican soap operas or on the legitimate stage. He has been a performer all his life. With the possible exception of Ronald Reagan, whose run on the world stage was considerably shorter than Fidel's, no other leader in modern times has been such a natural and versatile political thespian.

In his new role Fidel expunged his earlier and private selves. The man he had been—his past before Moncada—was submerged into the new, much more interesting persona. Negative impressions of him as *pistolero*, gangland hit man, grandstander, pseudo-anarchist, and unprincipled opportunist were supplanted by his ostensibly honorable new identity as the personification of the Cuban

Revolution. He presented himself as noble, moral, and principled. The appearance of all personal ambitions was obliterated. Everything he did now was for one purpose only: to advance and perfect the revolution.

Abandoning all evidence of a private life, he appeared to have joined a strict monastic religious order founded on vows of poverty, chastity, and humility. Without apparent family encumbrances, he could better act out his role as the revolution's selfless apostle. He would be its only focal point. So beginning in January 1959, nearly everything in his personal life receded, eventually falling out of sight entirely. He acknowledged no wife, no family, no significant relationships. He had no home, no personal needs beyond the most basic. He was not interested in honors or statues in his likeness. He was the revolution's servant, a secular clergyman.

As such, Fidel has never appeared in public escorting a woman. He is never seen embracing, kissing, holding hands, or even smiling endearingly at a female. He does not squire any of his children around in public. No intimate photos of him or them have been released. Wherever he has lived since the first year or two has been hidden, and no mention is made of an official residence. Beyond a small, trusted circle, no one is invited to the large, elaborately protected compound near Raul's, where Fidel has lived in recent years. The resulting impression in the public imagination is that Fidel is married to the revolution and that it is his only consuming interest.

Meanwhile, Raul's wife, Vilma Espin, the longtime head of the Cuban Women's Federation and in the past a member of the Communist Party Politburo, has been the nearest thing Cuba has had to a first lady. She studied chemical engineering for a year at MIT in Massachusetts before joining the Castro brothers, assuming the *nom de guerre* Deborah, after the biblical prophetess.

Like her husband, Vilma had strong ties to Cuba's "old communists" before she joined his Second Front in the Sierra Cristal. It was there that she was interviewed by an American reporter, probably for the only time. Working for a Philadelphia newspaper, the journalist traveled to the Sierra Cristal in the summer of 1958 to interview Raul but was more impressed with Vilma, finding her future husband unpleasant and taciturn.

"I could not think of him as one who I would like to have as a close friend. He was brash and cocky," the reporter observed.[11]

Dalia Soto del Valle, the mystery woman with whom Fidel has lived since the early or mid-1960s, remains out of sight with their five sons. She does not attend Fidel's public appearances, unless in disguise, and she does not accompany him to diplomatic receptions or official functions or on foreign trips. She is known only to a limited circle of senior Cuban officials and a few foreigners who are especially close to Fidel.

Dalia was a small town schoolteacher when Fidel met her. Later, when their sons were old enough to begin elementary school, she began to direct a small, ultra-elite academy for them and just a few other carefully selected children. The boys also studied in the Soviet Union. Dalia and her sons might as well have been consigned to a witness protection program, so elaborate are the security precautions that surround them.

Their very existence was top secret until just a few years ago. They were not known even to CIA analysts. I had never heard of Dalia or her family until I read of her in Georgie Anne Geyer's biography of Fidel and viewed, in late 1999, a Cuban government documentary, which had been screened for limited audiences in Cuba. The film and some accompanying press coverage were the first open acknowledgments that Fidel actually had a private life, an intimate relationship, and a brood of children. But just as that window was briefly opened in Cuba, it was promptly slammed shut. Dalia and her sons returned to obscurity.

Even within the large Castro clan in Cuba, they have been strangely invisible. Raul's wife Vilma and their four children also had little if any contact with Fidel's clandestine family. Fidel's daughter Alina Fernandez has never met Dalia. In a conversation I had with her in a Miami radio studio before she went on the air for her regular program, Alina shared a number of previously unpublicized Castro family stories with me.

In 1980 Vilma traveled to Moscow to attend the Summer Olympic games. She was in the spectator's area during an event with a Cuban team competing, and was surprised to notice a few of Fidel's personal bodyguards seated nearby among the other Cuban fans. The men were there guarding three young boys Vilma had never seen before. She concluded the children were the sequestered sons of Fidel and Dalia. Understanding Fidel's pathological need for privacy, she made no effort to approach them.[12]

The fortifications that Fidel has built around his family have resulted in even stranger incidents. Vilma and Raul's only son, Alejandro, told his cousin Alina of a chance meeting he had when, for the first time, he encountered another of his cousins, one of Fidel and Dalia's sons.

Alejandro was working out at an elite gym operated by the armed forces ministry's Special Troops. Antonio Castro Soto del Valle, rumored to be Fidel's favorite among Dalia's sons, was there too and they struck up a conversation as total strangers. These first cousins, both eighteen or nineteen years old at the time, may have been only vaguely aware of each other's existence. They bonded, however briefly, and driven by long repressed curiosity, wanted to stay in touch. Alejandro later told Raul about the meeting. He and his cousin wanted to get to know each other and their families better. Raul temporized, understanding it was not a decision he could make and finding it difficult to discuss with his son. When he did talk to Fidel about it, he was told the boys must be kept apart.[13]

This pathological denial of family and personal life is key to the heroic, unencumbered persona Fidel projects. It also reflects a fundamental element of his psychological composition. All his life he has demanded absolute personal autonomy.

When I taught at Georgetown University in Washington, I challenged every new class of students to name a political figure in modern times—besides Fidel Castro—who never had a boss. I told my students, that with the possible exception of the Cayo Confites affair, Fidel never spent a day in his life working for someone or taking orders. He has never subordinated himself to the will of another person. He has never said, "Yes, sir," not even to his father or the Soviet leaders when, at different times in his life, they were paying the bills. For more than thirty years, Raul paid public and private obeisances to the Kremlin, but Fidel always managed to keep his distance and maintain considerable independence even while in the bear's hug.

After pondering my own question for many years, and soliciting other opinions, there is only one additional prominent political figure in modern times who indisputably also fits in this strange category—Vladimir Lenin, the leader of the Russian Revolution, never had a boss either.[14]

Fidel may not be familiar with a memorable line attributed to the Irish-born playwright and wit Oscar Wilde, "The first duty in life is to assume a pose," but since 1959 he has lived by that dictum. An actor playing a part must faithfully express his character's essence and composition. If there are lapses or inconsistencies, if the performer falls out of character even briefly, credibility is undermined. Fidel has always understood this. Acting out his revolutionary persona for more than forty-six years, he has never allowed himself to slip out of character.

First, there is the familiar visage. He started growing his beard in the Sierra Maestra. Up there it had practical advantages he has occasionally spoken about. Men who shaved came under suspicion as possible spies and infiltrators, so beards defined the guerrilla brotherhood. Shaving gear was in short supply. When he was coaxed into discussing this with *Playboy* magazine in 1985, he put yet another spin on it. With pen and paper in hand, he calculated for his interviewers exactly how much time was saved in the sierra by not shaving. Certainly vanity was a factor. Photos taken before the guerrilla days show him with the beginnings of an unflattering double chin, soon overgrown and masked forever.[15]

During the insurgency and the early years, the beard invited biblical imagery that Fidel astutely encouraged. He was a thirty-two-year-old Christ-like figure when he came down victorious from the sierra, and it was not long before religious and superstitious Cubans, especially poor rural folk, were muttering about a second coming. Commentators were not discouraged from making comparisons to the Twelve Apostles. After the *Granma* landing, it was said that Fidel and only a dozen of his followers had survived.

His phenomenal charisma took on mystical and religious qualities that he did his best to encourage. He had miraculously survived so many close encounters with death, it was believed, that surely some divine authority was watching over him. Lee Lockwood told one such story, perhaps apocryphal. During one of the early guerrilla skirmishes, a man standing by Fidel's side was shot through the head and died instantly. Fidel was unharmed.[16]

After victory the beard became his quintessential emblem. Many of the other guerrilla veterans also sported beards after victory, but eventually nearly all of them shaved, yielding proprietorship of that particular symbol to Fidel. The few who have kept their beards trimmed them into goatees or Van Dykes. Beginning in his sixties, and now in his late seventies, Fidel's beard has been immaculately molded, tinted, and seems to gleam with pomade. It is an indispensable element of the imagery of his revolutionary persona. Without that thick, dark growth he would be like a shorn Samson, politically debilitated and emasculated.

Cunning CIA agents were onto this in 1960. With a mandate from the Eisenhower administration to destabilize the Cuban regime, they brainstormed ideas for covert actions that might neutralize Fidel's charismatic appeal. One plot that later came to light was intended to be carried out when he traveled abroad. An undercover agent would be tasked with sprinkling thallium powder, a depilatory, on his boots. The idea was that when Fidel put on the boots the next morning, he would transfer the powder to his hands and then to his beard when he stroked it. And if the cockamamie scheme worked, his whiskers would fall out! The idea was not really considered seriously and never tried, but is colorful confirmation of the iconic status of the beard.[17]

It complements his standard costume too. The guerrilla attire—combat boots, khaki uniform, military cap, and often a holstered pistol—is calculated to project the image of an ardent, lifelong revolutionary. It distinguishes him from the preening civilians of the preceding era, the corrupt politicians who could afford the best of everything. Wearing the fatigues, Fidel appears as neither a civilian nor a traditional military chieftain but a revolutionary hybrid, even though typically his boots are imported and made of fine patent leather.

However, he has occasionally compromised with the costume. In the 1990s, while attending presidential inaugurations in Latin American capitals or regional summit meetings, he appeared on a few occasions in business suits. It was a surprising development for those of us who have followed him so closely, but it did not signal any lasting adaptation of the public persona he plays.

He had not been seen in civilian clothes since the early 1950s, but he had grown increasingly sensitive to criticisms that he was the only head of government among the thirty-five independent nations of the Western Hemisphere who was not democratically elected. The occasional costume change, when he was traveling abroad, was intended to deflect criticism that he presided over a military-style dictatorship. Then, when Pope John Paul II visited Cuba in 1998, Fidel made his first appearance before his own people in a business suit.

A reporter for an Italian newspaper once asked him why he always dresses in guerrilla fatigues. He took umbrage and slipped into a bit of grandiosity that he is usually good at concealing.

"It is clothing I have worn all my life, comfortable, simple. It costs little and it never goes out of fashion. . . . But excuse me, during your interview with the Pope did you ask him why he always wears white?"[18]

For many years a sidearm was a necessary accessory to the uniform. When Fidel met in Havana with Ben Bradlee and Sally Quinn of the *Washington Post* in 1977, Quinn wrote that after their conversation, which extended into the early morning hours, Fidel insisted on accompanying them in a government car back to their hotel. As they were preparing to leave his office, he reached into the bookcase behind his desk for his cap and then strapped on a belt with a holstered pistol. When the three of them got into the back seat of the awaiting car, their feet were resting on a Soviet-made AK-47. Quinn wrote that it was one "that he carries with him always."[19]

In the context of his public persona, Fidel has always played the part of the ingratiating everyman. All over the world and for generations, he and no one else he could possibly be confused with has been known simply as Fidel. In the salons of the international intelligentsia, in university classrooms, at dinner parties in cities in dozens of countries for four and a half decades, there has been only one Fidel. And he loves it that way: "The people look on me as a neighbor, one more person," he told two American interviewers. "No one ever calls me Castro."[20]

In formal and bureaucratic settings he is referred to as Cuba's president, the *comandante*, the commander-in-chief, and most frequently in recent years simply as the chief. Raul and other subordinates, address him as "Chief." Meanwhile, he eschews another title—First Secretary of the Cuban Communist Party—except at the now-infrequent party conclaves.

In the heady early years he was Fidel to just about everyone, Cuban or foreign, *guajiro* or government minister. But as he has aged and expected more elaborate deference, his direct contact with the masses has diminished as his need for formality and ceremony in dealings with subordinates has increased. No bureaucrat or party official would presume to use the informal *tu* or *you*, in conversation with him. Cubans now in exile who had official dealings with the Castro brothers have said there were periods when even Raul deferred to Fidel, using the formal *usted* or *you*, the pronoun never used by family members speaking to each other.[21]

Fidel likes all the obvious connotations of his name: faithful, fidelity, loyalty, devotion. After he won power and stood before large audiences, he appreciated hearing its two staccato syllables so easily chanted by crowds of supporters and gatherings of ranking military officers. "Fee-del! Fee-del!"

Most importantly Fidel is a suitable, commanding name for a charismatic leader. Other memorable twentieth-century revolutionaries changed their names to enhance their celebrity. Stalin, Trotsky, and Lenin all adopted those names seeking more dramatic public auras, an easier familiarity with their followers. Stalin began life as Iosof Dzhugashvili. Trotsky originally was Lev Bronstein. And Lenin, probably the other most recognizable revolutionary two syllable brand name, was the *nom de guerre* of Vladimir Ilyich Ulyanov. None of that was necessary for Fidel, and his name has always pleased him.

"I like it. I have never been unhappy about having that name," he once told an interviewer.[22]

Personal valor is an essential component of Fidel's heroic image, but the reality, like so much in his character, is actually quite contradictory. There is no disputing that throughout his career he has acted courageously, beginning at Cayo Confites and Bogotá. He is not known to have flinched or lost his nerve in any of the innumerable crises he has experienced. He was sharp and in command during the Bay of Pigs, moving Cuban forces around the island like chess pieces. He made all the strategic decisions during Cuba's military interventions overseas. And he seems to have been no less capable as he aged into his sixties and seventies. In the summer of 1994, for example, during the worst anti regime rioting that has ever occurred in Cuba, he went to the scene at Havana's seaside Malecon boulevard in an effort to calm the protestors and personally direct the security response.

But because he considers his own survival more important than the lives of the men who fight under him, the chances he takes are calculated with exceptional cunning. His performance in action at Moncada and during all but the first few months of the insurgency was anything but personally heroic. He led no charges, was never in a fighting vanguard, and came through all the years of conflict physically unscathed. His view of the proper balance between leading fighting men and fighting at their sides was synthesized in a note he sent by messenger to Che in the early months of the insurgency: "I strongly recommend that you be careful. As a final order, you should not fight. Take charge of leading the men well. That is what is indispensable at the present time."[23]

Confident in his destiny yet unwilling to tempt his fate, he has followed his own advice. Throughout the insurgency he stayed relatively safe in the rear, away from the most dangerous action. He avoided the line of fire or, as he did when he was on the slopes of Monserrate mountain in Bogotá, managed to fire from a safe distance. He believed he was indispensable, and in fact he was essential to the cause. If he had been killed at any time during the struggle against Batista, his highly personalized movement probably could not have triumphed under any successors.

In the most tense final hours of the missile crisis in October 1962, Fidel invited the Soviet ambassador to withdraw with him to his bomb shelter burrowed out of a cave near Havana, just in case a nuclear war erupted. According to his British biographer Leycester Coltman, there is a bunker under Fidel's house, maintained by elite uniformed personnel.[24] When he travels abroad, he is accompanied by security details sometimes numbering in the hundreds, and all of his food is brought from Cuba. The survivor of a number of assassination attempts, he takes few chances with his personal security.

The only undisputed first-hand account of Fidel himself actually killing another man is described in Che Guevara's memoirs. The incident occurred at Arroyo del Infierno, a remote spot in the Sierra Maestra during the first weeks of the insurgency. Fidel, Che, Raul, and others, in what was then a guerrilla band of fewer than twenty, launched a surprise attack on a smaller group of soldiers. Che wrote, "Fidel opened fire, hitting a soldier, who fell crying out something that sounded like, 'Oh Mother!' and lay still."[25]

Fidel's favorite weapon was a rifle with a telescopic sight that he kept through the insurgency. He had apparently fired it at the soldier from a considerable distance.

After that firefight, there is no clear record of his engagement in combat again. As his guerrilla forces grew, Fidel spent most of the rest of the campaign at a headquarters encampment that was relatively safe, perhaps even idyllic. Celia Sanchez, his secretary and confidante, could have been speaking for him as well when she recalled after the victory that the days in the Sierra Maestra "were the best times. We were all so happy then. Really, we will never be so happy again."[26]

Unlike Che, who was wounded in the sierra, Fidel bears no known physical scars from his lifetime of conflict. The only time he is known to have been bloodied was during a demonstration at the university. He had learned critical survival lessons during his gangland days there, when, by his own accounting, his life was in greater danger than it has been at any time since.

Apparently he never fired a shot at Moncada, managing to stay at a relatively safe distance from the action in which many on both sides were killed. What he really intended to achieve with that incompetently planned assault is still disputed. He may have hoped, as he has always claimed, to spark a *bogotazo*-style uprising and to seize a large arsenal of weapons to carry on the fight against Batista. But a University of Havana professor who knew Fidel well had a different impression that seems much closer to the truth.

Herminio Portell Villa talked to Fidel in Havana just a few weeks before Moncada. Fidel told him of his plan for the attack and asked the professor if he thought it could be successful. When the older man said success seemed unlikely, Fidel's rejoinder was chilling: "Nevertheless, the plans have been laid. There is no turning back. We need a rallying point and if necessary we shall provide the martyrs."[27]

Beginning with the men who fell in that suicidal mission, thousands of other Cubans have died as martyrs fighting for Fidel, in Cuba and during internationalist missions in Angola, Ethiopia, Nicaragua, and other countries. Martyrdom for the revolution is the highest calling for real revolutionaries, even in missions Fidel prescribes that defy all apparent reason and require unthinking kamikaze loyalty.

He typically demands that. One of the most extreme examples occurred in October 1983 when the Reagan administration ordered American military forces into the small Caribbean island nation of Grenada. About eight hundred Cuban personnel were there at the time, and Fidel's instructions to them provide rare and reliable glimpses into his martyrdom complex and messianic leadership style.

Many of the Cubans on the island were construction workers, building an airfield for the friendly, socialist government that had seized power in a coup a few years earlier. The workers all had some military training and many were armed forces reservists. Active duty military and intelligence personnel were also there, and on the eve of the American intervention, Fidel dispatched a trusted colonel, Pedro Tortolo, to command the Cuban contingent. Back in Havana, it was Fidel who was calling all the shots, sending and broadcasting communiqués to the Cuban personnel.

As the American forces were landing, he ordered all of the Cubans, civilian and uniformed, to fight to the death. He instructed them to hold their positions, to resist attack, and to refuse under any circumstances to surrender.

Soon Colonel Tortolo informed him that he had spurned requests from the Americans to surrender. The response from Havana, in all likelihood drafted by Fidel himself, was ecstatic.

"We congratulate you on your heroic resistance. Cuban people are proud of you. Do not surrender under any circumstances."

Tortolo responded directly to Fidel.

"Commander-in-chief, we will fulfill your instructions and not surrender."

There was intense fighting between the Cubans and the American landing force. It was the first and only time that military personnel from the two countries engaged in combat, and there were casualties on both sides. Twenty-four Cubans died, martyrs in the struggle against American imperialism, just as their commander-in-chief had demanded.

To his horror, however, all of the remaining Cubans, more than seven hundred fifty of them, surrendered. Colonel Tortolo took asylum at the Soviet embassy, deciding to save himself so he could fight for the revolution another day. He soon got that chance. After he and the other Cubans who had defied their chief were safely returned home, the colonel was disgraced. He was stripped of his rank, reduced to the lowliest enlisted status, and shipped off to the wars in Angola. He later died there. Twenty-two other Cuban military officers had also been in Grenada. A few of them were among the Cuban dead, faithful to the end to their commander-in-chief. But all those who surrendered were also sent as privates to fight in Angola.[28]

For the Cuban leadership Grenada was a bitter and twisted morality tale. Fidel had expected all of the Cubans there to die heroically in the equivalent of a mass suicide and to take a large number of Americans down with them.

Perhaps, he calculated, if the fighting was savage and protracted, a chorus of international denunciations and opposition to the intervention in the U.S. Congress might have forced a cease fire. Win or lose, he wanted the world to witness the ferocious loyalty of Cuban revolutionaries to their commander-in-chief. He wanted more martyrs to help build up popular morale at home during a difficult period. And, he wanted to inflict as much pain as possible on the hated Reagan administration.

Florentino Aspillaga was a high level Cuban counterintelligence officer before he defected to the United States in 1987. He had intimate knowledge of the events a few years earlier in Grenada, and of Fidel's mindset at the time. In an interview with Georgie Anne Geyer, Aspillaga said that Fidel was shocked because so few of the Cubans had "died for him. . . . He didn't care about the dying, he cared about them dying for him."[29]

I have asked a number of American military officers of different ranks, including general officers, about the moral implications of Fidel's performance. Most responded that in any modern democratic society, "no surrender" orders like those Fidel issued would be illegal and immoral. Fidel's martyrdom obsession put him in the company of the most fanatical leaders of the world's worst pariah regimes and of terrorist organizations.[30]

Rugged masculinity is essential to Fidel's public imagery. But sexuality is not. Maintaining his public persona with discipline, he always manages to separate the two. In the early days, he was referred to as *el Caballo*, the horse, a sexually charged allusion. Cuban and foreign women used to flirt outrageously with him. When he is in character, however, nothing remotely sexual or affectionate filters through his performance. Readers of FBIS transcripts of his appearances could labor endlessly to find a sexually explicit comment or innuendo. In private he is spectacularly profane. But it is doubtful that even one swear word has ever passed his lips in formal public appearances.

When Sally Quinn interviewed Fidel, she noticed that "he never touches a female visitor." That contrasts with the many casual and impulsive forms of physical contact he has with men when talking and being interviewed. Quinn had the feeling that he was "looking through her rather than at her, the way he looks at a man."

She wrote in the *Washington Post* that Fidel's "posture changes when he talks to a woman. The confidence and assurance diminishes."[31]

Certainly he is not a revolutionary Calvinist or sexually repressed Puritan, yet, many anecdotes from people close to him since his adolescence indicate a strong streak of prudishness and awkwardness where women are concerned. He was appalled by the "brothels, nightclubs, and other lurid amusements" when he traveled through Panama City on his way to Bogotá in 1948. And when training in Mexico, he objected so strenuously to the bikini a girlfriend wore that he bought her a more modest swimsuit.

In all the words Fidel has spoken on the record, there are few that reflect on the individual behind the heroic mask. His inner feelings and emotions are rarely shared. Fears, guilt, doubts, remorse, any hint of his psychological inner workings or vulnerabilities are never revealed. He has seldom admitted to making a mistake. He told television journalist Barbara Walters in an interview that he had never made a strategic mistake, only some inconsequential tactical ones.

He has never acknowledged any kind of internal emotion or conflict. To do so would breach the performance imperative and in any event would be contrary to his nature. He must always be in control of his feelings when in public. The anger and melodrama that he often acts out in speeches, most frequently his anti-American tirades, are pure theatrics. He is always in control when he feigns those high emotions. Through all the years he has been on stage, there have been no incidents when he choked up, shed a tear, or was seized even momentarily by the invisible pull of underlying personal emotion. Employing the royal "we," he abstracts himself personally and in the same way absolves himself of any blame for errors made in the name of the revolution.

Studying his entire public record one would be hard pressed to find examples of genuine introspection or self examination. He has insisted many times that all the executions in the sierra and during the first months after victory were justified and necessary, once positively comparing what he condoned in Cuba to the Reign of Terror during the French Revolution and to the French revolutionary leader he admires the most: "The few months of the terror were necessary to do away with a terror that had lasted for centuries. In Cuba we need more Robespierres."[32]

Barbara Walters once pressed him about a number of personal matters that he generally refuses to talk about. She surprised him by asking if there was something that could cause him to weep: "There are many moments of emotion. I am not going to say that we cried real tears. . . . There are of course occasions when we have to hold back our tears. As for weeping copiously, for strictly sentimental reasons, I don't know. I have not had an experience of that kind for a long time."[33]

Any such acknowledgment of inner turmoil or sentimentality might suggest weakness, and Fidel could never admit to that. But the flesh-and-blood man hidden under the mask of the hero of course feels pain and emotion, and on occasion, out of public view, he has been stressed, even traumatized. As he suggested to Barbara Walters, he has cried too, at least in his previous life. He has admitted that he did so once at the university, when he feared for his life. Several credible sources who were close to him at different times before he won power remember crying episodes in a variety of settings. But when he responded to Walters's question, he was in character. The hero he plays, the persona who embodies the revolution, cannot admit to an interior life or to normal human emotions.

The Cuban poet Heberto Padilla, who knew Fidel in the early 1950s, wrote of his "inexplicable abandonment of self."[34] K. S. Karol, the European Marxist who also knew him well, commented that he hates to reminisce. What matters to him is the present.[35] Fidel himself admitted in one interview in 1985 that he is "allergic" to discussions of personal matters.[36] None of this has softened in the intervening years. If anything, in his old age he has become even more intractable about protecting his privacy and hiding his true feelings.

Considering how much he has spoken for the record, it is not surprising, however, that his shroud has parted or torn slightly on a few rare occasions. Inadvertently or not, that has occurred only in interviews with especially adroit and perceptive questioners. Barbara Walters coaxed him into talking briefly about how lonely he must be, even as he surrounds himself with crowds of admirers: "I really detest loneliness, absolute loneliness," he said.

"In other words, being alone?" she asked.

"Yes, yes," he muttered.

She persisted, asking, "Why?"

"Perhaps because of man's need for companionship . . . I spent many months in solitary."

And then, trying to get back in his impervious, heroic character, he said: "The fact that I detest solitude does not mean that I am not capable of withstanding it."[37]

CHAPTER NINE

The Moral and Political Duty

During the summer of 1975, in the months between the American retreat from Vietnam and the massive Cuban military intervention in Angola, I began drafting my first national intelligence estimate, NIE–85-1-75, *Cuba's Changing International Role*. By then I had about eleven years of experience as a Latin America analyst at CIA and as an air force intelligence officer, and I was completing my doctorate in Latin American history. Writing a difficult estimate was a welcome professional challenge.[1]

Whether they turn out to be right or wrong, prescient or mere iterations of the obvious, NIEs have rightly been considered the ultimate in intelligence analysis since the early 1950s. The various collection and analytic entities of the intelligence community participate as an estimate is drafted and coordinated and as evidence from all possible sources is brought into play. When that is done, agency heads gather to review and approve the text or offer dissenting opinions. The process is formal, often protracted, and cluttered with checks and balances. In the end, the CIA director takes personal responsibility for the facts and judgments compiled; estimates are his assessments, produced for the president and the senior national security team.

Like many NIEs, that one on Cuba was scheduled in support of urgent policy requirements. Top secret talks with the Castros' government had been undertaken by Secretary of State Henry Kissinger with the objective of reducing bilateral tensions and moving toward a comprehensive rapprochement. Entirely an American initiative, it turned out to be the most serious effort until then to repair relations that had been veering between badly strained and conflictive since early 1959.

The first feelers, made directly to Fidel, had actually been extended in June 1974 two months before Richard Nixon yielded the White House to Gerald Ford. The earlier rapprochement with communist China was the model for what, it was thought, might be possible with Cuba too. Arms control and other negotiations with the Soviet Union had also brought results considered advantageous by both sides. It seemed reasonable, therefore, that if Mao and the Kremlin could engage constructively at the negotiating table, Fidel would also see some benefit in talking. Kissinger and his Assistant Secretary of State for Latin America, William Rogers, managed the process under a thick cloak of secrecy. At first, only a few of us in government were involved.

Ironically, nonetheless, the first round of official talks was conducted out in the open in a crowded cafeteria at LaGuardia Airport in New York, in January 1975. Lawrence Eagleburger, then one of Kissinger's top deputies, huddled with two ranking Cuban officials to begin exploring the possibilities. He told them that ideological differences should not prevent the resolution of bilateral problems and that Washington was prepared to discuss everything of concern to Havana. The time for this initiative seemed propitious. Most Americans were tired of the long, acrimonious standoff, and many members of Congress from both parties were publicly advocating greater flexibility in the relationship.[2]

The pace quickened as I drafted the estimate. Exploratory meetings were held in Washington and New York, and the State Department went public, announcing that the United States was prepared to enter into serious discussions with Havana. In August, Fidel made a conciliatory gesture, returning ransom money obtained from the hijacking of an American airliner. Kissinger's project seemed to be gaining some traction, and therefore the need for a comprehensive national intelligence estimate was unmistakable. There was a lot the American negotiators wanted to know.

Was Fidel really interested in improving relations? If he were to negotiate seriously, what would he demand and concede as the talks proceeded? What would his priorities be? Would he put any issues of concern to the United States off limits? What minimum concessions would he expect to receive? After the missile crisis, he had laid out a set of five demands, and in the early 1970s he was still stubbornly insisting they were his non-negotiable bottom line. In one appearance he stated the five succinctly: "We have demanded an unconditional end to piracy, blockade, infiltration, and airspace violations, and let them return the Guantanamo base."[3]

The overarching issue for him was the economic embargo, which he has always referred to as a "blockade." He insisted it would have to be lifted as a pre-condition for any real negotiations. But would he hold to that? There were hints of some flexibility.

No one doubted that the American naval base at Guantanamo, a prize left over from the Spanish–American War, would have to be returned to Cuba, and at that time—when, of course, there were no Al Qaeda terrorists detained there—even the Navy and the Pentagon probably would not have objected too strenuously. Fidel's other three core complaints could easily be handled in ways that would assuage him.

Rereading a copy of the estimate years later, blank spaces obliterating a few sentences that were expurgated by CIA censors, I was pleased with how well it had aged. Most of what was predicted turned out to be right on the mark.

We were not sure that Fidel really wanted to engage in serious negotiations. If he did, we were confident he would drive a hard bargain. We even warned the Ford administration that he "probably calculates that, with the passage of time, pressures on the U.S. to accommodate him will continue to grow," and that he would thus expect to "get a better settlement with a new U.S. adminis-tration." It was hard to imagine him foregoing the anti-American bombast and vitriol that had been the rhetorical glue cementing his domestic and foreign policies for so long. Blaming the United States for nearly all of Cuba's problems was second nature by then. Fidel would not be Fidel without the American enemy to berate.

It was the most challenging of the many national intelligence estimates I would write on Cuba and other countries in later years. It would have been much easier had we been tasked with, say, describing the strength and capabilities of Raul's armed forces. Technical sources would have provided hard evidence of that. Writing about how the Cuban political system was evolving or how the economy was faring would have been easier, too, because reliable reporting from defectors and covert agents would be available.

Those were observable problems. But our task was to estimate abstractions— Fidel's reasoning and intentions. I needed to get into his boots and try to think like him. Reading his and Cuban government public statements helped, but how flexible might he be once the initial diplomatic posturing had been played out? And as always when assessing him, the actual had to somehow be separated from the artifice. It was always safe to assume that elaborately interwoven substrata of deception lay beneath nearly everything he said and did in public.

Raul figured only marginally in the estimate, getting less coverage even than "old communist" Carlos Rafael Rodriguez, who was described as the third most powerful figure in the leadership. There had been no reason to believe that the brothers had feuded since their confrontation in April 1959 in Houston. All the evidence indicated they were working together harmoniously. Furthermore, the estimate was concerned with Cuban foreign policy decision making, and we knew that was Fidel's bailiwick.

On the American side of the negotiating ledger, many thorny matters would be raised with the Cubans if serious talks developed. Havana's military relationship with the Soviet Union was still neuralgic in Washington, more than a dozen years after the missile crisis, though the estimate emphasized it would be non-negotiable. Cuba's commitments to exporting its revolution to other countries was a high American policy priority. We were confident, however, that Fidel would remain adamant about this. In the estimate, we concluded, "It is highly unlikely that Castro will renounce the right to support 'wars of national liberation.' " That critical subject would be off limits in bilateral talks, with the exception, we believed, of Puerto Rico.

That self-governing American commonwealth appeared to be Fidel's latest target as aggressive Cuban maneuvering in support of its independence intensified. More ink in the estimate was devoted to the island than to any other single subject because Fidel's intentions there were the hardest nut we had to crack. Was supporting Puerto Rican independence a higher priority for him than improving relations with Washington? If so, there could be no progress toward rapprochement, probably no sustainable negotiations at all.

Puerto Ricans after all, are citizens of the United States. They vote democratically to choose their governor, mayors, and other local officials. A non-voting delegate in the House of Representatives stands for the island in Washington. For at least the last fifty years support for independence has been miniscule, rarely reaching more than 5 or 6 percent of the vote, and in recent years it has been falling even lower. Puerto Rico would be granted its independence in no time at all if that were the democratically expressed wish of the majority there. The issue had almost no salience anywhere else in Latin America, where even in the most nationalistic circles it was viewed as one of Fidel's more peculiar obsessions.

The Cuban involvement in promoting independence was therefore difficult to understand. I knew that as a university student Fidel had been involved in bloody street demonstrations and that in his very first press conference after the guerrilla victory in January 1959 he had called for Puerto Rican independence. And the evidence was plentiful in 1975 that he was vigorously brandishing the matter again.

The estimate indicated that "over the past year or so the issue has been pressed with unprecedented intensity at the UN and other international forums, Havana was the site of an international conference in early September to generate support for that cause, and top Cuban officials increasingly have become identified with it." I noted too in the text that Fidel himself had said publicly, just a few weeks before we completed the estimate, that Cuban solidarity with Puerto Rican independence was a matter of principle that he would never renounce—not even to improve relations with the United States.

Was that his hardened position, or would he be flexible once engaged in negotiations? Like all the others involved in producing the estimate, I thought Fidel would see greater advantages in putting the Puerto Rico matter aside for the sake of getting relief from the economic embargo and achieving tangible benefits from improved relations. So I wrote in the estimate that "Despite the strong public statements of its leaders, we believe that there is some flexibility in Cuba's position on Puerto Rico."

That judgment was one of the two embarrassing mistakes we made in that exercise. It demonstrated starkly the perils of misreading the intentions of a leader as idiosyncratic as Fidel Castro. In Washington the thinking was that the rational choice was for him to downplay his interest in Puerto Rican independence for the sake of the economic and diplomatic rewards that would come with rapprochement.

But that was not *his* calculus. Certainly he was thinking rationally by his unique standards. His third-world interests and allies, not better relations with the United States, were his top priorities. We had been guilty of the classic analytic trap known as mirror imaging.

We made a second major error too, an oversight or failure of imagination. There was only one anodyne sentence in the estimate about Angola. But just as work on that estimate was being completed, contingents of Cuban military advisers were secretly arriving in Angola. They were sent to help the Marxist liberation movement there consolidate power as centuries of Portuguese colonial rule was expiring. That fall more Cuban advisers, and then troops, began pouring in, and by the end of the year as many as fifteen thousand were on the ground in that large southwest African country, engaged in combat operations.

The intervention came as a complete surprise. Cuba had never done anything like it before, and I don't think that any of us involved in thinking through the content of that estimate even considered the possibility. We were not the only ones surprised. Kissinger later wrote in his memoirs that it had been unimaginable Fidel "would act so provocatively so far from home."[4]

As the drafter of the estimate, I got to present the coordinated text to the chiefs of the nine main foreign intelligence agencies. On October 19, William Colby, the CIA director, chaired the session in the unpretentious little conference room near his office that has served all the Agency's directors since Allen Dulles. An American flag stood in one corner. A large photograph of President Ford hung on the wall to Colby's left. Plaster seals of all the intelligence agencies, each about a foot and a half in diameter, were arrayed on the other two walls. The FBI's plaque hangs among them, but it was the only principal agency that did not participate that day, or at any time during the process. I would not know until later how much its absence had damaged the collective effort.

What the FBI knew but the CIA did not was that Fidel had been supporting Puerto Rican terrorists for years. The hardcore Puerto Rican revolutionaries he backed and encouraged were not like the guerrillas of the so-called national liberation movements Fidel had helped in other countries because they had virtually no popular support.

They engaged in criminal activities on the island and the American main-land, and were responsible for a number of murders, bombings, and other felonies. Cuban intelligence agents, reporting to Fidel himself, worked with them for twenty years or more, their collaboration apparently beginning in the early or mid-1960s. What the Bureau must have known in 1975 about this Cuban support for terrorism within the borders of the United States was not conveyed to us foreign intelligence analysts. Had we known, even in just the broadest outline, of the Cuban government's activities, the estimate would certainly have reflected a harder line than it did.

Sadly, in those days, not long after the death of J. Edgar Hoover, the CIA and the FBI operated as rival intelligence services. What little cooperation there was occurred mostly on the margins, the two bureaucratic cultures rarely find-ing any common ground. To some extent the tensions were understandable. Law enforcement and foreign intelligence collection missions do not easily meld. FBI agents above all seek to prosecute criminals by using all the available evidence against them. By law, however, CIA officers must protect foreign intelligence sources and methods, so they are loath to go to court or to have their sensitive agent reports used as evidence.

There was a missed opportunity for greater cooperation back in 1975 that would have helped us avoid the intelligence failure on Puerto Rico, which paled, of course, in comparison to subsequent ones. The rivalries and opposing cultures persisted for many more years and contributed significantly to the inability of American agencies to predict or prevent the September 11 calami-ties. It is to be hoped that the new director of national intelligence will begin to rectify those problems and ensure that the CIA and FBI are really working in tandem.

By the time the Cuban-sponsored Puerto Rican terrorist groups finally played themselves out in the late 1980s, they had taken more American lives and inflicted more damage within the United States than any other international terrorists operating in the homeland other than the 1994 and September 2001 Al Qaeda attacks on the World Trade Center in New York

City. The Puerto Rican operations were all mounted with concerted Cuban support.

In the 1970s and early 1980s, the two principal groups—the Macheteros and the Puerto Rican Armed Forces of National Liberation, known by the initials FALN—conducted extensive, carefully planned, professionally directed, and well-funded campaigns in a number of American cities. They were well armed and trained by their Cuban mentors. Much of what they did would not have been possible if not for sustained clandestine Cuban government encouragement and support.

Machetero terrorists were responsible for the deaths of two American servicemen and the wounding of nine others when a navy bus was ambushed in Puerto Rico in 1970. They fired on their unsuspecting targets with Soviet-made machine guns. Numerous bombings on the island and in New York and Chicago were their work. Macheteros killed a Puerto Rican policeman and took credit in 1981 for the destruction of eleven Puerto Rican National Guard jet aircrafts at an island airbase.[5]

On September 12, 1983 a group of them implemented the well planned Operation *Aguila Blanca*, White Eagle. They assaulted a Wells Fargo armored car terminal in Hartford, Connecticut, stealing more than $7 million. It proved to be a perfect crime because the Cuban intelligence service was so involved. Much of the money and Victor Gerena, the main Puerto Rican perpetrator, were covertly exfiltrated to Havana in a series of typically proficient Cuban operations.[6]

After the robbery, Gerena hid in a secret compartment of an old motor home as it was driven from Texas across the border into Mexico. There he was met by Cuban agents and escorted to a safe house in Mexico City. Later he was provided with a false Argentine passport and smuggled to Cuba where he disappeared and probably still resides under Cuban government protection. Most of the Wells Fargo money also wound up in Havana, sent via the Cuban diplomatic pouch. Some reports indicate that the Cuban government kept a substantial portion of it for its own use in promoting revolution in other Latin American countries.[7]

Gerena was officially identified for the first time as a terrorist in December 2004, when the FBI announced an increase in the reward for his capture to one million dollars. At a Connecticut press conference, Bureau officials noted that

Gerena and Osama bin Laden were then the only two terrorists on the FBI's Ten Most Wanted List.[8]

Edmund Mahony, a Connecticut investigative reporter with the *Hartford Courant*, has written extensively about the Wells Fargo case and its Cuban intelligence connection. In a groundbreaking series of articles in November 1999 he described the web of ties between Cuban agents, the Macheteros, and the FALN. He found that the two terrorist groups, "created in consultation with Cuban intelligence agents," bombed a total of more than 120 targets beginning in the 1970s and possibly earlier.

Mahony quoted an unidentified retired FBI counterterrorism specialist familiar with tapes of conversations between Machetero leaders and Cuban intelligence agents:

"They were talking about Fidel. This was being decided at the highest levels in Cuba."[9]

That was consistent with the recollections of the Carter administration's senior Latin America specialist at the National Security Council. Robert Pastor, who consulted with Fidel and other ranking Cuban officials in Havana, later wrote about Fidel's Puerto Rico fixation.

"In discussing Puerto Rico in separate conversations with Cuba's highest officials, I found that only *one* could be said to be genuinely obsessed with the issue, and that person was Fidel Castro."[10]

Two former Cuban intelligence officers now living abroad also have divulged details of Cuban involvement in Puerto Rican terrorism inside the United States. Jorge Masetti defected in 1990 after many years of working in European and Latin American countries for Cuban intelligence. He named Jose Antonio Arbesu, a ranking Cuban intelligence official who later served as the top Cuban diplomat in Washington, as one the masterminds of the exfiltration operation through Mexico City.[11]

Domingo Amuchastegui, another former Cuban operative now living in the United States, described for the *Hartford Courant* Puerto Rico's special status in Fidel's calculus, and he later reiterated these thoughts in a conversation with me in the Washington area.

"Puerto Rico is different. For us in Cuba this was a part of a sacred policy or principle. For us, until this day, Puerto Rico is a colonial case." He added, "Fidel

Castro has stated privately many times that the day in history when only two people in the world advocate the independence of Puerto Rico, one of those two persons will be him."

Amuchastegui remembered his former leader's thinking accurately. Fidel told Barbara Walters almost exactly the same thing.

"So long as there is one Puerto Rican, just a single one, who wants independence for his country, so long will we have the moral and political duty to support him. Even if there is just one! If some day there are none, then that will cease to be our commitment to Puerto Rico."[12]

As Cuban intelligence agents were busy assisting Puerto Rican terrorists, they were also on the watch for sympathetic individuals who might be recruited as spies for Havana. The highest ranking Cuban mole ever apprehended in the United States was a Puerto Rican woman who worked over a period of seventeen years for Fidel. Ana Montes, a ranking Latin America analyst and a specialist on Cuba and Nicaragua, in DIA, the Pentagon's Defense Intelligence Agency, admitted her guilt and was sentenced in 2002 to twenty-five years in prison. She was such a loyal adherent of the revolution that at her sentencing she boasted of the moral obligation she felt to Cuba because American policy has been so "cruel and unfair."

Montes did enormous damage, and some sensitive information she provided the Cubans reportedly was then shared with the intelligence services of other countries.[13] Her crimes would have become progressively more damaging to American interests had she not been apprehended when she was. She stood a good chance of becoming the ranking Latin American analyst at DIA. She had access to highly sensitive intelligence and defense information. And because of her seniority she exercised considerable influence over more junior analysts, including some at SOUTHCOM, the Pentagon's unified military command in Miami that has operational responsibility for most of Latin America and the Caribbean.

When I was National Intelligence Officer for Latin America from 1990 to 1994, serving as the most senior analyst for that region in the dozen or so agencies of the intelligence community, Montes participated in the coordination of a number of assessments, including at least one national intelligence estimate. I never trusted her competence as a Cuba analyst, when, in retrospect, I ought to have registered a counterintelligence red flag. She was perhaps the most sour and unpleasant person I have ever worked with, but unfortunately it never occurred to me during the entire time I knew her that she was diligently working for Fidel.

I remember speaking to a veteran CIA Cuba analyst after Montes was convicted. "Everything we wrote on Cuba during those years was for nothing," the analyst bitterly complained. She assumed, no doubt correctly, that all of our most critical assessments on Cuba were promptly transmitted by Montes to Havana. I expect that Fidel was the most enthusiastic reader of her drops and that he personally supervised her handling as he does with most high-level intelligence cases, and many lesser ones as well.

I know that I was an important collection target for Montes. I had first come to the attention of Cuban intelligence in the early 1970s, and by the time I became National Intelligence Officer for Latin America in 1990, a thick dossier had been compiled on me. During my two official visits to Havana in the early 1990s, I was under blanket surveillance by my Cuban counterparts. I have no doubt that their files on me include a large quantity of photographs, videos, and audio tapes. I know that they have transcripts or recordings of lectures on Cuba that I delivered when I was an adjunct university professor, I assume from one or more of my students who reported to them. They also retain copies of many articles and book chapters I have written about Cuba. I sometimes wonder what else they might have.

On a few occasions my opposite numbers in Havana have delighted in taunting me, but in one instance it was in a fanciful fashion. In the summer of 1993, when I was serving as National Intelligence Officer, I chaired the process of producing my last Cuba national estimate. On July 21, Havana Radio broadcast a report summarizing a story that appeared that day in *Granma*, the Cuban Communist Party daily. They knew I would be more likely to read the FBIS transcript of the broadcast than the newspaper report, and they wanted to make sure I was aware of the story. I suspect, given the tendentious relationship I have had with him, that Fidel himself wanted it to run, and may even have dictated much of its language.

Even though there had been no public acknowledgment that an estimate was in production, he and Cuban intelligence knew about it from Montes.

The Cuban government reporter was quoted as saying the estimate "could have as its point of departure, the same old erroneous considerations that have induced earlier US administrations to err: that is, reports plagued by narrow, unrealistic views, and lacking in strategic content.[14]

Their final shot was to comment on some of my travels in and near Havana during my two visits to Cuba.

"The incomprehensible thing is for those men to think they can find out what the true feelings of almost eleven million people are by taking pleasure rides through the Vedado section of Havana or while seemingly on summer vacation on the beaches. . . ."

Overall, Cuban intelligence is one of the five or six best such organizations in the world, and has been for decades. It is narrowly focused on the Washington policy community, including Congress and the Miami Cuban exile community, as well as anyone who can provide useful information about either. Like all intelligence services it has had its share of failures, and following a series of morale-shattering purges of the parent Ministry of Interior in the summer of 1989, it has been rebuilding much lost competence. But it is very good still, and judging from its snide commentary on my visit to Cuba, even seems to exhibit a certain sense of humor.

CHAPTER TEN

The Corpse of Imperialism

Havana's Palace of Conventions overflowed with jostling, pontificating foreign dignitaries from about a hundred countries, the largest assemblage of national leaders that had ever gathered in Cuba. From the Middle East, Asia, Africa, the Caribbean, Latin America, and the Mediterranean they clogged the hall, chattering in a babel of tongues. International celebrities and infamous dictators among them, they were the full, polychromatic representation of third-world humanity. Nearly all had come to honor Fidel. His lifelong quest for fame and glory had reached its zenith.

As technicians struggled to keep the sputtering air conditioning system running on that muggy, hot afternoon, September 3, 1979—Fidel strode to the podium amid prolonged, exuberant applause. He looked more satisfied than he had in years. Many setbacks and embarrassments had befallen him in the 1960s and early 1970s, but on that late summer day his stars were in alignment. He was at the top of his form. Pausing at the lectern, dramatically fondling the microphones, he looked out over the large room full of his admirers and sycophants. Several of them would not even have risen to power in their countries were it not for Cuban help. He was among adoring friends, a multitude of them. And they were about to bestow the most improbable honor he has ever received.

This reliable ally of the Soviet Union was assuming the presidency of the non-aligned movement. That evening Fidel would be elected by acclamation to lead all of the countries and liberation movements that supposedly were free of binding entanglements with either the United States or the Soviet bloc. It was the culmination of the most remarkable foreign policy juggling act he has ever carried off. He had achieved what should have been impossible. Cuba was aligned yet non-aligned, closely tied to the Kremlin yet simultaneously the new leader of the non-aligned movement.

There was no denying his affiliation with the Soviets. They provided about $5 billion annually in economic subsidies. The 1975 estimate concluded there were five to eight thousand Soviet civilian advisers working in the Cuban government, trying to jump start the still chaotic economy. Every year Moscow also gave another $1 billion worth of free military supplies, including everything from berets and bullets to tanks and fighter aircraft. Several thousand Soviet military advisers and trainers were posted on the island. Cuban troops had fought in 1978 under the command of Soviet generals in the Horn of Africa, in support of the revolutionary Marxist regime in Ethiopia during its war with neighboring Somalia. To his enemies Fidel was a mercenary Soviet pawn.

But in most of the third world, in Africa, Asia, Latin America, and the Middle East, his dependence on Moscow no longer mattered much. He was one of them. He was an original, an audacious revolutionary hero unlike anyone else on the world stage. The Cuban troops in Angola had secured the revolutionary Marxist regime and then, late in 1975, at the end of a long, dangerously stretched supply line, they had met the racist South African army on dusty battlefields and triumphed. It was the South African dictatorship's Bay of Pigs. The Cubans fought with incredible ferocity, true to their commander-in-chief's uncompromising demands. They "rarely surrendered and, quite simply, fought cheerfully until death" according to South Africa's leading historian of the conflict.[1]

More than forty thousand Cuban troops were still in Angola at the time of the non-aligned meeting, doing most of the fighting to contain a stubborn rural rebellion. Another ten to fifteen thousand were stationed in Ethiopia and there were discussions in the Cuban leadership about deploying some to help the insurgents in neighboring Sudan.[2] Contingents of Raul's best—military, security, and intelligence specialists—were bolstering friendly governments and revolutionary groups in at least another dozen countries. In all, twenty-eight of the non-aligned nations represented that week in Havana were benefiting from the services of Cuban doctors, teachers, and advisers who helped with everything from agronomy to presidential security.[3]

Cubans had been bravely dying in distant insurgencies and national liberation wars since the mid-1960s. Such "internationalist service" was a badge of honor in Raul's armed forces, and a number of his top generals had survived one or more such tours. Nine Cubans had died fighting covertly in just one tiny West African country, once a Portuguese colony, and now known as Guinea-Bissau.[4]

The cumulative human toll was staggering, especially for a country of just 10 or 11 million. The true number of casualties is still a sensitive state secret known to only a few in Havana. But Rafael del Pino, a distinguished Cuban air force general who defected in May 1987, believed that ten thousand Cubans had fallen overseas by that time pursuing Fidel's internationalist dreams.[5]

In Southeast Asia, Fidel had made no secret of Cuba's enthusiastic support for the Viet Cong insurgency. He dispatched as many as two thousand Cuban advisers and during a visit to Vietnam in 1973, delivered a militant speech at the ruins of an American military base, predicting the bloody defeat of U.S. forces.

"Friends, you have given the imperialists a great lesson. They considered themselves invincible. However, friends, you were able to defeat them. We are gathered here today in the South Vietnamese liberated area, at a place where the imperialists built a strong military base which they thought no enemy force could occupy."[6]

For about a year in the late 1960s, American prisoners of war held by the North Vietnamese were tortured by English-speaking Caucasian foreigners they believed to be Cubans. The most vicious, nicknamed "Fidel" by the POWs, inflicted beatings with rubber truncheons, and used water torture, and other brutal punishment on about twenty Americans, nearly killing at least two. Eventually all of them were broken. The Cubans' identities have never been established despite exhaustive efforts by American defense and intelligence specialists. There can be little doubt that the Castro brothers authorized what came to be known among the abused prisoners as "the Cuban program."[7]

When Viet Cong and North Vietnamese armies overran Saigon in April 1975, it was just the first of a series of similar victories that bolstered Fidel's non-aligned credentials. During the four years between the 1975 intelligence estimate and the non-aligned summit, at least eight countries in Africa, Southeast Asia, and the Caribbean basin came under the control of revolutionary Marxist–Leninist or Marxist-oriented regimes. Every one of them owed a debt of gratitude to Fidel. He was the rare leader who did not just talk. For years he had been saying that it was his duty to assist other revolutionaries anywhere, and he was true to his word.

The crowd in the Palace of Conventions fell silent as he began a measured hour-and-a-half-long speech, a carefully scripted one by all indications. Brutal despots and the commanders of nearly all of the world's remaining guerrilla and insurgent groups were there, shoulder to shoulder with the presidents and prime ministers of fifty-three other countries, many of them democratically elected.

They came from India and Tanzania, Malta and Jamaica, and from Equatorial Guinea, Cape Verde, and other newly independent African nations few had yet heard of. The octogenarian Tito of Yugoslavia and Pham van Dong, the Vietnamese prime minister, attended. United Nations Secretary General Kurt Waldheim was there, not because the function in any way required his presence, but as a courtesy to the large number of UN member states that were represented. Nearly all expected private meetings with Fidel, though most had to settle for talks with other Cuban officials. Raul, however, was not in evidence at all, as has always been the norm during diplomatic occasions. Every hotel room in the city was booked as Cuban officialdom turned out en masse to tend to their visitors' needs.

Iraq's Saddam Hussein was there. So was the Syrian dictator Hafez al-Assad, a swaggering Yasir Arafat, head of the Palestinian Liberation Organization, and the Iranian foreign minister, all of whom delivered foaming speeches denouncing the United States and Israel. The Egyptian delegate, a future United Nations Secretary General, was barraged with criticism for his government's part in the recent Camp David accords brokered by the Carter administration. With Cuban military advisers providing training for Palestinian and other Arab guerrilla and terrorist groups, Fidel enjoyed strong radical Middle Eastern support.[8]

His two new allies in his own neighborhood, the first sibling revolutionary regimes Cuba had finally been able to boost into power in the backyard of the United States, were represented by their top leaders. Daniel Ortega of Nicaragua and Maurice Bishop of Grenada, both in office for only several months, and already in Havana's orbit, were among the most ecstatic participants. To them, and many of the Africans, Fidel was a virtual deity.

The leader of the Marxist Puerto Rican independence party was there, a favorite stepchild of the Cuban hosts during the week-long proceedings. In his speech to the delegates Fidel placed Puerto Rico first on the short list of oppressed nations, along with apartheid South Africa, colonial Rhodesia, and Palestine. He told the delegates, Puerto Rico "deserves our support without hesitation or weakness."

He was in a triumphal mood. I had written in the 1975 estimate that he actually was beginning to believe "imperialism is in eclipse," and a few years later he had even more abundant reasons to conclude that. As preposterous as it sounds today, years after the collapse of the Soviet bloc, by the middle of the 1970s Fidel was convinced that he was on the right side of an historical divide. Repeatedly using a standard Marxist term, he claimed that the "correlation of international forces" was shifting to the side of revolutionary, Cuban-style Marxism–Leninism.

It was not just classic *fidelista* hubris. Yanqui imperialism seemed to be experiencing a debilitating crisis in the second half of the 1970s. Watergate, Nixon's resignation, the retreat from Vietnam, the congressional exposés of CIA wrongdoings, and legislation restraining intelligence and military capabilities were all encouraging signs for Fidel. Anti-war sentiment in the United States and hostility to any more interventions in third world-conflicts resulted in what has been called the "Vietnam syndrome." Taking advantage of the opportunities that new pacifist mood in the United States provided, Fidel embarked on promising new internationalist ventures.

A large number of young revolutionaries from El Salvador would soon receive advanced guerrilla training in Cuba. Fidel persuaded the leaders of five feuding revolutionary groups there to join forces under a single guerrilla banner that he could then support even more generously. He believed that Nicaragua's small neighbor, where Latin America's newest insurgency was taking hold, was just about ripe to drop out of the imperialist tree. With Nicaragua under the control of his Marxist allies, the Sandinistas, El Salvador became Havana's next highest priority.

Nicaragua was the model. The Sandinistas had won power in July, just two months before the summit meeting, with massive, covert Cuban military assistance. To them Fidel was almost kin, a godfather or favorite uncle who had been providing encouragement, help, and advise for years. The Somoza dynasty they had overthrown together had been one of the original prime targets of Cuban subversion, beginning in the first weeks of the revolution. In his first large press conference after winning power, Fidel goaded Nicaraguans to take to the mountains and fight for justice as he had done.[9]

Twenty years later, he finally had the opportunity to help deliver the coup de grace to the dictatorship. Applying all his powers of persuasion, he enlisted the support of several other Latin American governments and leaders as revolutionary co-conspirators. He and Raul, along with their military and intelligence chieftains, masterminded a complex multinational covert action to provide the Sandinistas with a huge quantity of modern armaments. Cuban intelligence and paramilitary advisers poured into Nicaragua along with the equipment.[10]

They fought side by side with raw young Sandinista recruits, helping to plan and execute the final military offensives against Somoza's National Guard. It was no coincidence, therefore, that a Cuban general from the Ministry of Interior—where all the intelligence, police, and security functions are centered—was the first to storm into Somoza's bunker as it was being overrun by Cubans and Nicaraguans. The dictator had managed to escape, eventually finding asylum in Asuncion, the steamy capital of Paraguay, where a kindred dictator ruled.

But he was not safe there either. On September 17, 1980, a small multinational team of paramilitary operatives, undoubtedly carrying out a plan devised in Havana, was waiting as he was chauffeured about the city. The second shot from a bazooka, from fairly close range, incinerated the vehicle in an instant. It was just the kind of operation of which Fidel, the grandmaster of Cuban intelligence, loved to conceive. Another of his long-time nemeses—Somoza had provided critical support for the Bay of Pigs operations in 1961—finally was gone.[11]

These bold Cuban initiatives in so many countries were reminiscent of one of the most memorable, if macabre, revolutionary dicta that Fidel has put on the record. It first appeared in a speech late in 1961—and subsequently in a rallying document known as the Second Declaration of Havana—as he was aggressively ratcheting up Cuban support for the first waves of Latin American guerrillas. He exhorted Cubans and all those in the region aspiring to emulate the Cuban guerrilla experience to be fighting zealots.

Just as he had insisted as a youth in Bogotá, he maintained that it was their duty, their obligation to fight as revolutionaries. They must help conquer imperialism and not just sit idly by watching the fight. He said, "The duty of every revolutionary is to make a revolution . . . a revolutionary must not sit at his door and watch the corpse of imperialism go by." The non-aligned movement's headquarters would be in Havana for the next three years. Cuban officials and intelligence agents would constitute its bureaucracy and it would be among Fidel's highest personal priorities, perhaps second only to his unceasing vigil aimed at preserving his political hegemony at home.

He could now roam the globe challenging the rich nations of the industrialized world and demanding that they concede more to underdeveloped countries. He would be the secular pope for the world's poor and exploited. And he would do all that with legitimacy, ironically, because he had been elected to the movement's presidency in a relatively open process. No one could deny that he was the overwhelming popular choice to lead the non-aligned nations.

Fidel did not wait long to begin asserting these new prerogatives. Just a month after the Havana conference he traveled to New York to speak again at the United Nations. This time he would talk for less than two hours, making no effort to break the record he set there in 1960. And unlike that earlier, vitriolic performance, he did not insult prominent Americans or any of those present.

He spoke calmly, still for the most part employing the familiar royal "we" rather than the first-person singular "I." In the past, "we" had meant Cubans and the Cuban Revolution. Now, in his new, much grander international role, "we" stood for the hundreds of millions of non-aligned, oppressed or exploited people of the third world. His theme was familiar, but now it was being applied on a global scale.

"We want a new world order based on justice, equality, and peace to replace the unfair and unequal system that prevails today . . ."

He demanded that a new international economic order and monetary system be established and that rich creditor nations cancel third-world-country debt. The wealthy nations, he said, should contribute a total of $300 billion to the underdeveloped countries during the decade of the 1980s. He said that was how much was being spent every year on armaments. He was in earnest but provided few specifics. It was a thoroughly unrealistic, poorly conceived concept, immediately dismissed in Western capitals and financial centers. But he had every intention of leading that crusade wherever it might take him. When he finished he was applauded wildly, many in the UN audience sprinting to the speakers podium to embrace and congratulate him.

During that fall of 1979 Fidel was at the pinnacle of his extraordinary career. It would never be so good again. Even the victories over Batista in 1959 and Kennedy two years later at the Bay of Pigs paled in comparison to what he had accomplished during the second half of the 1970s. He did not want or need better relations with the United States. The Kissinger initiative of 1975 had withered on the vine after Cuba's intervention in Angola.

But a few years later the Carter administration just as seriously took up the possibility of rapprochement again. Limited diplomatic relations were restored and serious talks conducted. They broke down in 1978, however, as Cuban troops were pumped into Ethiopia. Once again it was clear that Fidel placed a higher priority on his internationalist interests and duties than on better relations with the United States. Jimmy Carter was the last American president to engage in a serious effort to work out the full spectrum of bilateral issues.

Fidel's triumphalism, the giddy conceits that surged in him after all the Cuban victories in the late 1970s, culminating at the non-aligned summit and his UN speech, infused him with an unprecedented hubris. He had become self-absorbed in his own grandiosity.

Florentino Aspillaga, the Cuban intelligence defector, recalls Fidel's visit to a Cuban military installation in Angola after the first major victories there in late 1975. The commander-in-chief arrived like a conquering Roman general, intent on parading before his troops and basking in the glow of his triumphs.

Aspillaga, who was present for Fidel's speech, recalls that about six hundred Cubans, all trusted military and intelligence personnel and ranking officials, also heard him that day. He said Fidel spoke candidly; for once, the CIA was not listening. Fidel proceeded arrogantly to expound on his exceptional leadership qualities, glorying in how much he and his small country had achieved all over the globe. He was behaving like a *gallego*, not a Cuban, Aspillaga thought to himself.

The defector believed it was the first time Fidel had ever spoken to any sizeable audience that way, boasting about his own exceptional leadership qualities. Fidel was uninhibited. He said his charisma was one of his most impressive characteristics. "But his greatest virtue," Aspillaga remembered Fidel saying, "was that he could move the multitudes," not just Cubans but many other nationalities as well.

Fidel was obviously in his own thrall, experiencing a narcissistic high as one victory followed another through the fall of 1979. Aspillaga, a tough and worldly intelligence veteran, who had seen so much action in many arenas, was appalled by his chief's performance. "It was sheer euphoria."[12] Fidel was acting out childhood fantasies and dreams of exalted destinies.

After the military victories in Africa and Nicaragua, he was able to think of himself as a Cold War Julius Caesar, a tropical Napoleon, or, more in keeping with his personal favorite hero, a contemporary Alexander the Great.

On several occasions Fidel has ruminated about those three "event making" men. He has said in interviews that it is Napoleon who deserves the greatest admiration. Unlike Alexander and Caesar, he was the only one to rise from humble origins. So in his own mind, Fidel is one part Alexander and one part Napoleon.

Fidel's uncontrolled hubris was out in the open in the autumn of 1979. As president of the non-aligned movement he was at his personal summit, intoxicated with visions of how he would transform the position into one of the world's most important and visible international offices. He expected Cuba would now win a coveted seat on the UN Security Council. He probably fantasized that he would negotiate with the president of the World Bank, the UN Secretary General, the head of the International Monetary Fund, and leaders of the wealthy nations. He would do it for the world's exploited and poor.

But for reasons beyond his control, Fidel would have only a short time more to enjoy the glory.

About ten weeks after the New York speech, as he was developing specific plans for transforming the non-aligned movement, the unstable contraption of his foreign policy came crashing down around him. In one shocking day Fidel's legitimacy as the non-aligned leader was shattered forever. A large airlift of invading Soviet troops landed in Afghanistan on Christmas Eve in 1979, followed by motorized rifle divisions.[13] The Muslim president of the country was killed in the fighting. Under military occupation, this previously non-aligned nation became another Soviet satellite. Fidel, of course, had not been consulted.

He had to decide whether to endorse or denounce the intervention, to be either aligned or non-aligned, but he did not have much of a choice considering the extent of Cuban dependence on the Kremlin's largesse. Nearly every other non-aligned government condemned the intervention, but Fidel cast his vote at the United Nations with Moscow. Professor Jorge Dominguez, the dean of Cuban political studies in the United States, has written "In the choice between the non-aligned movement and the USSR, there was no doubt: Cuba was a communist country first and foremost, under Soviet hegemony."[14]

Fidel later admitted the obvious, that he had been conflicted. He was pressed by an American broadcast journalist about whether he had "privately and personally" approved of the invasion.

"No," he said, squirming a bit, but then, as he so often does, he tried to shift the onus.

"We were not going to place ourselves on the side of the United States and so we were on the side of the Soviet Union."[15] And then, because it was so unpleasant, he changed the subject.

The leader of the non-aligned countries could be forgiven for nearly everything else in his relationship with the Soviets, but not for approving their invasion of another member state. Despite everything Fidel had done to earn the presidency of the movement, his legitimacy in that position evaporated the minute those first Soviet invading forces landed in Afghanistan.

He would not be able to travel the world as he had planned. Cuba could not attract enough votes to win the UN Security Council seat. For the rest of his three-year term as non-aligned president, Fidel was unable to take any significant initiatives or convene any meaningful meetings in that capacity, and he could no longer even press for the global economic restructuring he had demanded at the United Nations. The exotic non-aligned rug had been violently wrenched out from under him.

Psychologically, it was such a devastating blow that his behavior in the aftermath demonstrated how profoundly traumatized he was. The manic optimism of the triumphal years faded into a brooding, downcast fury that affected his judgment and caused him during the first half of 1980 to commit some of the worst leadership errors he has ever made. His judgment seemed to have been temporarily impaired.

There was a deadly military confrontation when two Cuban MIG jets sank a Bahamian patrol boat inside the territorial waters of that neighboring country. Many of its crew were killed in a blatant act of Cuban aggression. Fidel fairly openly supported a new urban guerrilla group in Colombia, in part to retaliate against the government in Bogotá that had played a key role in denying Cuba the UN Security Council seat. He miscalculated, seriously blundering while under the stress of rejection by his third-world friends and betrayal by the Kremlin.

Wayne Smith was the chief American diplomat in Havana at the time. He has written that Fidel "seemed not to be himself." He was "drawn and preoccupied," and following the death of Celia Sanchez that January, his decision making "reflected a certain irrationality."[16] In fact, there has been no other period during the history of the revolution when its leader has behaved so erratically, obviously under the pressure of emotional distress.

The worst was yet to come. A Cuban policeman on routine guard duty at the Peruvian embassy in Havana was killed on April 1 as a group trying to gain political asylum crashed through the gates. Fidel was so enraged that he withdrew the remaining guards and let it be known that any disaffected Cubans who wanted to leave the country could freely do so via the embassy. He thought just a small number would go, but he was out of touch with the mood in the streets.

Economic problems had worsened considerably while he had been preoccupied with his international feats, and with little regard for their plight, he had been demanding greater sacrifice and harder work from the populace. He made the mistake of publicly reprimanding the Cuban people, telling them to tighten their belts and work harder because it would be many more years before the economic hardships would be ameliorated. It was the last straw for many who had been suffering extreme hardships for the last twenty years.

Given the unexpected chance to emigrate, Cubans soon were rushing to the Peruvian embassy from all over the island. *Guajiro* and urban working-class people, the revolution's main beneficiaries, went in large numbers. Entire extended families huddled in hasty consultations around kitchen tables and then fled together as fast as they could to the embassy grounds. Policemen roared up to the gates on motorcycles, threw them down, and joined the throngs seeking asylum.

It was not long before about ten thousand desperate Cubans had congregated there, occupying every tiny patch of open space, perching on tree limbs, squatting precariously on the roofs of the buildings, children and the elderly sitting on top of relatives. For the regime it was a scene of horrible, humiliating bedlam.

About two weeks later Fidel devised a standard solution; he would transfer the problem to the United States. The Mariel boatlift began. It was the second of the massive seaborne migrations from Cuba to southern Florida with Americans, mostly Cuban émigrés, piloting small craft to that port on Cuba's north coast. There they took relatives and friends, as well as Peruvian embassy refugees, on board.

But Fidel's fury was still out of control and beyond reason. In response to an unspeakably cruel decision that no other leader in Cuba could have made, mental institutions and prisons were emptied and the inmates brought to Mariel to be forcibly placed on board boats headed to Key West and Miami. Murderers, rapists, and criminally insane patients were cynically removed from their families and medical treatment and disposed of in this fashion. The Cuban government has refused to take them back ever since, and almost all remain in the United States today.

The boatlift dragged on until September 1980, when Fidel, more and more embarrassed and concerned about deteriorating security conditions on the island, abruptly ended it. More than 125,000 people had departed. During the exodus Fidel was told by the Minister of Interior, his top security adviser, that at least another two million Cubans were also anxious to get on the boats and leave for Florida. He was enraged.[17]

Cuban society was in turmoil. Rafael del Pino, the air force general who had defected in a MIG fighter in 1987, had been among the many military commanders who were horrified by the spectacle and by their commander-in-chief's performance. For him and many others it was the beginning of their final disillusionment with the revolution.[18]

My own disenthrallment had begun in the aftermath of the 1975 intelligence estimate and would be complete within another year or so. I finally came to understand that Fidel was pathologically hostile to the United States and that this hatred could never be assuaged. He needs and wants the American enemy so that it can be blamed for his and the regime's failures. He will never retire his guerrilla uniform, shave the beard, or abandon his anti-Americanism because they are all essential elements of his revolutionary persona. He will go to his grave as that revolutionary.

His internationalist obligations will always be non-negotiable. He will never renounce support for terrorism or lethal violence, even though the issue of Puerto Rican independence has finally all but evaporated as the movement on the island has as well. There is little chance that he will ever be willing to enter into serious counterterrorism cooperation with Washington intelligence and homeland security agencies. What would a rapprochement mean without that critical element? After all, in May 2001, Fidel traveled to Iran—like Cuba, also certified by the Department of State as a state sponsor of international terrorism— and proclaimed publicly, in the presence of radical mullahs, "Together we must bring imperialism to its knees."

The absolute personal power Fidel exercises, the brutal suppression of all dissent, the egregious human rights violations committed in the name of revolutionary ardor will never be open to compromise. As long as he is physically and mentally able, he will run Cuba the way he has for more than four and a half decades, with an iron fist, an unyielding will, and a malign gaze on the hated United States.

To employ the kind of language used in national intelligence estimates, it is highly unlikely that a rapprochement involving mutual concessions on issues of importance to the United States and Cuba will be possible as long as Fidel is in power.

I wish it were not so.

CHAPTER ELEVEN

My Brother Twice Over

Arnaldo Ochoa was probably Raul's closest friend. They had worked together in the defense ministry for thirty years, sharing in spectacular successes. The bronze-skinned two star general was affectionately referred to as "el Negro" by his boss. Their friendship enjoyed a level of easy informality that only a few other top officers in the rigidly hierarchical armed forces experienced. Ochoa's first wife and Raul's wife Vilma were good friends. The four were like family.

On the night of Ochoa's birthday Raul had showed up at his home with a couple of others for an intimate surprise celebration. As usual, there was lots of drinking and camaraderie. It was the kind of spontaneous socializing Fidel abhors, but that Raul takes pleasure in. Raul gets to know his colleagues' families, he drinks with the men; they tell war stories, and occasionally he reveals personal demons, even secrets from his past. That is how he came to admit the murder he committed in Mexico.

Ochoa's natural, unrehearsed charisma and warm personality appealed to the taciturn Raul. The general was gregarious and self-effacing. He was six foot two—a little taller than Fidel—and from a *guajiro* background, strong and seemingly without an enemy in the world. He was admired up and down the military chain of command, equally by raw recruits and hardened veterans, and as well by leaders and counterparts in every country where he had performed internationalist military service.

He wore more decorations than any other officer, including the most coveted, Hero of the Republic. His exploits and swashbuckling demeanor while commanding Cuban troops in Angola, Ethiopia, and Nicaragua elevated him to a level of international fame perhaps second only to that of the Castros. He had fought against Batista as a teenager and with Venezuelan guerrillas in the 1960s. Most of his adult life was spent abroad in pursuit of Fidel's dreams of glory. He was the incarnation of Cuban internationalism and epitomized the selfless "new revolutionary man," living unpretentiously with no interest in luxuries or perquisites.

Ochoa was irrepressibly exuberant, like so many Cubans, but he had been putting Fidel on edge for years. In 1971 during a group boating excursion in Chile, he had infuriated the commander-in-chief by making fun of his underwear.

"Chief, you look really sexy in that underwear!"[1]

No one else would have dared joust with Fidel's vanity that way, but under Raul's protection he was seemingly untouchable. Ochoa sometimes presumed to use the informal *tu* when speaking to Fidel, making no effort as others do to be deferential. He was always joking, making light of sacred cows.

Raul's former chief of staff Alcibiades Hidalgo, who was a member of the Communist Party Central Committee, told me in Miami during extended interviews that he is convinced Fidel's long simmering irritations with Ochoa came to a boil as he learned in the mid and late 1980s that the general was losing respect for him.

Hidalgo said Ochoa "discovered that Fidel is not a great man" after all. For the proud and paranoid commander-in-chief who gradually became aware of that, it was the equivalent of betrayal.[2]

The general had been indiscreet in private conversations that had been captured by military counterintelligence wiretaps and bugs. Such surveillance, even of trusted high level officials, had been routine for years, but Ochoa no doubt was singled out for more searching scrutiny because of Fidel's deepening doubts. Later, the Ministry of Interior intelligence agent who had collected the most incriminating evidence used against Ochoa was himself promoted to general officer rank as a reward and given a choice assignment in Cuba.[3]

Tensions with Fidel spilled over during Ochoa's last tour as chief of the military mission in Angola. The general bristled as Fidel, ensconced in the defense ministry in Havana and communicating daily with him via a Soviet satellite hookup, second-guessed nearly every tactical order he issued. Raul's aide Hidalgo remembers that the face-off with South Africa in Angola in late 1987 and early 1988 became Fidel's "personal war." He was making every decision down to platoon level-operations.

He had done the same during the insurgency against Batista and would have done so in Grenada if he could have. Huber Matos, the former Sierra Maestra guerrilla leader, told me in Miami how Fidel had micromanaged everything during the insurgency.

"He was a brilliant strategist. He had a grand vision. But he was never involved in the actual fighting, and even from afar, he wanted to direct all the details of the battles . . . I wanted to take actions and not wait to receive little papers from Fidel, which was his way of directing all the details of the war."[4]

Fidel frequently reprimanded Ochoa in Angola for failing to follow such instructions. In one cable he complained: "I am very angry over your unexpected, inexplicable ideas that clash with my concept of the struggle. . . ."[5]

Ochoa seethed, but the last straw for Fidel—and the one that probably sealed the general's fate—was apparently the fruit of a surreptitious recording of Ochoa's last private conversation with Raul in his office at the defense ministry. It was a tense session. The general knew by then his career had run off the track and he lost his temper, protesting in an angry outburst that Fidel had been sending Cuban boys off to distant third world battlefields to die heroically, sometimes under orders never to surrender, while always managing to avoid any life-threatening situations himself. It was clear he had come to view Fidel as a bully and a coward.[6]

But Raul continued to "love Ochoa like no other friend." His aide Hidalgo—who defected on a moonless night in the Marquesas, mangrove islets in the Gulf of Mexico between Key West and the Dry Tortugas—told me Raul remained "extremely close to Ochoa."[7]

The Castro brothers' disagreements about Cuba's most accomplished general came to a head during the summer of 1989. For Raul, those were days of Old Testament anguish and ordeal. It was as if he were Abraham, instructed by God to slay his son Isaac as a demonstration of his faith. Raul had to choose between his best friend and his brother. There could be no splitting the difference, no neutral ground. Fidel decided what had to be done and it was then

Raul's responsibility to explain the virtually inexplicable to the rest of the military.

He had to tell the army's top officers that their most revered colleague was suddenly in disgrace, under arrest, and suspected of treason. It was Raul's job to do that persuasively enough so that the officers' loyalty to the regime would not falter. The brothers were so concerned about a backlash that they barricaded themselves in Raul's offices for days on end, sleeping little while monitoring key officers and units.[8]

As Fidel has done on other occasions, beginning in Mexico in 1956, he insisted that a colleague who somehow came to doubt him must be eliminated. He had to be certain that Ochoa would never defect to the United States, as General del Pino and the intelligence agent Aspillaga had done two years earlier. Fidel knew from bugged conversations that Ochoa had actually muttered about that possibility.

Most importantly, Fidel wanted to preclude any possibility that Cuba's most popular troop commander, who was attracted to the reform movements proliferating at that time in the Soviet Union and Eastern Europe, could ever become a rallying point for reformist critics of the regime. Ochoa had commanded a total of more than three hundred thousand Cuban troops in his different overseas assignments, and remained enormously popular. That alone was cause for concern. For Fidel it has always been axiomatic that a popular and charismatic troop commander would be the greatest threat to his hegemony.

As always since he took over as defense minister, Raul had no choice but to do Fidel's ruthless bidding. If it had been up to him, the whole Ochoa affair would have been resolved quietly, swept under the rug. His friend's indiscretions did not seem that serious. Ochoa was guilty of nothing more than inappropriate talk—mostly bluster, and bluster was Ochoa's style. There was no evidence that he was plotting against the regime and it was inconceivable to Raul that he would.

Furthermore, purging him might provoke an upheaval in the officer corps. Ochoa, Raul believed, could have been forced into retirement, one more out-of-favor official in what is known half-humorously in Cuba as the *Plan Pijama*, the Pajama Plan, former top officials in home exile, metaphorically living out the rest of their years in pajamas. But Fidel was adamant. He wanted the death penalty for Ochoa.

Hidalgo recalled that Raul "appeared to be destroyed personally." Executions were second nature to Raul, but the men condemned in the past had not been close to him.

He faltered under the pressure. That strange, rambling speech to the army officers he delivered in mid-June 1989, when he said Fidel "is our father," was just the first of two highly emotional performances. In each of them Raul admitted implicitly to his audiences that he felt pain and trauma for what he had to do.

Hidalgo does not believe Raul was inebriated when he spoke to the officers, as many suspected, but that his erratic, tortured display was the result of stress. Hidalgo is also convinced that Raul made no concerted effort to dissuade Fidel, to argue strenuously that his friend's life be spared.

"I think Raul always submits to Fidel's decisions."

Raul knew that Fidel had made up his mind, and, like the biblical Abraham, he faithfully complied, except that in the end Ochoa was not spared as Abraham's son was. There were many who did plead with Fidel to change his mind. Sandinista leaders in Nicaragua, the head of the Soviet military mission in Cuba, and others tried their best to persuade him to spare the general. But despite how he really felt, Raul, it seems, did not join in that chorus.[9]

On the eve of the execution, in his second strange performance, a nationally broadcast speech, Raul admitted to behavior unbefitting a senior military officer. He revealed that he had cried in his office at the ministry as he brooded about his friend's fate and family. He said that when he looked at himself in his bathroom mirror, "tears were streaming down my cheeks."

"At first I was angry with myself. I immediately got back my composure and understood that I was crying for Ochoa's children whom I have known since they were born."[10]

Most who knew him well understood that Raul was at war with himself. He agonized and suffered in ways that are beyond his brother's emotional competence. It is possible when he told of his crying episode that he wanted his misgivings to be obvious to his colleagues in the armed forces. Hidalgo, who probably knows the adult Raul better than any other Cuban in exile, says that he is given to occasional scenes of high melodrama.

Raul's sense of compassion conflicts with the image of "Raul the Terrible," a term he once used to describe himself. In January 1957, during the first days of the insurgency when defeat seemed likely, he scribbled out a last will and testament in his field diary. If he died fighting, he wrote, he wanted most of his substantial estate to go to the daughter of one of his colleagues who died in the Moncada attack. He also wanted some of his inheritance to be used to build a house for the mother and sister of a dead *Granma* expeditionary—hardly Marxist or tough revolutionary sentiments.[11]

A woman who knew Raul fairly well in the early 1950s in Havana told me with considerable feeling and shuddering gestures that Raul was "a serial killer." Yet, expressing contradictory impressions of him, as so many do, she added, "He is a pleasant serial killer."

She told me she learned from one of Raul's sisters that in early 1959, shortly after the guerrilla victory, that he took personal responsibility for bringing a number of young war orphans from the countryside to Havana, where they were boarded at a military base under his control.

Many anecdotes about his cruelty and implacability circulate among people who have known him. But those stories coexist with others illuminating his gentler side. He forgives and can be generous, even to those whom his brother would have mercilessly dispatched to prison, exile, or the execution wall in an unblinking instant. When he succeeds his brother in power, these opposing sides of Raul's personality undoubtedly will continue to be in conflict as they have since he carried out his first brutal acts.

Before dawn on July 13, 1989 Arnaldo Ochoa was roused from his prison cell, sweating in the mid-summer tropical heat. He was marched a short distance, and under bright lights illuminating a patch of the darkness, made to stand before a military firing squad. He knew better than to expect a last-minute reprieve.

It was the culmination of what had probably been the most painful personal crisis of Raul's life. His two vacillating performances before national audiences left the impression of a leader lacking in so many of Fidel's exceptional leadership qualities. Raul had appeared indecisive, inarticulate, fearful, and drained.

Fidel had never faltered as a leader, and some top Cuban officials wondered if his younger brother would be strong enough to survive for long after he assumed power in his own right. Yet, amid the crisis, the wily Raul managed to bolster his standing in the line of succession by securing control over an institution almost as powerful as the armed forces.

Additional executions, supposed suicides and accidental deaths, and the most dangerous political purges in the history of the revolution were all to follow Ochoa's demise in quick succession. Together they were the Cuban Revolution's nearly bloodless Tiananmen Square.

The slaughter of the pro-democracy activists in Beijing had occurred just a week or so before Raul's speech to the assembled officers and may well have been the critical turning point in Fidel's calculus about what he had to do. Always the strategic grandmaster, planning ahead for his next moves, anticipating not reacting, seizing initiatives, he meant to warn those in Cuba tempted to imitate the demonstrators in China that if they even contemplated action against the regime they would share Ochoa's fate.

The summer of 1989 in Cuba was the season of cataclysmic change throughout the Marxist–Leninist world. Coinciding with Beijing's Tiananmen Square, the Eastern European communist societies began hemorrhaging. The Berlin Wall was torn down in November, and with that the Cold War effectively was over. Soviet subsidies were drying up as Fidel imposed more draconian policies in defiant opposition to *perestroika* and *glasnost*.

In turn, he and the regime soon were being criticized in the alternative new Soviet media. This led him, only a few weeks after Ochoa's execution, to ban two popular Spanish language publications published in Moscow. He denounced them publicly as subversive, doing the bidding of Yankee imperialism. Fidel could never have imagined such a move in 1961 when he declared his undying faith in Marxism–Leninism.

The evidence linking Ochoa to Soviet, Chinese, or Eastern European style reform thinking is circumstantial, but I concluded at the time in a report I authored for the White House that indeed the general wanted the Cuban political system to be relaxed and opened. No evidence has ever surfaced, however, that Ochoa was organizing a dissident group or considered leading a military rebellion. But he probably was caught by eavesdropping operations while advocating reforms. Raul intimated as much in his speech to the army officers.

International communism was collapsing nearly everywhere. Fidel wanted to make sure that his regime would not also go down or be forced, as the Chinese leaders had been, to massacre large numbers of protesting civilians in the streets. He had to preempt potential crises, and Ochoa was the unfortunate scapegoat. Soon a new revolutionary motto was hoisted and heard everywhere, one with which Fidel and Raul would end all of their speeches. "Socialism or Death." It meant to convey that there would be no dilution of *fidelista* absolutism. Even to discuss the possibility of political reform would be a capital offense.

I completed my classified analysis of the Ochoa Affair coincidentally on the same day the general was executed. I was working then for the National Intelligence Council, the intelligence community organization that produces national estimates. I was asked by senior staff officers at the National Security Council to play devil's advocate because many new analysts, especially in the CIA, believed the Cuban government's explanation that Ochoa was guilty of drug trafficking, the fictitious charge the regime leveled against him. Ana Montes, the Cuban mole in the Defense Intelligence Agency, later did her best to promote that canard, no doubt under instructions from her Cuban intelligence handlers.[12]

I concluded in the assessment that was sent to the White House and other senior national security officials that "Castro deliberately engineered the crisis" and that "Ochoa's principal 'crimes' were in questioning the Castros' authority and contemplating defection." I believed then, and still do, that Fidel "concluded that Ochoa had to be convicted of truly heinous crimes . . . in order to preclude any backlash . . . in the military." The drug trafficking charges were a smoke screen.[13]

After years of studying Fidel, and having long before abandoned all romantic notions about his priorities and character, I was sure Ochoa was the victim of a Stalinist show trial. He appeared to many who watched Cuban television coverage to be drugged and dazed as he sat in the docket. His answers to the prosecutor's questions sounded scripted and false.

Many Cubans, military and civilian, came to the same conclusion. Several defectors have told me that they came to despise the Castro government after Ochoa's execution and set about arranging to emigrate. One young, previously loyal Soviet-trained field grade officer I know of came home from his job at the defense ministry the day the general was shot, sat at his dinner table, and wept for the man he so respected. Now living in Florida, he is one among many who were alienated in similar fashions.

Ochoa was condemned to death by a kangaroo court that obediently bowed to the dictates of the commander-in-chief. The sentence was ratified by Cuba's Council of State, the highest executive body in the government, and by a military tribunal of more than three dozen of the country's top generals, all of whom in the process became accomplices in the death sentence. Raul's wife, Vilma Espin, then a member of the Council of State, was among them and said in a firm voice, "Let the sentence be confirmed and carried out."[14]

In reality, other than Fidel, there was probably not another man or woman on the island who independently would have insisted on the death penalty.

Moments after the general was shot, senior intelligence officer and respected Ministry of Interior colonel, Antonio de la Guardia, followed in the geneval's footsteps to the execution line. De la Guardia's demise, and the subsequent unexplained arrest and supposed accidental death in prison of the Minister of Interior, signaled that the Castro brothers intended to use the crisis to solve another, unrelated set of problems. That is typical of Fidel's operating style. He has often provoked one crisis with the intention of justifying extreme actions for other political purposes.

In this instance, the country's intelligence and security agencies were purged and reconstituted under Raul's authority as a reward for his betrayal of Ochoa. Since the Sierra Maestra days, Fidel had always insisted on maintaining competing intelligence and special forces capabilities under different chains of command. Raul's defense ministry, officially the Ministry of the Revolutionary Armed Forces and known in Cuba by its acronym MINFAR, and the Ministry of Interior, known as MININT, had been rivals, often adversaries, for decades. It was as if a chastened FBI was suddenly put under the control of the CIA director or the Secretary of Defense.

Although Raul had been conniving for years to get control of MININT, he had previously scored only one major victory in those efforts. Four years earlier, he had persuaded Fidel to oust the powerful minister, Ramiro Valdes, who was a formidable personal rival. Valdes's revolutionary credentials were impeccable, and he commanded powerful, often sinister organizations that operated in towns and cities across the island and in numerous foreign countries. In 1985 Fidel finally agreed to remove him but, perhaps in another test of his brother's mettle, required Raul to personally deliver the news.

Valdes was summoned to Raul's office, and just in case he might become violent, Raul hid the chief of his personal security detachment in the bathroom that opens directly to his office. With his pistol drawn and cocked, the security man silently stood guard, listening to every word in the conversation as Valdes learned that his political star had fallen.

Some outside of Cuba believe the former minister could reemerge as a powerful rival to Raul in a succession struggle, and that possibility gained some credibility in 2003 when Valdes emerged from years of obscurity with an appointment to the Council of State. If he were elevated again by Fidel, say, to a seat on the party Politburo, speculation about his rehabilitation might prove to be accurate. But Alcibiades Hidalgo is convinced that "Raul completely defeated Ramiro" in that showdown in 1985.[15]

The rival ministries had some overlapping functions and comparable rank structures, and MININT also operated elite paramilitary forces that Raul and his generals resented. MININT personnel were adept at bugging the private conversations of army generals, even in their own homes. Intelligence officers generally enjoyed much higher living standards than their armed forces counterparts, and because of the undercover work that many did, they had easy access to illicit sources of enrichment. Hidalgo, who in Cuba was a civilian unassociated with either ministry, told me that before the 1989 purges an intelligence colonel typically lived a hundred times better than Raul's generals.

The most senior of them, Corps General Abelardo Colome Ibarra, then the only three-star officer, took over as Minister of Interior shortly before Ochoa's execution. Hundreds of career officials immediately were purged, including a number of the most senior and highly decorated. With those decisive strokes, MININT was converted into a free-standing branch of Raul's defense ministry. All foreign intelligence, internal security, and police functions were finally under his control through a trusted surrogate.

In his late sixties, Colome continues inconspicuously to run the ministry today. Known by his childhood nickname "Furry," he proudly states that he has been under Raul's command for almost fifty years, longer than anyone else. He was about sixteen when he ventured up into the Sierra Maestra in early 1957 and then went with Raul a year later to open the Second Front in the Sierra Cristal, where he served as his personal aide. He adores Raul, who he says saved him from what might have been a life of hard labor in a Santiago coffee warehouse.

Colome's resume reads like a history of the revolutionary armed forces, checkered with internationalist tours, police and intelligence work, and both staff and troop command responsibilities. He served as Havana police chief, later going under-cover in Algeria and Bolivia with a forged Algerian passport to support a failed insurgency in Argentina.

He demonstrated his revolutionary zeal and conformity with the Castros' leadership style by participating in a hangman's jury to condemn a young Argentine—a reluctant guerrilla—to death. "Furry" is among the few elite Cuban warriors to wear the highest decoration as Hero of the Republic. He was the first commander of the Cuban military mission in Angola and later was Raul's principal deputy in the ministry.[16]

Their relationship has been so close for so long that Colome essentially has been to Raul what Raul is to Fidel. This third most powerful man in Cuba—he is also a long time member of the party Politburo and the Council of State—will be one of the two or three most reliable and potent guarantors of Raul's succession after Fidel is no longer able to lead. And with Colome's hands on so many of the highest voltage-levers of power across the island, he will have the wherewithal to identify and neutralize anyone who might dare oppose Raul's ascension.

In short, Colome is the consummate *raulista*. The term applies to those ranking officers—and some civilians—who have long-standing, special relationships with Raul. The old guard *raulistas* are in their sixties and seventies, and served under him during the insurgency and in the early 1960s. Most worked overseas covertly as internationalists or commanders of expeditionary military forces, typically doing both.

They include many of the two- and three-star generals, as well as a number of others who retired from active duty but still have considerable influence. Like Colome, they identify more with Raul than with Fidel, though they know not to stray in the least from what the commander-in-chief expects of them. Ochoa's fate reminds them constantly of that. Nonetheless, these are men who Raul developed, encouraged, and promoted and who in turn reciprocate his trust.

A triumvirate of old guard *raulistas* in all likelihood will be just as determined as general Colome that Raul follow Fidel in power and that the process proceed smoothly. Julio Casas, Raul's principal deputy in MINFAR, and also a Politburo member, has been with him almost as long as "Furry" has. He heads the MINFAR holding company that operates about a dozen enterprises earning hard currency for the military, and he therefore controls a substantial flow of funds. The enterprises—the tourism conglomerate "Gaviota" is the largest—are run by senior army officers either retired or on detached duty, all reporting to General Casas. He was promoted to three-star rank in 2001.

Alvaro Lopez Miera, MINFAR chief of staff, is the next most powerful of the *raulista* old guard. The son of Spanish communist immigrants who were early supporters of the Castro brothers, the young Lopez went up to the Sierra Cristal to join Raul in the last months of the conflict. He was just fourteen, considered too young to fight, so he was assigned to teach peasant children in one of the schools run by the Second Front. Later, he saw action in Angola and Ethiopia as an artillery officer and studied for two years at one of the most prestigious Soviet military academies. He is Raul's right-hand man in day-to-day military affairs and was also promoted to corps general in 2001.[17]

Ulises Rosales del Toro, the third three star in Raul's powerful army triumvirate is another long-time colleague. He served as his chief of staff for more than fifteen years and now is the government minister in charge of the collapsing sugar industry. In the early 1960s he volunteered for combat in Vietnam and was also tempted to serve with several friends departing for the Dominican Republic to fight covertly against the dictator Trujillo, Fidel's old nemesis from the 1940s. Instead, he was sent to fight with Cuban-sponsored guerrillas attempting to overthrow the democratic government of Venezuela.

It gave him "tremendous joy," he says, when he was selected for that duty, though it turned out to be a harsh and disillusioning experience. He and three other Cuban guerrilla advisers were reduced to eating monkeys, burros, and poisonous snakes. One of them, gravely ill, wasted away to about one hundred pounds and could barely walk before they were all clandestinely exfiltrated back to Cuba. Not all of Fidel's followers in internationalist service found glory.

But Rosales was steeled by the experience and later become a Hero of the Republic and a Politburo member.[18]

The *raulista* old guard and the middle grade officers he has brought up through the ranks have confidence in Raul. His emotional performances during the Ochoa affair have not been repeated, and he is not known to have faltered again since then. His loyalists know that he would never make fanatical demands on them, as Fidel did to Colonel Tortolo in Grenada, or insist on making every tactical operational decision.

They appreciate that the pursuit of personal fame and glory has never been Raul's compelling motivation. His rhetoric is never apocalyptic as Fidel's has often been. His style is more relaxed, less confrontational. He delegates authority, maintains genuinely collaborative relationships, often acting on the advice he solicits from subordinates, and has worked with the same trusted associates for decades.

Under his leadership, the armed forces have always been the revolution's most stable and best managed institution. They alone have experienced a high degree of leadership continuity, due in no small part to Raul's success in insulating them from his brother's whims and micromanagement. He has been the only senior regime official who has been allowed a relatively free hand to run his organization. He has made the military into the nearest thing to a true meritocracy among Cuba's revolutionary institutions. Officer promotions and assignments up through middle ranks have been based mainly on competence and achievement rather than political, family, or other connections.

Fidel's managerial style could not be more different from his brother's. He regularly purges civilian officials with important portfolios, relegating most to the Pajama Plan. Since 1959, fewer than twenty top officials—out of thousands who have exercised real responsibility—have been able to hold on to their positions for extended periods. Fidel fears that if they stay in the same jobs too long they might develop independent power bases, become self-important, or linger in the limelight he refuses to share.

Very few officials manage to please Fidel for long, including even some of the most successful administrators. He does not welcome criticism or indulge doubts about policies he favors, and as he has aged into his late seventies he has become even more intransigent and sensitive to imagined slights.

Raul is also a tough disciplinarian, to be sure, but patient and willing to forgive honest human error. General Colome told an interviewer that Raul does not hesitate to reprimand subordinates, including himself, but that once the incident passes it is never brought up again. Fidel, in contrast, never forgets a slight or an error. Raul is detail-oriented and "profoundly respects his family," Colome added, perhaps consciously contrasting the brothers. He is more predictable and approachable than Fidel. "Raul inspires confidence," the general concluded; "you can discuss any kind of problems with him." Hardly anyone would say that about Fidel.[19]

The *raulistas* respect Raul's organizational and managerial skills. His successes in 1958, during the last year of the insurgency, exceeded those of any other commander, including his brother. He developed the largest guerrilla force, controlled the greatest expanse of territory with the largest civilian population, and he built extensive infrastructure—including airstrips—in his operating zone. He did all of that in less than a year. General Colome has lauded the "superior development" that Raul achieved, perhaps not mindful enough, however, of how Fidel might construe that comment.[20]

The commander-in-chief never volunteers to commend his brother's work. He does not like to admit that the military has been the one truly indispensable guarantor of the regime or that during difficult periods—including the last dozen years—it provided needed leadership in running critical sectors of the economy.

He tends to take Raul for granted and even seems jealous of his organizational abilities. Most of all, Fidel strives to give the impression that the military's successes have been the result of his own strategic vision and charisma, never mentioning—perhaps hardly considering—that those qualities do not keep the tanks and jet aircraft running or the troops fed and clothed.

Even when he is pressed by interviewers to talk about his brother's contributions, Fidel is generally evasive or noncommittal. He does not like to admit that Raul has steadily grown in stature and accomplishment or that the historic internationalist victories would not have been possible without him.

During the early years Fidel was sometimes cruelly dismissive of Raul. It must have been at a time of high tensions between the brothers when, in an interview in 1965 with Lee Lockwood, Fidel portrayed Raul as a glorified staff sergeant who takes orders but does not give them.

"He does not make decisions," Fidel said, "because he knows it is not his right to do so. He is extraordinarily respectful. He always consults me about all important questions."[21]

But Raul grew progressively stronger during the decades of the seventies and eighties, both politically and personally. And as he did, fraternal tensions not surprisingly, intruded periodically in their relationship, just as they did when Raul flew to Houston in April 1959 for the brothers' first known showdown. Stresses appear to have peaked again in late 1986 after Raul's triumph over Ramiro Valdes. Prominent *raulistas* had been granted unprecedented influence in the highest councils of the regime at that time, especially in the Communist Party after its Third Congress. They formed the largest single bloc in the Politburo and seemed so ascendant that Raul evidently felt it necessary to clear the air.

He scheduled one of his rare interviews, which was published the following January in a MININT magazine. Discoursing in a mostly desultory fashion, he seemed intent on raising what must have been the real irritant with Fidel. He denied that his Second Front had grown into "a state within a state" during the fight against Batista. It was a metaphor for the situation in the second half of the 1980s.

Rivals and critics probably had been bandying that term about, complaining that Raul and the *raulistas* had gained too much leverage, that they were eclipsing other elite groups in the party and government. Most likely the criticism originated in MININT among the disciples of Valdes. To dispel the impression they and other rivals of Raul were sowing, he did the only thing he could do. He heaped praise on Fidel's leadership.

"The type of organization" he had developed in his zone of operations "also existed in other fronts," Raul said of the guerrilla days. That was not true but surely helped to assuage the tensions. Bowing further to Fidel's sensitivities, he told the reporter that the "penal regulations we initially implemented in the Second Front had been drafted" under Fidel. It was a minor point, meant to show that what Raul had done in his operating area was mostly derivative and turned out to be successful because of Fidel's vision and leadership. That was not the case either, but Raul knew better than anyone that there could be no hint of a personality cult developing around anyone else, not even Fidel's acknowledged successor.[22]

Regardless of their periodic tensions, Fidel has never been known to muse about the possibility of any other heir. He does not like to discuss the dynastic succession either, especially for audiences in democratic societies.

He prefers to avoid the appearance that the revolution resembles a medieval Middle Eastern monarchy or the bizarre North Korean communist dictatorship where sons or brothers take over automatically when a leader dies. Thus, when he is pressed to discuss the succession, he usually insists it would not be automatic for Raul to replace him. The Communist Party and appropriate government institutions would have to ratify the choice, he says, and he has many "brothers" in the leadership.

Fidel employed this analogy in 1977 in the course of putting on the record perhaps his most enthusiastic endorsement of Raul's qualifications to succeed him.

"All those who died defending just causes in any corner of the world, they are my brothers," he told Barbara Walters. Then he paused for effect.

"Raul is my brother twice over: a brother in this entire struggle and a brother in ideas. But Raul does not have an office in this Revolution because he is my blood brother but rather because he is my brother in ideas and because he has earned that place through his sacrifice, his valor, and his capacity."[23]

No one, with the possible exception of former interior minister Ramiro Valdes, has ever seemed to have had a chance of supplanting Raul in the line of succession. Fidel has been consistent since January 1959 that his brother is the only possible heir, and that has been ratified a number of times by the top Communist Party and government institutions. Article 94 of Cuba's Marxist constitution makes it legal. It states that "in the absence, illness, or death of the President of the Council of State, the First Vice President replaces him in his functions." Raul has been the First Vice President since the position was created in the 1970s.

Assuming that he is in good health when his brother dies or is incapacitated, the odds will be negligible that others would lay claim to the succession or that they would have a chance of replacing him. Once confirmed, either as acting or permanent President of the Council, he will function as head of state and government as well as commander-in-chief of the armed forces. One of the three-star generals will take over the defense ministry, and Raul might also cede figurehead leadership of the Communist Party to someone else now serving on the Politburo.

Since the new leaders will want to minimize international perceptions that Cuba is governed by a praetorian guard, most of the civilians prominent today will continue to be influential, especially in economic and financial management and in foreign affairs. Carlos Lage, Secretary and First Vice President of the Council of Ministers and a member of the Politburo and the Council of State, has enjoyed Fidel's confidence—mostly in economic management—many years longer than all but a few other officials ever have. Evidently he also works well with Raul.

Ricardo Alarcon, the president of the rubber-stamp National Assembly, has performed a number of prominent roles as a diplomat and statesman and is a Politburo member. But like many of Fidel's other civilian subordinates who are obsequious and docile in his presence, he may not have earned enough respect with Raul and the generals to last long in a senior office. The abrasive young foreign minister, Felipe Perez Roque, has been one of Fidel's favorite sycophants for the last several years, and he too might be expendable. Initially, nonetheless, a key objective of the successor regime would be to maintain the appearances of as much continuity from the *fidelista* past as possible.

The *raulista* generals, five of whom serve on the Politburo, will be the king-makers. Leaders of no other institution, including the party, state and government entities, or the regime's large popular organizations, alone or in any combination, could effectively challenge the firepower, intelligence, and security resources the generals have at their disposal. Nor would anyone else be able to impose policies on the new regime that a united and disciplined military leadership opposed.

The most critical variable in every conceivable succession scenario will therefore be the extent to which Raul and the generals are able to uphold loyalty to the chain of command. The odds of that will be much in their favor, in the beginning at least. Since 1959, when Raul took charge of the new defense ministry, no military anywhere else in Latin America has remained so stalwart.

The 1959 and 1989 purges of respected senior officers were the only serious political shocks to the military establishment, and General del Pino was the only top officer to defect since the first unstable months of the Cuban Revolution. There have been no coup attempts, military rebellions, junior officer upheavals, or barracks revolts in Raul's armed forces. In any event, officers will have every incentive to collaborate in securing a peaceful succession in which their privileged statuses and prerogatives can be preserved.

They will be likely at first to enjoy the support of most among Cuba's civilian elites who will work constructively with them hoping too for a nonviolent transition in which they can also retain their privileges. Fear throughout Cuban officialdom that many in the exile community will lay claim to expropriated properties on the island and try to return to assert political leadership will help the elites to cohere. Fidel's successors will keep up the drumbeat of nationalistic rhetoric to distract the populace from the hardships they endure, to maintain morale and vigilance in the uniformed services, and to sanctify his memory as a unifying force.

But after a short honeymoon, the successors will have to choose between equally ominous sets of policy options. Fidel himself long ago recognized that the short term aftermath of his demise will be the most dangerous time. He told Herbert Matthews, a *New York Times* reporter, in an unpublished interview in May 1966 that "the first period after something happened to him could be the most difficult."[24]

Pent-up popular demand for meaningful change will probably soar once his titanic, intimidating hold is released. New leaders will be challenged then either to assuage or suppress those hopes, to permit the *perestroika* and *glasnost* type reforms that Fidel has rejected or to uphold his intransigence posthumously. The dilemma will get progressively worse as time goes on because Raul will not inherit Fidel's standing with the populace or his ability to communicate inspirationally with them.

His friend Che Guevara recognized this critical deficiency as early as 1960. He told Simone de Beauvoir during her visit to Cuba with Jean Paul Sartre, "I love Raul . . . enormously. He is a remarkable man, but he does not have the same direct influence on the country as Fidel."[25]

So how will Raul try to lead in the dangerous vacuum after Fidel? Would the compassionate Raul or "Raul the Terrible" predominate? Most of the populace will expect the latter. For so many years his was the most strident voice in the regime for cracking down ruthlessly on intellectual and cultural deviance. The respected Cuban poet Heberto Padilla, who was mercilessly denounced by Raul, and briefly imprisoned before going into exile, was earlier present at a meeting in Prague to hear one of his anti-intellectual tirades.

"In Cuba, fortunately, there are very few intellectuals," Padilla remembered Raul saying, "and those there are do nothing but get bogged down reinventing the wheel."

Padilla also quoted an American intellectual, otherwise blithely intoxicated with the revolution, who despised and feared Raul. "There is some deep abnormality in Raul. He is cold and cruel and is capable of any crime."[26]

It was the implacable Raul who acted as the regime's point man in carrying out massive political purges in the past. A defector from Cuba's foreign intelligence service told a congressional committee in Washington in 1969 that Raul personally gave the orders to state security for the harsh measures to adopt when the so-called microfaction was expelled from the Communist Party the year before.[27]

A few years earlier, savage campaigns were conducted with military precision to round up male homosexuals to perform forced labor. White-collar city workers, deemed insufficiently revolutionary or effete, were purged in large numbers in destabilizing "anti-bureaucracy" sieges.

In 1972 Raul spearheaded the campaign against "ideological diversionism," which was a catch all phrase for almost anyone who disagreed with the revolution or was merely disenchanted. The Nixon administration, long-haired "anti-social youth groups" in Cuba, foreign intellectuals including Fidel's one-time European traveling companion, K. S. Karol, and a prominent American anthropologist were denounced. The socialist Karol was a CIA agent, according to Raul.

It was the most infamous of his cutthroat speeches, delivered with the thundering repetition dozens of times of the phrase "ideological diversionism." The transcript excludes all of his histrionics, but it is easy to imagine that he pounded the lectern for emphasis time and again as he uttered the signature phrase. The real targets of the heightened repression that ensued were Cubans tempted by any of the forbidden thinking.

Raul has had some strange and sinister admirers too. The communist East German Markus Wolf, self-proclaimed as "communism's greatest spymaster," is notably in that company. For many years he headed his country's top notch foreign intelligence service, visiting Cuba, helping to train its intelligence agents, and running joint operations with them. He was critical of Ramiro Valdes, who was "less of a statesman than an adventurous operative."[28]

But Raul was "far more steady, well educated, and statesmanlike." Possibly alluding to Fidel, Wolf added that Raul, "unlike his more emotional colleagues took a cool strategic view of Cuba's situation." The East German was amazed that, unlike so many Cubans, Raul always turned up for appointments on time, leading him approvingly to tell how colleagues came to refer to Raul as "the Prussian." It was a supreme compliment from one tough intriguer to another.[29]

But on the other hand, Raul's softer side has been progressively more evident as the inevitable succession draws closer. Breaking with his hardline image, he has avoided close identification with Fidel's brutal suppression of human rights and pro-democracy activists in two major crackdowns since 1996. In the past it was expected that he would lead the charge against such groups.

He is also widely believed to have been the regime's most persistent advocate of liberalizing economic reforms in the years since the collapse of the Soviet Union. Although Fidel has stubbornly refused to agree, he has given Raul a freer hand to establish the hard-currency-earning enterprises run by senior officers.

During the same period, the two ministries that Raul controls have been waging a skillful campaign to portray him and the armed forces in the most favorable light. Their main targets are influential audiences in the United States.

He and Cuban generals have welcomed and squired visiting groups of retired American senior officers, most of whom return home advocating the establishment of military-to-military ties across the Florida Straits. In 1991 the Cuban National Defense College was created with the central purpose of fomenting ties with foreign military establishments.

Secretos de Generales, an attractively packaged book authorized by the defense ministry, and published in Spain in 1997, subtly makes the same case. Forty-one Cuban generals were interviewed about their lives and careers in a synchronized effort to put an appealing human face on the high command. All of them avoided the harsh and confrontational language about the United States that is still characteristic of Fidel's speeches and much regime propaganda. General Rosales, then the chief of staff and the highest ranking officer interviewed—and clearly authorized to speak for Raul—commented on the desirability of military to military discussions with the U.S. Defense Department.[30]

The most remarkable document in this public relations campaign was a little-known unclassified study written by Ana Montes, the Cuban mole in the Defense Intelligence Agency. Her study of the Cuban military was issued under the seal of that agency in August 1993 after she completed a fully paid sabbatical year supposedly to investigate the subject.

Montes was in the select company of about a half dozen other intelligence community analysts chosen competitively to participate in the Director of Central Intelligence Exceptional Analyst Program. Nearly all of those selected included relevant foreign travel in their research proposals, and it is likely Montes did as well.

It is reasonable to speculate, therefore, that she traveled to Cuba at American taxpayers' expense during her unsupervised year in that elite program, which was long after she betrayed the United States to work as a spy for Fidel. If Montes did in fact visit Cuba that year, her handlers no doubt took advantage of the opportunity to provide her specialized training in espionage and countersurveillance tradecraft with no fear of being detected. I had certainly been wrong about her all along. Indeed, she was an "exceptional" intelligence analyst.

No doubt taking her cue from Cuban intelligence, she wrote in her study of the military: "The armed forces believe that improved relations with the U.S. are a necessary component of Cuba's future economic stability and will continue to jump at the chance to improve communications with the U.S. The Cubans will be anxious to improve cooperation on operational issues, almost certainly would like to exchange military visits, and likely would accept U.S. military lecturers at (their National Defense College.)"[31]

In 1993 those were iconoclastic conclusions to say the least. No other intelligence analyst could have come to that view based on the available evidence. Some of her language in that passage, and throughout the paper, so faithfully, even adoringly reflected Cuban policy that it is surprising in retrospect she did not come under suspicion earlier than she did. The study is replete with pandering to the official Cuban line that ought to have at least raised eyebrows in American security and counterintelligence circles.

But Montes was not apprehended for another eight years as she continued to do terrible damage to American interests. The most curious, and to me still inexplicable, passage in her study was a cutting critique of Raul. Although in other places she cast him in a favorable light, here she wrote: "Fidel likely believes Raul has progressively become a poor judge of character, an advocate of too much economic change, and unable to handle sudden crises."

When she wrote it Raul was in overall charge of Cuban intelligence operations through General Colome. So it is difficult to fathom what, if anything at all, she was trying to achieve by undermining him. One obvious possibility is that lower ranking intelligence officers, still alienated by the Ochoa era purges four years earlier, were trying to discredit him.

On the cover of Montes's study there is a standard issue disclaimer that must have been deliciously ironic for her and her Cuban intelligence overseers. They probably shared some good laughs at the expense of all those in the American government who trusted her. It said: "The views expressed in this article are those of the author and do not reflect the official opinion or position of the Department of Defense, the Director of Central Intelligence, or the U.S. Government."

To survive in the game for long, a high level mole, just like a double agent, must do sleight-of-hand work with smoke and mirrors. There were no dead give-aways in her study and her critical observations about Raul may have been no more than a throwaway that Cuban intelligence agents approved believing they might add to her credibility among her peers.

She was right, of course, that Raul's prestige had been damaged by his speeches during the Ochoa crisis. He did not handle himself well, and Fidel probably does worry about how he will manage even more threatening challenges when he assumes power in his own right.

Raul's exceptional qualities all are best exhibited behind the scenes, where he has been most comfortable all these years. But without his brother's charisma, extraordinary intellect, vision, communications skills, ability to persuade and inspire, and strategic gifts in planning many moves ahead, he will be tested once in power himself as he has never been tested before.

Whatever her motives, the Cuban mole was actually right on this one point. It is appropriate to speculate about how well Raul will manage the inevitable crises on his watch. How decisive will he be under extreme pressure? Will he be as ruthless as Fidel when he is in charge, or will his compassionate side give enemies room to maneuver against him?

It cannot even be said with confidence that Raul will want to be more than a transitional leader. He has ruminated publicly about retiring to a favorite place in the countryside, and will not enjoy the pounding pressures and crises that make Fidel's adrenalin surge and typically induce his best thinking. And most critically for Cuba, Cuban Americans, and the United States generally, what kind of future for Cuba does Raul want?

The answers to these and similar questions are not likely to be known until after Fidel is gone. It won't be until then that the younger brother will begin to emerge in his own right. The puzzling juggling of his masks will finally come to an end, and he will be able to express himself without fear that he will disappoint Fidel.

CHAPTER TWELVE

More Than Enough Cannons

An Italian television journalist once asked Fidel what must have been the most impertinent question ever put to him on the record. Recalling that Fidel has often spoken admiringly of Ernest Hemingway's fiction, the journalist asked him about the Nobel Prize winning author's classic, *The Old Man and the Sea*.[1]

The story is set in Cuba. Hemingway's old man, Santiago, is a fisherman down on his luck, who goes out in a small skiff and hooks the biggest fish of his career. After Herculean struggles, the old man subdues the giant marlin and lashes it to the side of the skiff. But he is out of sight of the Cuban coast now and has to sail slowly back to port.

"He's my fortune," the old man thinks, the biggest, most valuable catch of his life.

But sharks begin to attack. At first it is one, then others, and soon a roiling, ravenous pack, methodically gnawing away at the giant fish. The old man is helpless as his greatest triumph is eaten away before his eyes.

Nothing but shreds of flesh and glistening bone are left hanging at the side of the small boat when the old man finally gets back to shore.

Talking to himself, and to what is left of the fish, he mutters, "I am sorry, I went too far out. I ruined us both."

The Italian reporter thought of Hemingway's tale as a metaphor for Fidel and the revolution.

"Aren't you afraid you will wind up like Ernest Hemingway's fisherman?," he asked.

Fidel was incredulous. No one had ever challenged him with such an offensive question before. The commander-in-chief hurriedly changed the subject, launching into a long, dissembling monologue.

It was true. The wasting of the revolution began to accelerate beyond Fidel's control in 1990 as the Soviet Union was going into its death throes. Deliveries of fuel and other essentials were no longer arriving on time, if at all. Shortages multiplied daily. Street crime reached such high levels that Fidel was complaining in speeches. Hungry Cubans waited in interminable ration lines as social tensions flared.

The internationalist glories of the past were also in shreds. In March, Daniel Ortega lost presidential elections in Nicaragua by a wide margin, a resounding repudiation of Cuba's only remaining socialist ally in the region. Fidel blamed the loss on the CIA but had been furious with the Sandinistas for agreeing to hold elections in the first place—a mistake he would never have made. Cuban advisers returned home.

It was the same in Angola. After nearly sixteen years of military intervention, American-led negotiations had forged a regional peace settlement. Cubans were coming home in a steady flow, and in May 1991 Raul welcomed the last of them accompanied by their commanding general. Fidel's last, best hope in Central America, the Marxist insurgents in El Salvador, were negotiating the end of their conflict as well. Puerto Rico still came up occasionally in the regime's rhetoric, but even that favorite flame was flickering out.

There was almost nothing left of Fidel's globe girdling internationalist triumphs. In one of the most difficult concessions he has ever had to make, he told the Cuban people their internationalist duty now was to stay at home and join together "in extraordinary efforts to save the revolution."

Soon he was talking about almost nothing but the economy. It continued to sink through the rest of 1990, and then plunged precipitously the following year as the Soviet Union disappeared and what was left of the massive subsidies ceased. The free fall continued through the next two years with a total economic implosion of between 40 and 50 percent from the 1989 level. It was the worst depression Cubans could remember.

The country was put on the equivalent of a war footing under the futuristic sounding Zero Option plan and the Special Period in Peacetime, terms adapted from Raul's contingency planning for invasion and war. The military was ordered to become self sufficient, meaning that soldiers went to work in the fields, planting, weeding, and harvesting their own food. It was a humiliating epilogue for the former internationalists to be reduced to the roles of peasant farmers and field overseers. Raul felt it necessary to state publicly that, under the circumstances, "beans are worth more than cannons."[2]

The impact on the civilian population was devastating. Unemployment soared to include more than half of the work force. Most factories had to curtail production or shut down, because fuel, spare parts, and materials were not available. Food shortages and distribution problems caused malnutrition and disease. Public health and sanitation deteriorated sharply.[3]

Without enough fuel to power electrical generators the lights literally were going out across the island. Blackouts lasted for up to sixteen hours a day, causing terrible hardships as food rotted without reliable refrigeration. Public transportation and farm machinery idled. Havana looked like a city at war or under siege.

"We are entering the bicycle era," Fidel told an audience in late January 1991. He meant it to be somehow reassuring.

More than 700,000 bicycles were purchased from China for assembly in round-the-clock shifts at a dozen technical schools turned over entirely to that task. Soon Fidel was talking incessantly about everything conceivable related to bicycles. He had been reading up and became the nation's premier bicycle expert.

"I can assure you that is easier to put together a Swiss watch than a bicycle. It is a complicated thing. I believe it requires three hundred forty-seven different parts."[4]

The era of the tricycle came later that year.

In December Fidel said that sixty thousand of the three wheelers had been purchased to "perform many of the activities for which motorized vehicles are now used."[5]

Then it was oxen to replace tractors and other farm vehicles.

"We are breaking in one hundred thousand oxen. And as soon as we are done we are going to break in another hundred thousand."

Civilians from the cities were moved to the countryside to perform stoop labor in the fields. In April 1991, Fidel spoke of that for the first time and later admitted that some, who he insisted were volunteers, would be gone for as long as two years.[6]

"Over sixty camps with room for two hundred thousand workers were built in a few weeks," he said, adding that "tens of thousands of people went from Havana to Pinar del Rio to pick tomatoes."[7]

He had previously commented in a speech about how much he liked the Roma tomatoes from Pinar del Rio in his salads. He wanted everyone to eat more fresh vegetables.

Cassava roots were a good source of protein, he lectured, and could be used instead of imported wheat to make bread. It was a comparison like another in the mid-1970s when he had talked endlessly about the nutritional value of a new Cuban beer as a substitute for rationed foodstuffs.

I was anxious to try Cuban beer myself the first time I visited Havana, but there was none to be had during that trip in early 1990. I remember entering a workingman's bar in Old Havana, near the wharves, walking up to the counter, and asking the big, gruff bartender for *una cerveza, por favor*. He glowered at me, probably thinking I was a Cuban or a Latin American. Ponderously, he placed his big hands on his hips, rubbed his broad stomach, and scowled. "You know perfectly well there is none of that to be had!"

I visited a second time, during the worst of the economic crisis, in the early spring of 1993, to assess conditions for myself. Fidel and Cuban intelligence had known of me for a long time by then, but the necessary entry visas were issued expeditiously by the diplomatic mission in Washington. I was an analyst, not an operative. My objectives were harmless: to consult with American diplomats in Havana and to get a sense of how much the situation had deteriorated. I had no clandestine or operational assignments, although Cuban officials could not be sure of that.

I had been warned by other American officials who traveled to the island that they had been harassed and intimidated, presumably by Cuban counterparts. There were abusive phone calls at three or four in the morning, near misses with menacing drivers on the roads, and I even heard that garbage was dumped between the sheets in the hotel beds of visiting CIA analysts.

One colleague woke up in his Havana hotel room in the middle of the night as two counterintelligence agents silently picked through all of his belongings. Wisely, he pretended to be asleep, and they left as surreptitiously as they had entered. I don't know why, but I was not bothered by Cuban intelligence in any way, although of course, I was kept under total, blanket surveillance.

It was after dark that Havana was most haunting. The dim light in the streets was penumbral, the few low-wattage bulbs here and there casting hazy shadows that quickly dissolved in the dark. People out and about mostly scurried, avoiding eye contact, saying nothing to each other. I remember how depressingly monochromatic almost everything seemed. Exterior paint and stucco had washed out and puckered over the years. It surprised me that Cuba and Cubans seemed to be all faded hues of brown and gray. I never heard laughter during any of my walks around the city.

Exploring Havana during those grim nights in 1993, I was reminded of fragments from a few of Fidel's speeches in the late 1980s and of the chokehold he has so long imposed on Cuban society. It was at a time when he was ranting against the liberalizing Soviet reforms, insisting that Cuba would never allow private initiative or what he disparagingly started calling "neo-capitalist" enterprise. He actually singled out for public denunciation a resourceful man who had briefly brought color and a bit of tawdry glamour to the lives of some Cubans, but who had been guilty, Fidel said, of illicit profiteering.

Somehow this unnamed individual managed to acquire a quantity of imported toothbrushes. It was probably in his kitchen where he melted and molded the plastic into bright red and yellow and green costume jewelry— simple necklaces and bracelets that he sold clandestinely for a few Cuban pesos. He brought some cheer to the streets, but he was branded a neo-capitalist exploiter and probably served a jail term.

Fidel denounced others like that man: one who bought chocolate bars in Havana's Lenin Park and later resold them for a small profit; others who salvaged interesting bits of refuse from the city dump to make into works of folk art to sell; and, according to the commander-in-chief, "people painting and selling paintings, even to state institutions, earning more than two hundred thousand pesos in a year." And after all, he complained, "these are not the works of Picasso or Michelangelo." Fidel feared that if these and other microentrepreneurs were allowed to continue, the revolution's egalitarian ideals would be compromised.

And as the revolution was being eaten away, Fidel increasingly resembled Hemingway's old fisherman. Until his seventy-fifth year, in 2001, questions about the succession had attracted only the vaguest hypothetical interest. He had always endeavored to project an image of indestructibility, unfailing robust health even as he aged into his sixties and seventies. He continued delivering interminable speeches, sometimes out in the hot sun. He met with foreign interviewers late at night, often talking nonstop until dawn.

It was all calculated to suggest longevity and superhuman vigor. Regime flacks liked to point out that his father had lived into his eighties, hinting he had died years later than he actually did just a few months short of his of eighty-first birthday. (Lina died just before her sixtieth birthday.) The appearance of perpetual youth was as essential to the projection of Fidel's revolutionary persona as the beard, the khakis, and the olive green cap.

He made quite a public show of giving up his trademark cigars in the summer of 1985 during a period when his speeches were peppered with peculiar allusions to health and mortality. The most remarkable of them was a telling allusion a few months earlier. More than an hour into a speech he muttered, in no particular context, that he was "being stalked by the grim reaper."

I noticed an unusually high incidence in his public remarks of what seemed like a dark preoccupation with his health that went well beyond the normal hypochondria he keeps well hidden. He had been pontificating to audiences so often and so knowledgeably about intricate medical matters that in one appearance he admitted that Cubans had been asking him, "Are you in your fourth year of medical studies?"

He soon felt compelled by the persistence of the rumors to dismiss—though not explicitly deny—that he had cancer. He may very well have undergone surgery, and it is not surprising that no doctors have ever come forward or leaked to the press that they treated him. By the end of 1985 whatever afflicted him had apparently resolved, and for the next fifteen years or so there would be no further signs of health problems.

That all began to change in the second year of the new century. In June 2001 he was filmed for the first time faltering during a speech. He appeared disoriented and dizzy, nearly collapsing before being carried off by aides. Nothing like that had ever happened before, and the international media reported he had briefly lost consciousness.

In two subsequent appearances that summer he became strangely incoherent for short spells, as members of the audience each time squirmed in embarrassment. Something clearly was wrong, but whatever it was remained top secret. He started wearing athletic shoes instead of boots when putting in a symbolic lap in mass demonstrations in Havana. He was slipping out of character.

More incidents followed. The worst of his known pratfalls occurred in October 2004 when he was televised tripping stiffly off a low platform after completing a speech. He crashed into a heap, breaking his left kneecap and right arm, and spent weeks in a wheelchair. Since then the broken arm seems to have withered.

As in all of his mishaps, he and the regime hastened to reassure the public that he had quickly rebounded, was well and fully in charge. But the reality is that many Cubans suspect the commander-in-chief is suffering from one or more life-threatening ailments. Rumors of recurring cancer, heart attacks, minor strokes, Alzheimer's, and Parkinson's disease have circulated.

A number of foreign visitors who have spent time with Fidel since 2001 have spoken of his mental lapses, strange verbal meanderings, and inability to concentrate. Some have been struck by how much he has declined physically just in the last few years. His skin has turned sallow; he is stooped and focuses poorly. His once characteristic striding gait has shrunken into a rigid shuffle.

The frequency and length of his public appearances have diminished, foreign journeys are not scheduled as they used to be, and even on the island he is uncharacteristically sedentary. He still manages to deliver speeches, but usually he is seated now, frequently lapsing into strange soliloquies. Observers increasingly wonder if he will live to celebrate his eightieth birthday on August 26, 2006, or if by then he might unravel into cognitive disarray. Meanwhile Raul is playing a larger role behind the scenes, perhaps already acting as a kind of regent, filtering and providing checks and balances on Fidel's instructions to other subordinates.

It was at the height of the crisis in the early 1990s that Raul began to assert himself, seemingly with the same kind of determination he demonstrated in Houston in 1959. This time, however, he was the more flexible, cautious brother, less wed than Fidel to ideological certainties. Impressed with the Chinese political-economic model, Raul pushed for the adoption of decentralizing open market reforms, though mostly without success. He did manage to win his brother's consent, probably grudging, to promote engagement between the Cuban and American military establishments and to let senior officers profit from running large sectors of the economy.

The tipping point for both Castros occurred in 1993 when street violence swept a Havana suburb in July, followed a few months later by disturbances in another nearby town. The most ominous rioting occurred in Havana, in August, 1994. Thousands of demonstrators took to the streets around the Malecon chanting "Freedom" and "Down with Fidel."[8]

Raul and his generals feared that social stability was breaking down and that military command and control might be put at risk. The institution he had spent his adult life building could not be allowed to rupture, and the surest way for that to happen would be if he had to order troops into a bloody Tiananmen Square situation. And Raul knew that if the police were unable to restore order, Fidel would insist that the military complete the job. But the armed forces are not trained for crowd control and have never fired on civilians. Most commanders would be loath to acquiesce in orders to do so.

The situation in the streets was so bad that Raul had to put the populace on notice that further disturbances would not be tolerated. The military would do whatever was necessary to preserve order, he proclaimed, warning "the revolution's enemies" not to "miscalculate," and adding that we "have more than enough cannons and other things to defend this land." This was "Raul the Terrible" laying down a line in the sand, but his threats only further undermined the limited popular support he enjoyed.[9]

Typically, too, Fidel sought relief by provoking another crisis with the United States. Following the 1994 rioting, he induced a third sea borne migration—this time of about forty thousand rafters—who set out from the north coast toward Florida with little more than paddles and jugs of drinking water.

Hundreds of thousands more would have taken their chances on any flimsy contraption that might float, but a negotiated settlement was reached providing for a legalized flow to the United States of at least twenty thousand emigrants annually. Some have described this as Cuban demographic blackmail. Still in effect today, the agreement relieved some of the pressure on the regime, and Fidel once again managed to find a silver lining in a domestic crisis.

Raul has eschewed public discussions of the 1965, 1980, and 1994 migrations, and it is therefore reasonable to infer that he was unenthusiastic in each instance. His thinking may well have been the same as that of General Rafael del Pino, who, after his defection, remembered that most honorable military officers considered Mariel a "Roman circus." Del Pino and other officers believed Fidel had unnecessarily stirred instability across the island. They were more concerned with preserving domestic stability than lashing out against the United States.

It was not just in Miami that observers became convinced in the early 1990s that the regime was not likely to survive much longer. I was among them. In August 1993 I chaired the final meetings of a working group of Cuba specialists from CIA and the other intelligence agencies to produce another national estimate. We concluded there was "a better than even chance that Fidel Castro's government will fall within the next few years."[10]

I still believe that we were right, that the odds then were stacked slightly against him. I learned later that top Cuban officials had reached a similar conclusion. One of them later admitted in a private conversation with a senior American government official that Cuba was "only about six months from an economic meltdown." They were preparing for hyperinflation and widespread instability.[11]

It was in the face of imminent upheaval that Fidel was persuaded that only a steady flow of hard currency from abroad could save him and the revolution. The situation was so dire that he was willing to compromise previously sacred revolutionary principles to maintain absolute power. There were only two realistic ways enough hard currency could be acquired: large-scale foreign tourism and dollar remittances from the Cuban diaspora.

The first—flinging open Cuba's doors to foreign tourists—was a bitter and dangerous pill. For decades it had been dogma that waves of tourists would contaminate and destabilize revolutionary society. Fidel had boasted that one of his greatest moral accomplishments had been to eradicate the prostitution, casino gambling, and mafia vice associated with the tourism of the Batista era. If multitudes of visitors were allowed to come again, they would bring most of that back. Drugs and the sex industry would proliferate. Crime would increase, and most alarming of all, Cubans would be exposed to the contagions of counterrevolutionary ideas and attitudes.

Since then tourism has grown into one of the two principal revenue sources, and with all of the feared consequences. But the regime's policy of tourism apartheid has been even more insidious and potentially destabilizing. The average Cuban is banned from the beaches, bars, hotels, and restaurants set aside for foreign tourists and regime elites. This segregation is bitterly resented by a populace that has been drilled for so many years in propaganda about its supposedly egalitarian society.

The regime's decision in July 1993 to begin legalizing foreign currencies has done even more to provoke social tensions. Until then it had been a crime for Cubans to possess American dollars, but the government needed to provide incentives for Cubans abroad to subsidize their relatives. Dollars have been heavily taxed, and most of the money received has to be spent in government-run stores that charge exorbitantly for food and other essentials. Dollarization has made it legitimate for Cubans providing services to foreigners to accept tips or fees as all manner of street solicitation and individual entrepreneurship have flourished again.

Crime, drug abuse, and prostitution have soared, as many Cubans see greater advantage in hustling foreigners for hard currency than in pursuing traditional careers. Doctors and physicists drive taxis. Unemployed scientists and engineers wait tables for tips. University enrollment is less than half what it was in 1990. What good is a degree, many youths ask, when there are so few jobs and ten or a hundred times more than a government wage can be made by providing services to foreigners?

Racial discrimination was supposedly expunged decades ago. In fact it has grown worse as Afro-Cubans are generally discriminated against for jobs in the tourist sector. And since comparatively few blacks have relatives abroad, they are less likely to receive hard currency remittances and therefore are confined to the hardships of the peso economy.

A caste system has resulted. Foreign economists have concluded that by the early years of the current century, wealth and income distribution had become more unequal in Cuba than almost anywhere else in Latin America. Ironically, the one country where grotesque inequalities supposedly were forever eradicated has now probably become at least as unequal as it was before the Castros came to power.

Parallel economies operate side by side. The rich and the regime's nomenklatura have access to hard currency and therefore to goods and services unavailable to the masses. The poor must do their best to subsist with worthless pesos while enduring long ration lines and shortages of almost all necessities. Animosities across these new societal faultlines are likely to intensify after Fidel leaves power and to confront Raul with grievous problems that will defy quick or easy solutions.

The revolution is literally in ruins. A University of Miami study found that in Havana alone an estimated three hundred buildings collapse every year, and that about one hundred thousand residents there live in unsafe structures.[12] Highways, communications and sewage systems, water mains, and other critical infrastructure are in advanced stages of disrepair. The rot has spread across the island in almost every civilian sector. Even many government and Communist Party officials now admit to each other, when they are sure they cannot be overheard, that the system has failed. Raul will inherit all of these problems. And he will have no alternative but to try somehow to alleviate them.

A praetorian regime dominated by Raul and the generals seems all but certain to succeed Fidel, though for how long is impossible to know. Preparations for a smooth succession have been underway for some time, and second- and third-tier officials have every incentive to stand together, if only as the best strategy for preserving their equities.

Civilian elites, individually or in any conceivable alliances, will be unable to challenge the military as long as it remains united. The Communist Party and popular organizations are hollow shells that have been allowed by the Castros to fade in importance. Opposition groups dedicated to advancing human rights and democracy are still small and scattered. Thus, in the short term, no others could effectively confront the *raulistas*. The main threat to stability will be that the country's new leaders will miscalculate as they deal with an increasingly restive populace desiring change.

With about fifty thousand to sixty thousand personnel, the military is the most powerful, competent, and influential institution in Cuba. It is also the richest. The many tourism and other enterprises controlled by active and retired senior officers are run from the fourth floor of the defense ministry. Raul's son-in-law and General Casas, the second in command at the ministry, manage these for-profit activities, apparently without any outside oversight. They take in about 60 percent of tourism revenues and two thirds of hard currency retail sales.[13] Several other government ministries and agencies are also run by ranking officers.

Raul was the lead architect of these adaptations in military missions. Like the concessions Fidel made to allow foreign tourism and dollarization, Raul had no illusions about the risks of giving selected officers access to substantial financial flows. But as the economy collapsed, he concluded there was no alternative if the military was to survive and the revolution was to endure. Nonetheless, the cost to the institution has been so great that it is no longer wise to assume that the high command will remain united when the new regime faces its first major tests.

Morale, discipline, and the once-strong sense of common national purpose have been eroding as resentments and jealousies among officers intensify. Faultlines run parallel to those in society at large, where some, who are favored by Raul and his top brass, thrive with access to hard currency, while others must manage on the margins in the peso economy. Younger officers, those stationed in the provinces beyond the tourist centers, and the non-commissioned cadre are probably mostly on the impoverished side of the divide. And it is likely that hardline traditionalists in the armed forces are appalled and angry as they see their once-proud institution turned into a hotbed of conspicuous consumption.

One of Raul's colonels is a good example. He controls a large and attractive apartment building in the Vedado neighborhood of Havana, not far from the American diplomatic mission. The colonel lives comfortably in the penthouse unit he is said to own. A former American diplomat in Havana who knows the building and one of its foreign tenants has described it to me.

It is ten to twelve stories high, with a fastidiously restored Art Deco exterior, and contains more than thirty apartments. A British businessman rents one of the units and pays the colonel a handsome monthly rent in hard currency. That apartment is like most of the others. It has a large balcony on which thirty to forty people can congregate and is fitted with imported fixtures and expensive details. All the other luxury apartments apparently are also rented to foreigners who pay the colonel in hard currency.

The poor Cubans who lived in the building before it was renovated were evicted in a coup of what might be termed neo-revolutionary gentrification. Surely the former tenants were not inclined to resist an elite and well-connected army colonel as they packed their belongings and moved on, though their options were bleak in a country with a deficit of 1.6 million housing units. It is difficult to imagine that such behavior by high-handed military officers has not generated severe animosities that will undermine stability in the post-Fidel era.

Only a few officers are known to have been dismissed for corruption. A general and two colonels were fired for especially egregious fraud a few years ago, yet Raul's ministry appears to tolerate all but the most blatant profiteering. No standards of conduct have been articulated and almost nothing is known outside the institution about how military entrepreneurs are managed, how they are selected, how long they serve, or what qualifications other than political acceptability they bring to their assignments. Not surprisingly, the praetorian enterprises are known to be inefficient and would be unable to compete in a free-market environment.

The short-term gains Raul achieved by granting these sinecures are likely to prove the longer term enemies of stability when he is in power. By giving favored officers access to higher living standards, he has secured their loyalty, but for how long will that be true as they become accustomed to the once-forbidden fruits of capitalism? Almost everything Raul has done to insert officers into the hard currency sector of the economy has deleterious implications. If the generals and colonels fall into conflict among themselves, the survival of the *raulista* regime would be immediately threatened. Several developments could shatter already brittle command and control.

The most dangerous possibility involves Raul himself. What if he were to die before Fidel? He is five years younger but is known to be an unreformed alcoholic. On occasion the stresses of his responsibilities have clearly weighed on him in ways that may have enduringly affected his health. Rumors that he is seriously ill periodically surface, in part because he often goes for lengths of time without appearing in public. In December 1991 persistent rumors that he had died forced him to talk to the local press.

"Every so often," he told reporters, "a rumor gets started that I died. During the Pan-American Games they were saying I was being kept in a freezer."[14]

Unlike his brother, Raul has a lively, often black sense of humor. He laughed, said he was in good shape physically, and that he walks several kilometers most days.

On June 3, 2006, he will be seventy-five. But if he were to predecease his brother, the succession plan would be thrown into chaos. A power struggle would be inevitable and Fidel's ability to control it in doubt. The most destabilizing scenario would be if Raul were to die at a time when Fidel's judgment was impaired by age or infirmity. The Castros' regime would then be on the verge of disintegration.

Raul's prior death would throw all three of the country's most critical lines of succession—in the Communist Party, the government, and the defense ministry—into contention simultaneously. Fidel would come under enormous pressure as rivals anxious to move up jockeyed for his favor and clashed with each other. He would be reluctant to name a new defense minister, who would then have the unchecked ability to mount a coup. Under the constitution, the Council of State would meet to select Raul's replacements in the government, but that body has always functioned as the Castros' rubber stamp and would be paralyzed by indecision and infighting if neither brother could call the shots.

If they remained united, the generals could easily prevail, but rivalries and animosities would break out into the open if Raul were not around to mediate them. Foreign observers acquainted with the high command believe there is no internal consensus about who should succeed Raul as defense chief. General Colome is the ranking three star, but the tough and taciturn interior minister is thought to be best suited for the job he holds. General Casas would probably be an even more polarizing choice because of the taint of corruption that has attached to his business dealings.[15]

There has never been a back-up succession plan, or anyone poised as third in line. No other leader in the party, government, or military has the stature to make a credible claim to be next after the Castros. The brothers have always made certain that no one else could acquire standing as a contender to succeed either one of them. Their strategy worked well for decades to guarantee their respective hegemonies, but now that the succession is drawing near, it is a time bomb waiting to go off.

A Tiananmen Square scenario could also sunder the military. Even if the survival of the revolution were at stake, many troop commanders would probably be unwilling to fire indiscriminately on protesting civilians. There are elite units, however—the Special Troops that were the first dispatched to Angola in 1975, and other paramilitary forces—that would be likely to obey such orders. But that could be the surest formula for civil war, pitting loyalist and dissident commanders and units against each other.

It is a nightmare scenario for both Cuba and the United States. Any widespread breakdown of law and order on the island inevitably would result in the fourth massive seaborne migration to Florida. Some in the exile community would probably return with the hope of further destabilizing the regime. There would be politically influential calls for an American or international intervention. And if the loss of life on the seas or in Cuba escalated, there might be no widely acceptable alternative to military intervention. That would be the worst possible outcome for both countries.

The fear of such a crisis is probably a key reason why Raul and the high command have lobbied, unsuccessfully so far, to engage with the American military. They want the legitimacy that such contacts would bestow. They calculate that their standing with the Cuban people would improve. And most critically, they would use sustained contacts with the Pentagon to create the sense that a successor *raulista* regime is inevitable and the best alternative for American interests. They hold out the prospect of cooperation across the Florida Straits in counternarcotics, immigration control, and other areas of mutual concern.

I know a number of active duty and retired Pentagon officers, as well as academic specialists, who advocate such engagement. The Bush administration is opposed, however, believing that military-to-military exchanges would bolster the prospects for a praetorian succession while undermining the chances for a transition to democracy after Fidel. As a result, the only regular contacts between the two militaries occur at "fence-line" talks at Guantanamo, where the American base commander and a Cuban general meet monthly. They discuss issues of local concern, such as cooperation in fire fighting and disaster relief, and with the goal of minimizing the possibility of cross-border incidents.

These talks reached a higher plateau in early 2002, when Guantanamo was being prepared for the incarceration of Al Qaeda terrorists. The Cuban government was informed in advance of the decision to use the base for that purpose, and military authorities in that area were advised about what their troops should expect to observe so that unfortunate surprises might be avoided. A few days later, Havana issued a favorable statement. And then, to the surprise of most international observers, Raul told reporters that if Al Qaeda detainees were to escape into Cuban territory, he would be sure they were returned to Guantanamo.

That was not the only indication in recent years of Raul's changing attitude toward the United States. I believe, as a result, that once in power in his own right, he will place an early and high priority on improving relations.

He will likely tap intermediaries to probe American interest while issuing conciliatory statements abandoning the decades of his brother's anti-American vitriol. To a considerable extent Raul has already softened his rhetoric about the United States. With the support of the generals, he probably calculates that his regime can survive over time only if the four-and-a-half-decade bilateral impasse can be overcome. Many clues already point in this direction, although as long as Fidel is alive, Raul will not openly acknowledge such an interest.

Unlike his brother, he has never been motivated by an ego-charged quest for fame and glory or internationalist gratification. He does not thrive on conflict and confrontation as Fidel has since childhood. He worries more about the economic hardships the Cuban people endure and has been the most influential advocate in the regime for liberalizing economic reforms. He is likely to be more flexible and compassionate in power. Fidel's daughter, Alina Fernandez, knows Raul well. She told me that "he is the practical brother."

Raul's anti-Americanism was unmistakable for decades, though it was probably never as intrinsic as Fidel's. When Raul commanded his own guerrilla forces in 1958 he kidnapped about four dozen Americans, including civilians and military personnel stationed at Guantanamo. Fidel spread the myth that his brother had acted on his own, encouraging the notion that it was Raul who was the anti-American brother. Later, during the only visit Raul has ever made to the United States, in April 1959 when he conferred with Fidel in Houston, his boorish behavior added to that reputation. And for decades Raul's infatuation with nearly everything Soviet put him in the forefront of Cuban hardliners. But his world view changed fundamentally when the Soviet Union disappeared.

By 1997 when the volume of candid interviews with forty-one Cuban generals was published, Raul's thinking about the United States clearly had evolved. That the book appeared at all was a remarkable development, given Fidel's paranoia and the historical secrecy at the top levels of the armed forces. But it was even more unusual that every one of the generals eschewed anti-American rhetoric at a time when Fidel was regularly ranting against the United States. The book was clearly orchestrated and reviewed in Raul's office and was meant to confirm earlier indications that the high command wanted better relations with the United States, regardless of what Fidel was saying.

No other departure from his brother's legacy would be as monumental for Raul as supporting a rapprochement with Washington. He would begin to move out of Fidel's shadow, asserting himself definitively as his own man. It would be a popular policy in the military, with most civilian leaders, and especially with the Cuban people. His main objective would be to win a significant reduction, or termination, of the U.S. economic embargo. But I suspect that unlike Fidel, he will be willing to negotiate in good faith and with no superseding priorities.

It is impossible to say how much Raul would be willing to yield in a process of reconciliation. Nonetheless, in light of the stand he took regarding the Al Qaeda detainees at Guantanamo, he might be inclined openly to embrace counter terrorism cooperation with the United States, a possibility that has been anathema to Fidel. Furthermore, Raul might be willing unequivocally to renounce the use of violence in Cuban international relations and possibly even to expel known terrorists and felons wanted for capital offenses in the United States.

If he did just those things, the stage would be set for a fast-moving process of normalization. Legislation signed by President Clinton in 1996, the Helms-Burton law, that tightened the economic embargo, would lose support in Congress and would probably be repealed or modified to take advantage of new opportunities. If military-to-military exchanges were formalized, counternarcotics and immigration cooperation would be likely to flourish. Popular and congressional support for the embargo, including restrictions on travel to the island, would likely evaporate.

But Raul's intent through such a process most likely would be to gain implicit American acceptance for a tough Chinese-style regime in Cuba. He realizes that if he were to permit a broad political opening, his government could be overwhelmed by spiraling popular demands for participatory government. The generals and the civilian elite alike would oppose any sudden political decompression, rightly fearing that they would lose most of their prerogatives. So the *raulista* regime will be keenly committed to maintaining order and keeping popular expectations for political change in check.

That will not be easy. Pent up demand for sweeping change will be powerful. A small and heroic dissident minority has been speaking out insistently and challenging the regime. Its numbers will probably grow exponentially after Fidel. Cubans want to be able to travel, study, and live abroad. They want the freedom to read whatever they want, to enjoy the media entertainments available in almost every other country in the world, and to express themselves without fear. More and more want to own property and businesses and be free from the eavesdropping and intimidation of the ubiquitous security services. The younger generations, who have known nothing but the rigors and sacrifices of the revolutionary years, are the most desirous of change.

Small but broadly representative dissident and human rights movements have coalesced around these needs. All involved are pacifists. They are Cuba's Gandhis and Martin Luther Kings seeking peaceful democratic change. Although they are not allowed any access to the media on the island, they are getting known by word of mouth.

Independent libraries have opened in the homes of many brave citizens who lend non-subversive books to neighbors. A small cadre of independent journalists is waiting in the wings for the time any modicum of free speech is allowed. Now they compose mostly social and literary stories that are phoned or mailed abroad for dissemination. Courageous human rights activists have been calling on the regime to free political prisoners. Osvaldo Paya's Varela Project, operating entirely within Cuban law, gathered many thousands of signatures from ordinary citizens on petitions seeking a democratic opening.

When these independent voices acquired real resonance in the spring of 2004, Fidel pounced ferociously. About seventy-five individuals were arrested and summarily imprisoned for terms up to twenty-eight years. They included one of the country's most prominent poets, independent economists, librarians, journalists, and leaders of the Varela Project. Books were seized and burned, fax machines destroyed. One activist was found guilty of sending information about human rights to Amnesty International. An independent librarian was jailed for sharing a copy of the Universal Declaration of Human Rights.

Whether a *raulista* regime will survive for just months or for many years will likely depend largely on how skillfully he and his associates deal with this coalescing independent civil society. Lacking Fidel's exceptional leadership qualities and credibility with the populace, Raul will be hard pressed to strike just the right balance. He will have to take tangible steps to assuage public discontent and raise living standards for the masses, but without opening the valves too much or too quickly. He will have to do better than he has in the past at communicating with the people. And he will probably have to be adroit at managing crises. It may prove to be too large an order.

If he is to have any chance of retaining power for long, he will have to overcome the ingrained popular image of "Raul the Terrible," the role he allowed Fidel to cast him in since the early 1950s. His government could not survive long, for example, if he resorted to the kind of brutal force in the streets that he threatened to employ in 1994. There are enough cannons in the military's inventory to maintain order, but they cannot be deployed or used against the people. Killing civilians in the streets or plazas would be all but certain to bring down his regime, or that of any other successor who ordered it.

Perhaps in his own twilight years, this complex, repressed younger brother will find his own independent political persona. Maybe then the real Raul, unencumbered by Fidel's uncompromising demands will come into focus. Their sister Juanita, and others who have known Raul are convinced that once he is freed of the need to please Fidel and honor his dictates, he will finally become his own person. Huber Matos, the former guerrilla leader who fought with the Castro brothers, told me, "Raul's traumas are the result of being Fidel's brother."

Perhaps, then, Fidel's death will be Raul's catharsis.

Notes

Prologue

1. NIE 85-2-60, *The Situation in Cuba*, June 14, 1960.

Introduction

1. Joseph North, "Raul Castro Tells Our Reporter of Cuba's Revolutionary Aims," *The Worker*, February 1, 1959, p. 7.
2. Nikita Khrushchev, *Khrushchev Remembers*, Little Brown, 1970, p. 489.
3. Aleksandr Fursenko and Timothy Naftali, *One Hell of a Gamble*, Norton, 1997, p. 14.
4. Rufo Lopez Fresquet, *My Fourteen Months with Castro*, World Publishing Company, 1966, pp. 110–111; and Philip Bonsal, *Castro, Cuba, and the United States*, University of Pittsburgh Press, 1971, pp. 64–65.
5. Teresa Gurza, "Cuba: Past, Present, Future of Socialist Revolution," *El Dia*, September 19, 1975. JPRS No. 65966, October 20, 1975.
6. Teresa Casuso, *Cuba and Castro*, Random House, 1961, p. 216.
7. Jeffrey J. Safford, "The Nixon-Castro Meeting of 19 April 1959," *Diplomatic History*, Vol. 4 (Fall 1980).
8. Interview with Ernesto Betancourt, Washington, DC, March 27, 2003.
9. Interview with Barbara Gordon, Washington, DC, April 11, 2002.
10. Hugh Thomas, *Cuba: The Pursuit of Freedom*, Harper and Row, 1971, p. 1211.
11. Jeffrey M. Elliot and Mervyn M. Dymally, *Fidel Castro: Nothing Can Stop the Course of History*, Pathfinder Press, 1986, p. 23.
12. Herminio Portell-Vila, "Quien Mal Anda, Mal Acaba," *Bohemia Libre*, January 1, 1961, p. 88.

13. Neill Macaulay, *A Rebel in Cuba*, Quadrangle Books, 1970, p. 14.

14. Carlos Franqui, *Family Portrait with Fidel*, Vintage Books, 1985, p. 30.

15. Bonsal, op. cit., p. 36.

16. Interview with Huber Matos, Miami, FL, February 24, 1986.

17. FBIS, January 22, 1959.

18. Rolando Bonachea and Nelson Valdes, *Revolutionary Struggle: The Selected Works of Fidel Castro*, The MIT Press, 1972, p. 285.

19. "Excerpts from the Appearance of Fidel Castro Before the Press," U. S. Department of State, American Embassy, Havana, March 13, 1959.

20. Interview with Ernesto Betancourt.

21. Harold Scarlett, *The Houston Post*, April 29, 1959, p. 1.

22. Betancourt, op. cit.

23. Thomas, op. cit., p. 1228.

24. Bonsal, op. cit., p. 108.

25. Richard Bissell. *Reflections of a Cold Warrior*, Yale University Press, 1996, p. 154.

26. *Revolucion*, January 29, 1959.

27. Interview with Jaime Costa, Miami, FL, February 25, 1986.

28. Gianni Mina, *An Encounter with Fidel*, Ocean Press, 1991, p. 230.

29. Pablo Diaz Gonzalez, "La Travesia Historia del Granma," *Bohemia*, December 3, 1961, p. 46.

30. Ernesto Che Guevara, *Episodes of the Revolutionary War*, Havana, 1967, p. 9.

31. Rene Rodriguez, "From Tuxpan to Las Coloradas," *Granma English Weekly*, December 6, 1981.

32. Interview with Alcibiades Hidalgo, Miami, FL, August 6, 2004.

33. Ibid.

34. Tomas Borge, *Face to Face with Fidel Castro*, Ocean Press, 1992, p. 143.

35. Thomas, op. cit., p. 1087.

36. Interview with Lucas Moran Arce, San Juan, Puerto Rico, February 27, 1986.

Chapter 1

1. Robert Quirk, *Fidel Castro*, W.W. Norton, 1993, p. 4.

2. Alina Fernandez, *Memorias de Una Hija de Fidel Castro*, Plaza y Janes Editores, S.A., Madrid, 1997, p. 11.

3. I am grateful to Juan Tomas Sanchez of the Cuban Sugarcane Growers Association in Florida, and Dr. Jose Alvarez, Professor of Food and Resource Economics, University of Florida, for sharing descriptions of the Cuban *zafra*.

4. Alina Fernandez, *Castro's Daughter: An Exile's Memoir of Cuba*, St. Martin's Press, 1998, p. 80.

5. Interview with Barbara Gordon, Washington, DC, April 11, 2002.

6. Rafael Diaz Balart, interview by Adriana Bosch, for *American Experience*, PBS, June 2, 2003.

7. Leycester Coltman, *The Real Fidel Castro*, Yale University Press, 2003, p. 5.

8. Harvey Cox, *Fidel and Religion: Castro Talks on Revolution and Religion with Frei Betto*, Simon & Schuster, 1987, p. 115. This is the most extensive autobiographical discourse that Fidel Castro has ever given.

9. Norberto Fuentes, *La Autobiografia de Fidel Castro* (Vol. 1), Ediciones Destino, Barcelona, 2004, p. 110.

10. *Fidel and Religion*, op. cit., p. 98.

11. Interview with Juanita Castro, Miami, FL, February 24, 1986.

12. *Fidel and Religion*, op. cit., pp. 128 and 138.

13. Interview with Armando Llorente, S.J., Miami, FL, February 25, 1986.

14. Interview with Jose Ignacio Rasco, Coral Gables, FL, February 24, 1986.

15. Lee Lockwood, *Castro's Cuba: Cuba's Fidel*, Vintage, 1967, pp. 16–17.

16. Ibid., p. 184.

17. Georgie Anne Geyer, *Guerrilla Prince*, Little Brown and Company, 1991, p. 23; Interview with Lucas Moran Arce, San Juan, Puerto Rico, February 27, 1986.

18. Juana Castro, "My Brother Is A Tyrant And He Must Go, *Life*, August 28, 1964, p. 27.

19. Interview with Manuel Romeu, Hato Rey, Puerto Rico, February 27, 1986. Teresa Casuso, *Cuba and Castro*, Random House, 1961, p. 131, repeats essentially the same account.

20. "Interview with *Musawwar's* Reporter," Unclassified enclosure, U.S. Embassy Cairo, February 11, 1966.

21. Alina Fernandez. *Castro's Daughter*, op. cit., p. 5.

22. Teresa Casuso, "I Saw Castro Change," *Look*, November 21, 1961, p. 128.

23. Betto interview, op. cit., p. 170.

24. Gerardo Rodriguez Morejon, *Fidel Castro: Biografia*, P. Fernandez y Cia, Havana, 1959, pp. 221, 223.

25. Interview with Alina Fernandez, Miami, FL, November 10, 2004.

26. Juan O. Tamayo, "Castro's Family," *Miami Herald*, October 8, 2000.

27. Lucas Moran Arce interview, op. cit.

28. Mario Parajon, "Fidel y Raul Vistos por Juanita," *El Mundo*, Havana, January 9, 1959, p. A7.

29. Elliott and Dymally, op. cit., p. 213.

30. Ibid., p. 23.

31. Ann Louise Bardach, *Cuba Confidential*, Vintage Books, 2002, p. 59.

32. Parajon, op. cit.

33. Tomas Borge, *Face to Face with Fidel Castro*, Ocean Press, 1992, p. 38.

34. Bardach, op. cit., p. 59.

35. FBIS, March 27, 1991.

Chapter Two

1. The letter is preserved in the Pino family collection.

2. Georgie Anne Geyer, *Guerrilla Prince: The Untold Story of Fidel Castro*, Little Brown & Co., 1991, p. 25.

3. Serge Raffy, *Castro el Desleal*, Santillana Ediciones Generales, 2004. His finding is confirmed in Katiuska Blanco, *Todo el Tiempo de los Cedros*, Casa Editora Abril, Havana 2003, an authorized volume of Castro and Ruz family history and genealogy.

4. Alina Fernandez, *Castro's Daughter*, St. Martin's Press, 1998, p. 7.

5. Both photos are included in Fidel Castro *Fidel, My Early Years*, Ocean Press, 1998.

6. Carlos Franqui, *Diary of the Cuban Revolution*, The Viking Press, 1976, p. 2.

7. *Fidel, My Early Years*, op. cit., p. 39.

8. Ibid., p. 44.

9. Franqui, op. cit.

10. Interview with Father Armando Llorente, Miami, FL, February 25, 1986. Teresa Casuso, *Cuba and Castro*, Random House, 1961, p. 131, wrote similarly of Fidel, mentioning "some hidden wound related to his childhood that had never healed."

11. Harvey Cox, *Fidel and Religion: Castro Talks on Revolution and Religion with Frei Betto*, Simon & Schuster, 1987, p. 110.

12. Franqui, op. cit., p. 88.

13. *Fidel: My Early Years*, op. cit., p. 44.

14. Geyer, op. cit., p. 51.

15. Franqui, op. cit., pp. 3 and 7.

16. Leycester Coltman, *The Real Fidel Castro*, Yale University Press, 2003, p. 49.

17. Raul Castro, Interview with *Moncada* magazine, translation by FBIS, February 27, 1987.

18. Interview with Norberto Fuentes, Coral Gables, FL, November 12, 2004.

19. Pedro Alvarez Tabio and Otto Hernandez, "From Llanos del Infierno to Epifanio Diaz' Farm (V)," *Granma Weekly Review*, January 1982, p. 3.

20. Alcibiades Hidalgo, *An Enigma Named Raul*, a presentation at the Center for Strategic and International Studies, Washington, DC, March 20, 2003.

21. *Granma Weekly Review*, op. cit.

22. Norberto Fuentes interview.

23. Franqui, op. cit., p. 4.

24. Interview with Ramon Mestre, Coral Gables, FL, February 25, 1986; and Armando Llorente interview, op. cit.

25. *Fidel and Religion*, op. cit., p. 120.

26. Juana Castro, "My Brother is a Tyrant and He Must Go," *Life*, August 28, 1964, p. 27.

27. Franqui, op. cit., p. 5.

28. Castro family letter in the Pino family collection; Franqui, op. cit., p. 84.

29. Blanco, op. cit., p. 528, quotes the official record of the christening on January 19, 1935, indicating that Fidel's name then was Fidel Hipólito Ruz Gonzalez.

30. *Fidel and Religion*, op. cit., p. 108.

31. Cancelled checks in the Pino family collection.

32. Raffy, op. cit., p. 616, and Blanco, op. cit.

33. A photocopy of the diploma appears in Blanco, op. cit., on an unnumbered page.

34. Pino family collection.

Chapter Three

1. Interview with Jose Ignacio Rasco, Coral Gables, FL, February 24, 1986.

2. Tad Szulc interview with Juan Rovira, October 27, 1984, Tad Szulc Collection, Cuban Heritage Collection, University of Miami Libraries.

3. Interviews with Father Quevedo, Aibonito, Puerto Rico, February 28, 1986; and Father Feliz, San Juan, Puerto Rico, February 28, 1986.

4. Rasco interview, op. cit.

5. Lee Lockwood, *Castro's Cuba, Cuba's Fidel*, Vintage, 1967, p. 23.

6. Fidel Castro news conference, FBIS, April 27, 2000.

7. One substantial reference to the New Deal appeared in a letter Fidel wrote from prison on the Isle of Pines on April 15, 1954. It reflected a mixture of appreciation for the impact of the New Deal's reforms but also Fidel's authoritarian and anti-free-market instincts as well as his misunderstanding of Roosevelt's "court packing" crisis. Fidel wrote: "The prosperity that followed, after years dominated by poverty, was not the byproduct of chance or the famous free play of supply and demand, but the result of the sound measures courageously taken by the government. He attacked the conservative spirit entrenched in the Supreme Court; he had to get rid of a few old men legally, by pensioning them off. Given the character, the mentality, the history of the people of the United States, Roosevelt actually did some wonderful things." Carlos Franqui, *Diary of the Cuban Revolution*, The Viking Press, 1976, p. 76.

8. Szulc interview with Juan Rovira, op. cit.

9. Franqui, op. cit., p. 76.

10. Interview with Luis Aguilar, Coral Gables, FL, October 22, 2002.

11. Gianni Mina, *An Encounter with Fidel*, Ocean Press, 1991, p. 171.

12. FBIS, March 27, 1991.

13. Telephone interview with Juan Grau, Mexico City, December 10, 2004.

14. Hugh Thomas, *Cuba: The Pursuit of Freedom*, Harper and Row, 1971, p. 876.

15. Alberto Bayo, *Mi Aporte a la Revolucion Cubana*, Impresa Ejercito Rebelde, Havana, 1960, p. 21.

16. Norberto Fuentes, *La Autobiografia de Fidel Castro*, Ediciones Destino, Barcelona, 2004, pp. 88–89.

17. Roger Miranda and William Ratliff, *The Civil War in Nicaragua*, Transaction Publishers, 1993, p. 52.

18. Leycester Coltman, *The Real Fidel Castro*, Yale University Press, 2003, p. 221.

19. Georgie Anne Geyer, *Guerrilla Prince*, Little Brown, 1991, pp. 32–33.

20. "Exclusivo: Diario de Campana de Raul Castro," *Revolucion*, January 26, 1959, p. 4.

21. Interview with Alina Fernandez, Miami, FL, November 10, 2004.

22. Interview of Raul Castro by Mario Vasquez, Rana, *El Sol de Mexico*, Havana, *Prensa Latina,* April 21, 1993.

23. Juanita Castro testimony, Washington, DC, House Un-American Activities Committee, June 11, 1965.

24. Interviews with Bernardo Benes, Surfside, FL, January 30, 2002, and Manuel Romeu, Hato Rey, Puerto Rico, February 27, 1986.

Chapter Four

1. Lee Lockwood, *Castro's Cuba, Cuba's Fidel*, Vintage Books, 1969, p. 156.

2. Alfredo "El Chino" Esquivel, interviewed by Adriana Bosch for *American Experience*, PBS, Miami, FL, unspecified date in 2003.

3. Robert Quirk, *Fidel Castro*, W. W. Norton, 1993, p. 22.

4. Quirk, op. cit., p 16; Pardo Llada, op. cit., p. 86; and Alina Fernandez, *Castro's Daughter*, St. Martin's Press, 1998, pp. 43, and 54 where she wrote that "he sat comfortably on the sofa and demanded his manicure."

5. See, for example, Lockwood, p. 72.

6. Speech at the University of Havana, September 4, 1995, in Fidel Castro, *Fidel, My Early Years*, Ocean Press, 1998, p. 82.

7. Quirk, op. cit., p. 23.

8. Tad Szulc interview of Jose Ignacio Rasco, Tad Szulc Collection, Cuban Heritage Collection, University of Miami Libraries; also Pardo Llada, *Fidel*, Plaza y Janes Editores Colombia, Ltda., Bogotá, 1976, p. 29.

9. Pardo Llada, op. cit., pp. 19–20.

10. Lionel Martin, *The Early Fidel*, Lyle Stuart, Inc, 1978, p. 46.

11. Gianni Mina, *An Encounter with Fidel*, Ocean Press, 1991, p. 36.

12. Esquivel interview, op. cit. See also, Pardo Llada, op. cit., p. 38, and Georgie Anne Geyer, *Guerrilla Prince*, Little, Brown & Co., 1991, pp. 54–58.

13. *Fidel, My Early Years*, op. cit., p. 87.

14. Pardo Llada, op. cit., p. 11.

15. Luis Conte Aguero, *Fidel Castro: Psiquiatria y Politica*, Ed. Jus., Mexico, 1968, p. 31, wrote that "Fidel could not accept the limitations of his country."

16. Quirk, op. cit., p. 18.

17. Geyer, op. cit., p. 61.

18. Pardo Llada, op. cit., p. 29.

19. Notes of meeting with Fidel Castro by Herbert Matthews, Herbert Matthews Papers, Rare Book and Manuscript Library, Columbia University.

20. Stephen G. Rabe, *The Most Dangerous Area of the World: John F. Kennedy Confronts Communist Revolution in Latin America*, University of North Carolina Press, 1999, pp. 36–39.

21. Interview by Barbara Walters, in *Bohemia*, July 1, 1977, translation by Cuban government Department of Stenographic Records, Havana.

22. Speech at the University of Havana, September 4, 1995, in *Fidel: My Early Years*, p. 86.

23. Walters interview, op. cit.

24. Philip Bonsal, *Cuba, Castro, and the United States*, University of Pittsburgh Press, 1971, p. 57.

Chapter Five

1. Hugh Thomas, *Cuba: the Pursuit of Freedom*, Harper and Row, 1971, p. 891.

2. Peter Bourne, *Fidel*, Dodd, Mead & Co., 1986, p. 48.

3. Interview by Arturo Alape, September 1981, in Fidel Castro, *Fidel: My Early Years*, Ocean Press, 1998.

4. Carlos Franqui, *Diary of the Cuban Revolution*, The Viking Press, 1980, pp. 9–19; Fidel Castro news conference in Cartagena, Colombia, August 13, 1993, FBIS, August 17, 1993; and Alape interview, op. cit.

5. Interview of Enrique Ovares by Jaime Suchlicki, Miami, FL, May 24, 1967, in Suchlicki, *University Students and Revolution in Cuba, 1920–1968*, University of Miami Press, 1969, p. 54.

6. Alape interview op. cit., p. 125.

7. Cartagena press conference, op. cit.

8. Ovares interview, op. cit.

9. Gerardo Gallegos, *El Bogotazo*, undated monograph.

10. K. S. Karol, *Guerillas in Power*, Hill & Wang, 1970, p. 122.

11. Lionel Martin, *The Early Fidel*, Lyle Stuart Inc., 1978, p. 64.

12. Ibid., p. 38 quotes a speech Fidel Castro delivered in Chile on December 19, 1971.

13. Betto, in *Fidel, My Early Years*, op. cit., p. 132.

14. Martin, op. cit., p. 72.

15. Karol, op. cit., p. 123.

16. Robert Quirk, *Fidel Castro*, W. W. Norton & Co., 1993, p. 29.

17. Pardo Llada, *Fidel*, Plaza y Janes Editores Colombia, Ltda, Bogota, 1976, p. 42.

18. Documentary evidence from the Pino family collection.

19. Pardo Llada, op. cit., p. 62.

20. Pino family collection.

21. Georgie Anne Geyer, *Guerrilla Prince*, Little Brown & Co., 1991, p. 100.

22. Interview of Rafael Diaz Balart by Adriana Bosch, Miami, FL, June 2, 2003, *American Experience*, PBS; and Geyer, op. cit.

23. Coltman, op. cit., p. 56. Also Geyer, p. 100; Rafael Diaz Balart interview op. cit.; and Pardo Llada, op. cit., p. 41.

24. Quirk, op. cit., p. 33.

25. Carlos Maria Gutierrez, "A Conversation with Fidel," *Marcha*, Montevideo, Uruguay, August 18, 1967. *Punto Final*, Chile, September 1–15, 1967, also carried much the same story.

26. Ibid.

Chapter Six

1. Rufo Lopez Fresquet, *My Fourteen Months with Castro*, World Publishing Co., 1966, p. 49.

2. Luis Conte Aguero, *Fidel Castro: Vida Y Obra*, Editorial Lex, Havana, 1959, p. 10.

3. Interview of Raul Castro by Mario Vazquez Rana, *El Sol de Mexico*, Havana, *Prensa Latina*, April 21, 1993.

4. Juanita Castro testimony before the U.S. House of Representatives Un-American Activities Committee, Washington, DC, June 11, 1965.

5. Juana Castro, "My Brother Is a Tyrant and He Must Go," *Life*, August 28, 1964, p. 28.

6. Teresa Gurza, "Cuba: Past, Present, Future of Socialist Revolution," *El Dia*, September 19, 1975, JPRS 65966, October 20, 1975.

7. Vazquez Rana interview of Raul Castro, op. cit.

8. Raul Castro, "VIII Aniversario del 26 de Julio," *Verde Olivo*, July 16, 1961, p. 4.

9. Jesus Montane in Carlos Franqui, *Diary of the Cuban Revolution*, The Viking Press, 1976, p. 54.

10. Herbert Matthews Papers, Rare Book and Manuscript Library, Columbia University.

11. Aleksandr Fursenko and Timothy Naftali, *One Hell of a Gamble*, W. W. Norton, 1997, p. 71.

12. Author unknown, "Youth in the Struggle for Their Rights," *Pravda*, March 24, 1953, no. 83, p. 3.

13. Jules Dubois, *Fidel Castro*, Bobbs-Merrill, 1959, p. 274.

14. *El Dia*, op cit.

15. Lee Lockwood, *Castro's Cuba, Cuba's Fidel*, Vintage Books, 1969, p. 163.

16. Nikolai Leonov, *Likholete*, Moscow, 1994, p. 29, Translations by Alexei Porfirenko.

17. Lester Rodriguez, "La Accion del Palacio de Justicia, *Verde Olivo*, July 25, 1971, p. 11.

18. Ibid.

19. Peter Bourne, *Fidel: A Biography of Fidel Castro*, Dodd Mead & Co, 1986, p. 82.

20. Hilda Gadea, *Ernesto: A Memoir of Che Guevara*, Doubleday, 1972, p. 98.

21. *El Dia*, op. cit.

22. Fursenko and Naftali, op. cit; and interview with Timothy Naftali, New York, NY, November 16, 2004.

23. Fursenko and Naftali, op. cit., p. 11.

24. Jon Lee Anderson, *Che Guevara: A Revolutionary Life*, Grove Press, 1997, pp. 194–195.

25. Ernesto Che Guevara, *Episodes of the Revolutionary War*, Guairas, 1967, p. 23.

26. Alberto Bayo, *Mi Aporte a la Revolucion Cubana*, Imp. Ejercito Rebelde, Havana, 1960, pp. 83–91.

27. Tad Szulc, *Fidel, A Critical Portrait*, William Morrow & Co., 1986, p. 360.

28. *Revolucion*, January 26, 1959.

29. "Dialogue with a Deputy of the Enemy," transcript of "Interview of Fidel Castro by Congressman Stephen Solarz," Havana, July 6, 1981.

30. Interview with Norberto Fuentes, Coral Gables, FL, November 12, 2004.

Chapter Seven

1. J. Niles Riddel, "National Security and National Competitiveness: Open Source Solutions," Remarks at the First International Symposium, December 2, 1992.

2. Teresa Casuso, "I Saw Castro Change," *Look*, November 21, 1961, p. 125.

3. Dispatch from the Embassy in Cuba to the Department of State, February 18, 1959, in Mark Falcoff, *The Cuban Revolution and the United States*, U.S.-Cuba Press, 2001, p. 83.

4. Juanita Castro, Speech at Meeting of the Information Council of the Americas, New Orleans, LA, January 18, 1965, from the Theodore Draper Collection, Hoover Archives, Stanford University.

5. Fidel Castro, *My Early Years*, Ocean Press, 1998, p. 141.

6. Herbert Matthews Papers, Rare Book and Manuscript Library, Columbia University.

7. Interview by Barbara Walters, in *Bohemia*, July 1, 1977, translation by Cuban government Department of Stenographic Records, Havana, July 1977.

8. Tad Szulc, *Fidel: A Critical Portrait*, William Morrow, 1986, p. 39.

Chapter Eight

1. Charles O. Porter, "An Interview with Fidel Castro," *Northwest Review*, Fall 1963, p. 82.

2. Gianni Mina, *An Encounter with Fidel*, Ocean Press, 1991, p. 12.

3. Telephone interview with Betty Whitehurst, December 7, 2004.

4. I. F. Stone, "Prefatory Note," in *Che Guevara, Guerrilla Warfare*, Vintage Books, 1969, p. viii.

5. Andres Suarez, *Cuba: Castroism and Communism, 1959–1966*, MIT Press, 1967, p. 52

6. Carlos Franqui, *Family Portrait with Fidel*, Vintage Books, 1985, p. 54.

7. Interview with Huber Matos, Miami, FL, February 24, 1986.

8. Jean Paul Sartre, *Sartre on Cuba*, Ballantine Books, 1961, p. 44.

9. Ibid., pp. 134–135.

10. Interview with Domingo Amuchastegui, Miami, FL, August 2004.

11. Charles Shaw, "A Visit to Raul Castro's Rebel Hideout in Cuba," *The Sunday Bulletin*, Philadelphia, PA, August 3, 1958.

12. Interview with Alina Fernandez, Miami, FL, November 10, 2004.

13. Ibid.

14. I am grateful to Professor Harold Shukman of St. Antony's College, Oxford University for his assistance with this interpretation of Lenin.

15. "Playboy Interview: Fidel Castro," *Playboy*, August 1985, p. 58.

16. Lee Lockwood, *Castro's Cuba, Cuba's Fidel*, Vintage Books, 1969, p. 6.

17. Evan Thomas, *The Very Best Men*, Simon and Schuster, 1995, p. 208.

18. Interview by Jas Gawronski, *La Stampa*, FBIS, December 28, 1993.

19. Sally Quinn, *The Washington Post*, March 27, 1977.

20. Jeffrey M. Elliot and Mervyn M. Dymally, *Fidel Castro: Nothing Can Stop the Course of History*, Pathfinder Press, 1986, p. 202.

21. Former Cuban government officials now residing in Miami.

22. Mina, op. cit., p. 245.

23. Rolando Bonachea and Nelson Valdes, *Revolutionary Struggle*, MIT Press, 1972, p. 372.

24. Anatoly Dobrynin, *In Confidence*, Random House, 1995, p. 85; Leycester Coltman, *The Real Fidel Castro*, Yale University Press, 2003, p. 220.

25. John Gerassi, ed., *Venceremos: The Speeches and Writings of Ernesto Che Guevara*, Simon and Schuster, 1968, p. 35.

26. Lockwood, op. cit., p. 74.

27. Herminio Portell Villa, *Dallas Morning News*, July 25, 1963, as cited by Ward M. Morton, *Castro as Charismatic Hero*, Occasional Publications Number Four, The University of Kansas, January 1965, p. 7.

28. Rafael del Pino, *General del Pino Speaks*, Cuban American National Foundation, 1987, p. 12.

29. Florentino Aspillaga interview by Georgie Anne Geyer, April 14, 1988, undisclosed location in Virginia, Georgie Anne Geyer Collection, Hoover Institution Archives, Stanford University.

30. The Grenada analysis is based on my previous work, "Castro and the World: The Dilemmas and Anxieties of Cuba's Aging Leader," in *Cuban Foreign Policy: The New Internationalism*, ed. Jaime Suchlicki and Damian Fernandez, University of Miami, 1985.

31. Sally Quinn, op. cit.

32. Carlos Franqui, *Diary of the Cuban Revolution*, Viking Press, 1980, p. 73.

33. Interview by Barbara Walters, in *Bohemia*, July 1, 1977, translation by Cuban government Department of Stenographic Records, Havana, July 1977.

34. Heberto Padilla, *Self Portrait of the Other*, Farrar, Straus, Giroux, 1990, p. 20.

35. K. S. Karol. *Guerrillas in Power*, Hill and Wang, 1970, p. 467.

36. Elliott and Dymally, op. cit., p. 219.

37. Walters Interview, op. cit.

Chapter Nine

1. National Intelligence Estimate, 85-1-75, *Cuba's Changing International Role*, October 16, 1975.

2. Peter Kornbluh and James G. Blight, "Dialogue with Castro: A Hidden History," *The New York Review of Books*, October 6, 1994.

3. FBIS, December 23, 1971.

4. Henry Kissinger, *Years of Renewal*, Simon and Schuster, 1999, p. 816.

5. Cuban American National Foundation, *Castro's Puerto Rican Obsession*, Publication 21, 1987, p. 18.

6. Edmund Mahony, " 'Aguila Blanca': The Wells Fargo Robbery," *The Hartford Courant*, November 11, 1999.

7. Edmund Mahony, "A Rocket Attack, An FBI Revelation," *The Hartford Courant*, November 12, 1999; also Jorge Masetti, *In the Pirate's Den: My Life as A Secret Agent for Castro*, Encounter Books, 1993, pp. 75–77.

8. Edmund Mahony, "Wells Fargo Reward Soars," *The Hartford Courant*, December 8, 2004.

9. Edmund Mahony, "Clemency Granted Despite Havana Connection," *The Hartford Courant*, November 7, 1999.

10. Robert A. Pastor, "Puerto Rico as an International Issue," in Richard J. Bloomfield, ed., *Puerto Rico: The Search for a National Policy*, Westview Press, 1985, pp. 116.

11. Masetti, op. cit.

12. Interview by Barbara Walters, in *Bohemia*, July 1, 1977, translation by Cuban government Department of Stenographic Records, Havana, July 1977.

13. Bill Gertz, "DIA Fears Cuban Mole Aided Russia, China," *Washington Times*, February 1, 2003.

14. FBIS, July 22, 1993.

Chapter Ten

1. Cited in Piero Gleijeses, *Conflicting Missions*, University of North Carolina Press, 2002, p. 316.

2. Interview with Alcibiades Hidalgo, Miami, FL, November 10, 2004.

3. FBIS, September 4, 1979.

4. Gleijeses, op. cit., pp. 212–213.

5. Rafael del Pino, *General del Pino Speaks*, The Cuban American National Foundation, 1987, p. 15.

6. FBIS, September 18, 1973.

7. Stuart I. Rochester and Frederick Kiley, *Honor Bound: American Prisoners of War in Southeast Asia, 1961–1973*, Naval Institute Press, 1999, pp. 394–409.

8. National Intelligence Estimate, 85-1-75, *Cuba's Changing International Role*, October 16, 1975.

9. *Foreign Relations of the United States*, Vol. VI, p. 383, Cable of January 23, 1959, from the embassy in Havana to the Department of State.

10. Jorge Masetti, *The Pirate's Den*, Encounter Books, 1993, pp. 49–56.

11. Ibid., pp. 66–67; and Claribel Alegria and Darwin Flakoll, *Death of Somoza*, Curbstone Press, 1996, pp. 131–135.

12. Florentino Aspillaga interview by Georgie Anne Geyer, April 14, 1988, undisclosed location, Georgie Anne Geyer Collection, Hoover Archives, Stanford University.

13. Bruce D. Porter, *The USSR in Third World Conflicts*, Cambridge Univesity Press, 1984, p. 34.

14. Jorge Dominguez, *To Make a World Safe for Revolution*, Harvard University Press, 1989, p. 105.

15. Fidel Castro interview with Robert McNeil, FBIS, February 20, 1985.

16. Wayne Smith, *The Closest of Enemies*, W. W. Norton, 1987, pp. 206–207.

17. Manuel Sanchez Perez interview, FBIS, January 2, 1986.

18. Del Pino, op. cit.

Chapter Eleven

1. Andres Oppenheimer, *Fidel's Final Hour*, Simon & Schuster, 1992, p. 77.

2. Interview with Alcibiades Hidalgo, November 10, 2004, Miami, FL.

3. Ibid.

4. Interview with Huber Matos, February 24, 1986, Miami, FL.

5. FBIS, July 13, 1989.

6. Philippe Clarence and Jacobo Machover, "It Isn't Always Necessary to Tell the Truth," *The Globe*, November 10, 1989.

7. Hidalgo interview.

8. FBIS, June and July 1989.

9. Ibid.

10. FBIS, July 11, 1989.

11. Pedro Alvarez Tabio and Otto Hernandez, "From Llanos Del Infierno to Epifanio Diaz' Farm (II)," *Granma Weekly Review*, April 1981, p. 5.

12. A. B. Montes, "The Military Response to Cuba's Economic Crisis," Defense Intelligence Agency and CIA Center for the Study of Intelligence, August 1993.

13. "An Assessment of the 'Ochoa Affair' in Cuba," National Intelligence Council, July 13, 1989.

14. FBIS, July 19, 1989.

15. Hidalgo interview.

16. Luis Baez, *Secretos de Generales*, Editorial Losada, Barcelona, 1996, pp. 21–32; and Jon Lee Anderson, *Che, A Revolutionary Life*, Grove Press, 1997, p. 554.

17. Baez, op. cit.

18. Ibid., pp. 123 and 567.

19. Ibid., p. 31.

20. Ibid., p. 25.

21. Lee Lockwood, *Castro's Cuba, Cuba's Fidel*, Vintage Books, 1969, p. 170.

22. "Interview with Armed Forces Minister," reprinted in *Granma*, January 11, 1987.

23. Interview by Barbara Walters, in *Bohemia*, July 1, 1977, translation by Cuban government Department of Stenographic Records, Havana, July 1977.

24. Herbert Matthews interview with Fidel Castro, May 2, 1966, Herbert Matthews Papers, Rare Book and Manuscript Library, Columbia University.

25. Simone de Beauvoir, "What is the Situation of the Cuban Revolution?" *France-Observateur*, Paris, April 7, 1960.

26. Heberto Padilla, *Self-Portrait of the Other*, Farrar, Straus, Giroux, 1990, p. 143.

27. Orlando Castro Hidalgo testimony, "Communist Threat to the United States Through the Caribbean," October 16, 1969, U.S. Senate, Subcommittee to Investigate the Administration of the Internal Security Act and Other Internal Security Laws of the Committee on the Judiciary, p. 1427.

28. Markus Wolf, *Man Without a Face*, Random House, 1997, pp. 310 and 312–314.

29. Ibid., p. 311.

30. *Secretos de Generales*, op. cit.

31. A. B. Montes, op. cit.

Chapter Twelve

1. Gianni Mina, *An Encounter With Fidel*, Ocean Press, 1991, p. 249.

2. FBIS, August 5, 1994.

3. *Cuba: The Outlook for Castro and Beyond*, National Intelligence Estimate, 93–30, August 1993.

4. FBIS, January 31, 1991.

5. FBIS, December 23, 1991.

6. FBIS, May 2, 1991.

7. FBIS, April 5, 1991.

8. *Economist*, September 3, 1994.

9. FBIS, August 5, 1994.

10. National intelligence estimate, op. cit.

11. Interview with a senior U.S. government official who learned this from a ranking Cuban government official in 2004.

12. Eric Driggs, "Deteriorating Living Conditions in Cuba," Institute for Cuban and Cuban American Studies, University of Miami, October 14, 2004.

13. *Cuba Facts*, Issue 9, March 2005, Institute for Cuban and Cuban American Studies, University of Miami.

14. FBIS, December 20, 1991.

15. Portions of this discussion and others about the armed forces are derived from my study, *The Cuban Military and Transition Dynamics*, Institute for Cuban and Cuban American Studies, University of Miami, 2003.

Index